HOW THEN SHOULD WE CHOOSE?

CONTRIBUTIONS BY:
HENRY & RICHARD BLACKABY
GARRY FRIESEN • GORDON T. SMITH

HOW THEN SHOULD WE CHOOSE?

Three Views on God's Will
and Decision Making

Douglas S. Huffman
editor

Kregel
Publications

How Then Should We Choose? Three Views on God's Will and Decision Making

© 2009 by Douglas S. Huffman

Published by Kregel Publications, a division of Kregel, Inc., P.O. Box 2607, Grand Rapids, MI 49501.

Library of Congress Cataloging-in-Publication Data
How then should we choose? : three views on God's will and decision making / edited by Douglas S. Huffman.
   p. cm.
   Includes bibliographical references and indexes.
1. God—Will. 2. Providence and government of God—Christianity.
3. Decision making—Religious aspects—Christianity. I. Huffman, Douglas S.
BT135.H6685   2009   231.7—dc22   2008042677

ISBN 978-0-8254-2898-2

Printed in the United States of America

09 10 11 12 13 / 5 4 3 2 1

TABLE OF CONTENTS

PREFACE

How Then Should We Choose?

Whether it is personal or national, individual or corporate—many would suggest that one of the things valued most by humans in all times and places is freedom. Indeed, from arguments between parents and children to wars between nations, battles have been fought in the name of freedom. The dilemma in such engagements—sometimes not fully considered until after the battle is won—is that the possession of freedom entails not only the privilege to make one's own decisions but also the responsibility for the consequences resulting from those decisions. Often at the individual level as well as at the corporate and national levels, the external battle for freedom is quickly followed by an internal battle over responsibility. With the privilege and freedom to choose comes the weight of responsibility with regard to those choices.

In a sense, this book is about how Christians face the weight of responsibility for their choices. We recognize that life is filled with decisions for which we are both free *and* responsible. Thus, we find ourselves asking, "How then should we choose?" As Christians, we recognize that we are not left alone to make choices but that Jesus has promised to be with us in our living of free and responsible lives (cf. Matt. 28:20; Luke 24:48–49; Acts 1:7–8). Nevertheless, we recognize that decision making is more complex than "God-is-with-me" platitudes, and the contributors to this volume want to engage that complexity more fully.

Specifically, as its title reflects, this book is about Christians making decisions in the light of God's guidance, that is, in accordance with God's will. But, as the title also indicates, we recognize that different Christians have different views on how God's will relates to the decision making for which believers are responsible. Thus, we have asked key representatives from each of three different schools of thought on this subject to present their perspectives and to engage one another on the matter of God's will and decision making. Of course, this means that the readers of this volume will be asking yet again, How then should we choose between these models for making choices?

While the presenters disagree with one another in key areas, all agree that the purpose of this volume is more than the mere academic presentation of their views, more than modeling cordial Christian exchange, and more than making accessible the complexities of the discussion. This volume is about encouraging Christians toward greater freedom in their decision-making responsibilities to the glory of the God who is with us. May your reading of this volume and your reflection on its discussion be helpful toward that end.

I would like to acknowledge here my gratitude to several people involved in the production of this volume. First, I offer my thanks to Jim Weaver, director for Academic and Professional Books at Kregel Publications, for his idea for this book (after seeing my Trinity Evangelical Divinity School masters thesis on this topic) and for his belief in me to head it up. Second, I am indebted to the contributors for their willingness to participate in this complex and collaborative project, despite their otherwise busy schedules. Their work on this volume included shorter presentations of their views in a three-hour interactive series of sessions at the fifty-ninth annual meeting of the Evangelical Theological Society in San Diego, California (November 16, 2007). That series of sessions was only a glimpse of the thought and interaction that reaches its climax with the book you are now holding. Third, I am grateful for the support of my home institution, Northwestern College in St. Paul, Minnesota, particularly the encouragement of my colleagues in the Department of Biblical and Theological Studies, but especially the labors of our administrative assistant, Ruth Olson. Ruth gathered dozens of books for me on God's will and decision making, typed pages of notes for me, and helped me get the manuscript into shape. Finally, I am thankful for the support of my wife, Deb, who encouraged me in this work as she does in the rest of my life.

DOUGLAS S. HUFFMAN

CONTRIBUTORS

Douglas S. Huffman, professor of biblical and theological studies at Northwestern College, St. Paul, Minnesota, earned his PhD at Trinity Evangelical Divinity School and has written several scholarly articles and coedited and contributed to *God Under Fire: Modern Scholarship Reinvents God* (Zondervan, 2002). He is a member of the Evangelical Theological Society, the Institute for Biblical Research, and the Society of Biblical Literature. Huffman researched the subject of decision making and God's will for his MA thesis in Christian thought (Trinity Evangelical Divinity School), in which he identified the three different schools of thought featured in this volume.

Henry Blackaby is the internationally renowned author of dozens of popular and best-selling books on Christian living. He earned his BD and ThM from Golden Gate Baptist Theological Seminary and has received four honorary doctorates. He has served as a pastor and as a denominational leader, has spoken in over one hundred countries as well as at the United Nations and the White House, and has regularly counseled the top Christian CEOs in America.

Richard Blackaby, the eldest child of Henry and Marilynn, serves as president of Blackaby Ministries International. He earned a PhD in church history from Southwestern Baptist Theological Seminary and has been a pastor as well as a seminary president. He works with CEOs, speaks internationally on spiritual leadership, authors books, and served as general editor/contributing author of *The Blackaby Study Bible* (Nelson, 2006). Henry and Richard have coauthored ten books, including *When God Speaks: How to Recognize God's Voice and Respond in Obedience* (LifeWay, 1995), *Hearing God's Voice* (Broadman & Holman, 2002), and, with Claude King, the revised edition of *Experiencing God: Knowing and Doing the Will of God* (LifeWay, 2007), making them well-known representatives of the specific-will school of thought for this volume.

Garry Friesen, professor of Bible at Multnomah Bible College, Portland, Oregon, earned his ThD at Dallas Theological Seminary. His dissertation was on the subject of God's will. Friesen's work presenting the wisdom view caused a significant stir among evangelicals when it was published in 1980. The revised and expanded edition of *Decision Making and the Will of God* (with J. Robin Maxson) released in 2004 (Multnomah). Friesen maintains a Web site where he reviews books on God's will and decision making (see www.gfriesen .net). A member of the Evangelical Theological Society, Friesen is arguably the leading representative of the wisdom school of thought in the evangelical world and represents that view in this volume.

Gordon T. Smith, president of ReSource Leadership International, was formerly academic dean and associate professor of spiritual theology at Regent College in Vancouver, British Columbia. Smith earned his PhD at Loyola School of Theology and continues to teach at Regent University in Canada. He is a member of the Evangelical Theological Society. Among the books he has authored are *Listening to God in Times of Choice: The Art of Discerning God's Will* (InterVarsity Press, 1997), *Courage and Calling: Embracing Your God-Given Potential* (InterVarsity Press, 1999), and *The Voice of Jesus: Discernment, Prayer and the Witness of the Spirit* (InterVarsity Press, 2003), which show his approach to the subject of God's will and decision making to be different from both the specific-will and the wisdom schools of thought, an approach we are calling the relationship view in this volume.

INTRODUCTION

Searching for the Will of God

DOUGLAS S. HUFFMAN

1. Important Questions

The most important thing in anyone's life is to know the will of God and to follow it.

—DEREK CLEAVE[1]

God does not want confused, bewildered, frustrated Christians wandering around anxiously searching for His will. He wants people who are walking confidently and peacefully in His will.

—J. GRANT HOWARD JR.[2]

The evangelical Christian world has produced thousands of pages on the subject of finding God's will for one's life. Those who desire to serve God in the best way possible and to enjoy all that God has in store for them naturally are concerned with making correct decisions. Some fearfully fret over the idea of God's plan for them, and, of course, most everyone faces hard decisions in life for which there seem to be no clear answers. Paul Little asserts that if Christians were allowed one question of the Lord Jesus Christ, it would have to do with knowing God's will for their lives. "After all, to a committed Christian this is really the only thing that counts. Our peace and satisfaction depend on knowing that God is guiding us. And the absence of that certainty leaves us fearful and restless."[3]

---

1. Derek Cleave, *How to Know God's Will* (Phillipsburg, NJ: P & R, 1985), 13.

2. J. Grant Howard Jr., *Knowing God's Will—and Doing It!* (Grand Rapids: Zondervan, 1976), 89.

3. Paul Little, *Affirming the Will of God* (Downers Grove, IL: InterVarsity Press, 1971), 3.

But are such fears and restlessness legitimate? In day-to-day living, to what extent are Christians required to find God's will for their lives? Is the Christian expected, obligated, or even commanded by God to discover His will? How is this discovery to be accomplished?

The last few decades has brought to life the disagreement between those who believe God has a specific will for which a Christian ought to search and those who believe God does not have any specific will for individuals. A third position proposes that God may indeed have individual plans for individual Christians but they should not be unduly stressed. These basic views represent the three main schools of thought on God's will toward which modern writers on the topic tend to gravitate or upon which they depend for various nuanced mediating positions. By way of a discussion among advocates of these three different approaches, this book sets out to explore the idea of God's will in relation to the Christian's responsibility to discover it.

2. Definitions Related to God's Will

The phrase is commonly used by Christians today. But few are certain just what is intended by "God's will" as it is used in the Bible, or when it is related to an individual's Christian experience.

—LAWRENCE O. RICHARDS[4]

Which Will?

Before pursuing these questions, it is necessary to define what is meant by "the will of God." This phrase may bring to mind a multitude of theological topics, including foreknowledge, predestination, free will, foreordination, providence, revelation, spiritual gifts, prayer, and divine attributes. While briefly touching on many of these topics, the focus of this work is on God's will as it relates to God's plan for an individual and to the individual's decision making.

---

4. Lawrence O. Richards, *Expository Dictionary of Bible Words* (Grand Rapids: Zondervan, 1985), 626.

Theologians deal primarily with the will of God as an attribute or capacity. God's will is His ability to choose to cause (or to allow) things to happen. Quite often, the phrase is used in reference to the results or objects of God's willing ability. The things (actions, events, etc.) that God chooses to occur are themselves called "God's will."

Generally, two aspects of God's will are distinguished—God's unchallengeable decrees (His "decretive" will) and His precepts (His "preceptive" will), which people often neglect or rebel against.[5] Other paired terms used to make this same sort of distinction, with slight variations, are His "hidden" or "secret" will and His "revealed" will;[6] His "irresistible" will and His "resistible" will;[7] His "sovereign" will and His "moral" will;[8] His "ultimate" will and His "intentional and/or circumstantial" will;[9] and His "determined" will and His "desired" will.[10] Howard briefly describes the distinction in this way: "The determined will of God is that which will happen. The desired will of God is that which God wants to happen. We do not know what will happen but we do know what He wants to happen."[11]

The relationship between these two basic aspects of God's will is somewhat of a mystery and perhaps separate discussions of them only confuse matters. It is important to note that God is not said to

5. See Lewis Sperry Chafer, *Systematic Theology* (Dallas: Dallas Seminary Press, 1947–1948), 1:209; Louis Berkhof, *Systematic Theology*, 4th ed. (Grand Rapids: Eerdmans, 1941), 77; R. A. Finlayson and P. F. Jensen, "God," in *The New Bible Dictionary*, 3rd ed., ed. J. D. Douglas, N. Hillyer, and D. R. W. Wood (Grand Rapids: Eerdmans, 1962), 418–20.

6. M. Eugene Osterhaven, "Will of God," in *Evangelical Dictionary of Theology*, ed. Walter A. Elwell (Grand Rapids: Baker, 1984), 1172–73.

7. John Theodore Mueller, *Christian Dogmatics: A Handbook of Doctrinal Theology for Pastors, Teachers, and Laymen* (St. Louis: Concordia, 1955), 171.

8. Garry Friesen with J. Robin Maxson, *Decision Making and the Will of God: A Biblical Alternative to the Traditional View*, rev. ed. (Sisters, OR: Multnomah, 2004), 220. Unless otherwise noted, page numbers for Friesen's work will be in reference to the 2004 edition.

9. Mack King Carter, *Interpreting the Will of God: Principles for Unlocking the Mystery* (Valley Forge, PA: Judson, 2002), 16–29.

10. Howard, *Knowing God's Will*, 15–21.

11. Ibid., 20. See the helpful discussion in Paul Helm, *The Providence of God*, Contours of Christian Theology (Downers Grove, IL: InterVarsity Press, 1994), 47–49 and 130–37.

have "wills" (plural); rather, distinctions such as these are considered different "aspects" of the one divine will. According to Finlayson and Jensen, the decretive/sovereign will is the more frequently referred to aspect in Scripture.[12] Ephesians 1:11 represents this aspect when it speaks of "him who works out everything in conformity with the purpose of his will" (cf. vv. 5, 9). In the midst of several moral instructions, Ephesians 5:17 is representative of the preceptive/moral aspect of God's will: "Therefore do not be foolish, but understand what the Lord's will is." Deuteronomy 29:29 appears to allude to both the hidden and the revealed will of God: "The secret things belong to the LORD our God, but the things revealed belong to us and to our children forever, that we may follow all the words of this law."

The two main aspects of God's will can be compared in chart form (see figure I.1).[13] The decretive will of God can be subdivided into two further aspects: the effective will and the permissive will. The first is exercised when God carries out, by whatever means, those things that are in conformity with His holy character. The latter is exercised when God permits evil things (those things not in conformity to His holy character), which in His sovereignty He

FIGURE I.1. THE WILL OF GOD

Decretive/Sovereign Will	Preceptive/Moral Will
1. God's plan, which determines everything that happens	1. God's revealed commands in the Bible
2. Inevitable—will happen	2. Desirable—may not happen
3. Cannot be "missed"—should be humbly accepted	3. Can be "missed" through ignorance or disobedience
4. Mostly hidden. Only what is revealed of it in the Bible can be predicted	4. All we need to know is revealed in the Bible (2 Tim. 3:16–17)
5. Its ultimate purpose is to glorify God	5. Its ultimate purpose is to glorify God

12. Finlayson and Jensen, "God," 418–20.

13. Figure I.1 is largely a conflation of charts by Garry Friesen and J. Grant Howard; see Friesen, *Decision Making* (1980 ed.), 229; Howard, *Knowing God's Will*, 113.

nonetheless, chooses to permit.[14] The effective aspect is that which God decrees and which conforms to His holiness. The permissive will is that which is not what God desires but what He permits to occur "by the unrestrained agency of rational creatures."[15] Both the effective will and the permissive will represent things that do happen and are, therefore, parts of God's decretive/sovereign will.

We can picture these aspects of God's will with a diagram of overlapping circles (figure I.2).[16] One circle pictures God's decretive/sovereign will (circle 1) and the other His preceptive/moral will (circle 2). The decretive/sovereign will represents what does in fact happen in reality, both good and evil (and thus the solid line in our diagram). The evil that occurs is represented in the diagram by area A and can be called God's permissive will. Acts against God's commands fall into this area. The whole of circle 2 represents the things God desires in conformity to His character. Area B (the effective will) represents God's preceptive will that is carried out, that actually happens (and is thus inside the solid line of circle 1). The good that God desires but that humans do not carry out is represented by

FIGURE I.2. GOD'S DECRETIVE WILL AND PRECEPTIVE WILL

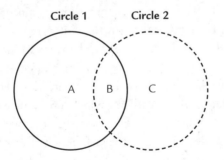

14. Heinrich Heppe, *Reformed Dogmatics: Set Out and Illustrated from the Sources*, with a foreword by Karl Barth, rev. ed. Ernst Bizer, trans. G. T. Thompson (London: Allen & Unwin, 1950), 89–90.

15. Paul D. Feinberg, "Will of God," in *Wycliffe Bible Encyclopedia*, ed. Charles F. Pfeiffer, Howard F. Vos, and John Rea (Chicago: Moody, 1975), 2:1810.

16. I owe much of this diagram to Garry Friesen's version of it in Friesen, *Decision Making* (1980 ed.), 232. Friesen revises his diagram to a series of concentric circles rather than overlapping circles in *Decision Making* (2004 ed.), 222.

area C (and is thus projected by the dotted line of circle 2 outside of circle 1). Only those things within circle 1 actually happen.

All that occurs in all of life and history happens according to God's sovereign will (within the bounds of circle 1). Howard summarizes humanity's relation to God's will: "Though we are always in God's determined will (His plan), we may or may not be in His desired will (His pleasure)."[17]

Free Will?

Interestingly, one of the things God has chosen (or willed) is that humans should be volitional beings. People have the ability to make choices—to determine (or will) things. People refer to this human ability when they speak of "the willpower to remain on a diet," the "strong will" of some children against their parents, or the legal document that describes how persons "will" to have their belongings distributed after death. This human ability to make choices is referred to as our free will.

Just how much freedom God has given in humanity's volitional ability is the subject of much debate. It is difficult to understand how the free will for which humans are responsible relates to the sovereignty of God. To what extent are things foreordained? To what extent does God limit His control/influence on humanity's destiny? Do people really have a choice in what happens to them, or are all their circumstances the result of divine manipulation? Across the centuries, theologians have leaned in both directions, some favoring the free will of humans and others giving more emphasis to the sovereignty of God. Despite many attempts to balance these paradoxical ideas, no one has described it to the satisfaction of everyone else.[18]

Regardless of where they stand in the free will debate, evangelicals recognize humanity's ability, however limited, to make decisions. A

---

17. Howard, *Knowing God's Will*, 21.
18. See the classic modern-day discussion of this issue in D. A. Carson, *Divine Sovereignty and Human Responsibility: Biblical Perspectives in Tension*, 2nd ed. (Grand Rapids: Baker, 1994), esp. pp. 201–22. One book that explores the complexity of this matter in relation to one aspect of Christian living is Terrance Tiessen's *Providence and Prayer: How Does God Work in the World?* (Downers Grove, IL: InterVarsity Press, 2000). Tiessen discusses no less than ten theological models in answer to his question and describes how differing people choose to pray depending on their model of providence.

person's free will is one of the things willed by God and therefore always functions within some aspect of the will of God. It can be said that humans are never able to exercise their wills outside of God's sovereign will (circle 1 in figure I.2). A person wills only because God wills it.

This book is not aimed at contributing to—much less proposing a solution for—the debate on human free will. Rather, it wishes to discuss Christian decision making. More specifically, it deals with the attempts of Christians to make better decisions by obtaining more knowledge from the omniscient God, that is, by discerning the will of God for their lives.

Wish or Will?

Evangelicals agree that God's Word is never to be disobeyed in the process of making decisions. God's desire in any situation is never contrary to His Word. This commitment, however, does not solve our decision-making dilemmas. "In fact it is possible for Christians to subscribe together to the authority, infallibility and reliability of God's word—yet, at the same time, differ strongly here, and to accept radically different views of how God guides us."[19]

After all, we must make decisions about many issues in modern life that are not specifically dealt with in the Bible, or at least not as clearly spelled out as many would like. Some of these issues have moral ramifications and are commonly called "gray areas" (because the Bible does not identify them clearly as wrong or right, i.e., "black or white"). Over the centuries, these issues have included such things as entertainment activities, food and beverage choices, political positions, economic theories, arms industry stances, and perhaps hundreds of other types of behaviors and stances depending upon the group of people asked (see Paul's discussion of this matter in the first-century church in Romans 14, where he terms them "disputable matters"). How does God really feel about an individual's decisions in these things? And, just as important, how does the individual find out?

---

19. Sinclair B. Ferguson, *Discovering God's Will* (Carlisle, PA: Banner of Truth, 1982), 27.

It is not difficult to know God's will when all but one of the options in a decision are contrary to God's Word. But it is most difficult to discern God's favored option when more than one is morally correct (or is simply non-commanded). As someone has said, "The most difficult decisions are always between rival goods."[20] In fact, most of a person's decisions fall into this area: what clothes to wear, what to have for dinner, where to purchase gas, how much to buy, and so on and so on. Likewise, some of life's big decisions are "plagued" with too many good choices: what career to pursue, whom to marry, what school to attend. Among all the "good" options, which one is "best"? Does God have a wish within His moral/preceptive will?

Dedicated believers want to make choices that are within God's realm of morality. But they not only want to make "good" decisions; they also want to make the "best" decisions. Some affirm that within the sovereign and moral will of God (area B of figure I.2) there is a detailed plan for each individual's life according to God's wishes, including His preferences in non-commanded matters. It certainly seems reasonable that an omniscient God would know all the minute details of all the options in a decision and thus be able to judge one of them better, even if only slightly better, than all the rest.

As M. Blaine Smith writes, "It is hard to imagine that a God who sees the minutest intricacies of all human events in precise detail would ever perceive two alternatives as having absolutely equal value for his purposes. He would surely see that one of them would help tilt the balance of history at least slightly better toward the accomplishment of his mission."[21] Some decisions of far-reaching effect may have several good options, none of which is prohibited in Scripture and more than one of which may even be encouraged by Scripture. It is in these types of situations that believers want to know more of God's design and thus search for the will (or wish) of God. Unless otherwise defined, the writers in this book use the

---

20. See R. C. Sproul, *God's Will and the Christian* (Wheaton, IL: Tyndale, 1984), 43, where he writes of the donkey that starved to death unable to decide between the hay and oats that lay before it.

21. M. Blaine Smith, *Knowing God's Will: Finding Guidance for Personal Decisions*, 2nd ed. (Downers Grove, IL: InterVarsity Press, 1991), 238.

phrase "the will of God" in this sense of God's plan for an individual, especially regarding non-commanded decisions.

3. The Search for God's Will Through History

We may be startled at realizing that the New Testament has next to nothing to say about the ways of ascertaining God's will for one's life—a major concern for us, yet one seemingly unknown to the early Christians.

—EMILE CAILLIET[22]

Compared to the modern level of Christian concern, it appears that relatively little was written on the idea of discovering God's specific plan for one's life prior to the twentieth century. Indeed, the writers who touched on the subject in previous centuries tended to speak of God's will more in its moral/preceptive aspect than in a specific individual sense, that is, more in terms of one's relationship with God than of a revelation of a plan. Augustine (354–430) spoke of living well when seeking God.[23] Martin Luther (1483–1546) encouraged focusing on the person of Christ as revealed in Scripture: "It is impossible for you to fail to meet the Father's will if you hold to the Man Christ; in this Man you will encounter the Father. There is no other will, neither in heaven nor on earth nor in hell."[24] John Calvin (1509–1564) emphasized God's providential control over all of creation, also focused on the moral aspect of God's will as revealed in Scripture, and spoke of the leading of the Spirit.[25] John Flavel (1627–1691) stressed God's ability to control circumstances.[26]

---

22. Emile Cailliet, "God Never Gives a Blueprint," *Eternity*, August 1960, 6.

23. See esp. Augustine's *The Happy Life*.

24. Martin Luther, *Luther's Works*, ed. Jaroslav Pelikan and Helmut T. Lehmann, vol. 23, *Sermons on the Gospel of St. John Chapters 6–8*, ed. Jaroslav Pelikan and Daniel E. Poellot (Philadelphia: Fortress, 1953–86), 70–71.

25. See esp. John Calvin, *Calvin: Institutes of the Christian Religion*, ed. John T. McNeill, trans. Ford Lewis Battles, The Library of Christian Classics (Philadelphia: Westminster, 1960), 1:74, 201, 217–19, 360; 2:907, 923, 952–53.

26. John Flavel, *The Mystery of Providence* (1678; repr., London: Banner of Truth, 1963), esp. 188–90.

Jonathan Edwards (1703–1758) emphasized God's providential control of all circumstances to the point of making a specific-will idea viable.[27] John Newton (1725–1807) and John Wesley (1703–1791) more clearly wrote with a specific-will-of-God idea. Newton warned of wrong methods to discover God's plan.[28] Wesley spoke of making sensible decisions.[29] But it was after George Müller (1805–1898) that the "how-to" approaches began to multiply, and such approaches flourished in the last half of the twentieth century, spilling over into the twenty-first century.[30] Modern writers on the topic of finding God's will frequently refer to Müller. While some prior to his time had given principles or rules for discerning God's will (e.g., Flavel), Müller was the first to give a step-by-step method for discovering God's specific will.[31]

But we must take care not to dismiss concern over good decision making as a recent fad. Rather, it is a particular kind of methodological concern that seems to have become more the issue in recent decades. Indeed, this becomes part of the discussion among the contributors to this volume.

4. The Options

You can find a book about God's will that says exactly what you want to hear if you look long enough. You have to decide, however, which view really reflects biblical teaching and is a sound evaluation of the way God has designed life to work.

—GARY T. MEADORS[32]

---

27. See Jonathan Edwards, *The Works of Jonathan Edwards*, with a memoir by Sereno E. Dwight, revised and corrected by Edward Hickman (Carlisle, PA: Banner of Truth, 1974), 1:70–71.

28. See John Newton, "How God Guides . . . and How He Doesn't," *Eternity*, November 1977, 40–41, 53–54.

29. See John Wesley, *The Works of John Wesley*, vol. 2, *Sermons II: 34–70*, ed. Albert C. Outler, Bicentennial Edition of the Works of John Wesley, ed. Frank Baker (Nashville: Abingdon, 1985), 53–55.

30. See the sampling of books in this volume's bibliography.

31. See esp. George Müller, "How I Ascertain the Will of God," *Eternity*, July/August 1981, 16.

32. Gary T. Meadors, *Decision Making God's Way: A New Model for Knowing God's Will* (Grand Rapids: Baker, 2003), 133.

Just how detailed God's plan is for each individual person has become the subject of much debate in the last few decades. Scores of contributions to the discussion have perhaps muddied the waters of our understanding of the issues at stake. As mentioned above, among the plethora of approaches to this subject, this volume brings together representatives of the three primary positions in this debate in order to conduct a dialogue regarding the Christian's responsibility to discover God's will. I briefly introduce these three differing schools of thought here.

The Specific-Will View

> *Once again, we need divine guidance because* **God has a purpose for each of us such as no one else has.** *One of the most arresting and dignifying truths of Scripture revelation is, that for every human being there is a preconceived divine plan and intention.*
>
> —J. Sidlow Baxter[33]

Certainly there is biblical evidence for a specific will, especially if God sovereignly "works out *everything* in conformity with the purpose of his will" (Eph. 1:11, emphasis added). That is to say, it makes sense for God's sovereign will over all things to entail specific plans for each of us within that overall plan. God knows everything and controls everything (Ps. 135:6; Rev. 4:11). A look at the marvelously detailed order of the created world demonstrates God as a detailed designer. Scripture states that He knows the number of hairs on one's head and that a single sparrow cannot fall to the ground apart from the heavenly Father's attention (Matt. 10:29–30).[34] This seems quite specific.

There are biblical examples of God directing individuals very specifically (e.g., Abram and Lot to move, Gen. 12:1–4 and 19:12–22; Elijah where to hide, 1 Kings 17:2–6; Philip and Peter where to go to witness, Acts 8:26–29 and 10:9–24; Paul and Barnabas to be missionaries, Acts 13:1–4). Indeed, it is reasonable to conclude that

---

33. J. Sidlow Baxter, *Does God Still Guide? Or, More Fully, What Are the Essentials of Guidance and Growth in the Christian Life?* (London: Marshall, Morgan & Scott, 1968), 23 (emphasis in original).

34. The NIV translation of Matthew 10:29 has "apart from the will of your Father."

the designer of the universe would have a specific will for each person, even as David indicates in Psalm 139, "All the days ordained for me were written in your book before one of them came to be" (v. 16). Thus, it seems that the all-knowing and all-powerful God of the whole universe would have plans for each part and each person in the universe. We are calling this school of thought the specific-will view.

As one supporter of the specific-will view remarks, "God doesn't want us to be confused. He wants us to know his plan for our lives. For people who want to discover his will, there are several avenues to follow." The means by which to discover God's will often include things like Scripture, prayer, circumstances, and counsel from fellow believers.[35]

This view is sensible enough and, as mentioned already, very common in the evangelical world. It is the view believers often hear from the pulpit and from media preachers. But is it the correct view? Our contributors representing the specific-will view are Richard Blackaby and Henry Blackaby. As they say in one of their full-length books on the subject of divine guidance, "There is nothing more important in life than understanding when God is speaking to you. If you are disoriented to God's voice, your life is dangerously vulnerable. The Bible indicates conclusively that God does speak to people and that he does guide them to his will. The problem of not hearing from God never lies with God. He does communicate his will. It is not a matter of us searching in vain for God's hidden will. He readily reveals it to those who show themselves obedient to do it."[36] Thus, the Blackabys will present their case here, arguing that all Christians should adopt the specific-will view.

The Wisdom View

We must face the fact: "How do you know the will of God in making life's decisions?" is not a biblical question! The Bible never tells us to ask it. The Bible never gives us direction in answering it. And

---

35. Roger C. Palms, *God Guides Your Tomorrows: How to Be Confident That God Is Leading Your Life*, rev. ed. (Downers Grove, IL: InterVarsity Press, 1987), 33.

36. Henry T. Blackaby and Richard Blackaby, *Hearing God's Voice* (Nashville: Broadman & Holman, 2002), 264.

the pursuit of some personalized version of the "will of God" often leads us toward disobedience. When we find ourselves facing the tough choices in life—those day-in, day-out decisions that make up the very fabric of our existence—we shouldn't seek special messages from God. Instead, we should ask, "How do we develop the skills necessary to make wise and prudent choices?"

—HADDON W. ROBINSON[37]

Despite the popularity of the specific-will view, some challenge the concept of a specific will of God for every individual. They claim that the view of God's specific, individual will results from misinterpreting biblical examples of exceptional guidance to be normative for Christians today.[38] The specific-will idea is said to stem from "a misguided effort to reconcile the sovereignty of God with the free will of man." "Too often we fail to marvel at the mysteries of God, but seek to reduce them to the understanding of man" (cf. Rom. 11:33–36).[39]

Lillian Harris Dean, in an article entitled "Do We *Have* to Find God's Will?" says that most Christians would like to believe that God has specific plans for both important and minor areas of their lives, but the bases for such beliefs are all too frequently found in immaturity and result in guilt and frustration. "One thing mature spiritual children have to do is make decisions they would rather have God make for them. Most of us are spiritual adolescents and, like teenagers, we want the authority without the responsibility."[40] James Coggins is careful to say that God certainly can give specific direction if He so chooses, but he also says clearly that Christians cannot be demanding of individual guidance.[41] As Bruce Waltke puts it, "God gave each of us a brain, and He expects us to put it to good use."[42]

---

37. Haddon W. Robinson, *Decision Making by the Book: How to Choose Wisely in an Age of Options* (Wheaton, IL: Victor Books, 1998), 54–55.

38. E.g., Friesen, *Decision Making*, 73–76.

39. James R. Coggins, "Finding God's Will for Your Life," *The Presbyterian Journal*, November 28, 1979, 9.

40. Lillian Harris Dean, "Do We *Have* to Find God's Will?" *The Christian Herald*, February 1968, 35.

41. Coggins, "Finding God's Will," 10.

42. Bruce K. Waltke, *Finding the Will of God: A Pagan Notion?* (Grand Rapids: Eerdmans, 2002), 143.

The champion presentation of what has come to be known as the wisdom view is the work by Garry Friesen. His Dallas Theological Seminary doctoral dissertation on the subject of God's will caused a significant stir among evangelicals when it was published in a popular format in 1980 entitled *Decision Making and the Will of God: A Biblical Alternative to the Traditional View*.[43] Friesen agrees that God's sovereign will and God's moral will exist, but he asserts that a specific individual will for every detail in a person's life is a teaching not found in Scripture. If this contention is correct, "many believers are wasting a great deal of time and energy searching for something that does not exist."[44] He argues that God does not have any real preferences between options in non-commanded decisions, but that it is the Christian's responsibility to make wise choices. Friesen seeks to alleviate the guilt and frustration associated with attempts to identify God's ideal will and to motivate Christians to make decisions in areas of God-given freedom based upon spiritual wisdom and usefulness. "*In the area of freedom, the believer's goal is to make wise decisions on the basis of spiritual usefulness*," which basically means that the believer should choose "what works best to get the job done—within God's moral will, of course."[45] "If God has revealed only the actuality of His sovereign will and the content of His moral will, we may expect them to be fully adequate for our decision-making needs."[46] Along these lines, then, Friesen will argue in this volume for the validity of the wisdom view for Christian decision making.

The Relationship View

The will of God is not a mysterious set of sealed orders we search for and receive if we happen to hit on the right formula. Rather, the will of God is a relationship with Him in which He

---

43. In addition to this volume, rereleased in 2004 in a revised and expanded edition, Friesen maintains a Web site where he reviews books on God's will and decision making (see www.gfriesen.net).

44. Friesen, *Decision Making*, 41.

45. Ibid., 174–75 (emphasis in original).

46. Ibid., 80.

discloses His purpose, power, and plan for our lives—and in that order.

—LLOYD JOHN OGILVIE[47]

The debate between the specific-will view and the wisdom view at times has been a heated and difficult one. And, of course, various scholars and writers have taken up various nuanced stances along the continuum of positions between these two views. But, in fact, life is messy enough to propose yet another school of thought on God's will for one's life. The third position represented in this volume— the relationship view, as we are calling it—is not at all a mediating view on the continuum between the other two positions. This third school of thought does not get caught up in the "how-to" question of finding God's will, and it does not argue against the existence of a specific will of God in favor of simply making wise choices.

Indeed, the existence of a specific will does not necessarily mean one's primary objective in life is to search for it. Nor is denying the existence of a specific will of God and insisting on wise decisions the only way to help Christians avoid feelings of guilt and frustration that accompany searches for God's individual will. Perhaps there is a specific will of God that believers need not be fretting over. Over against the other two schools of thought, the relationship view observes, "The 'blueprint' people look for signs and examine circumstances. The 'wisdom' people essentially trust their own capacities to make choices. But somewhere in all of this we must ask about God."[48]

Writes Ben Campbell Johnson, "The question of the will of God for each of us must be dealt with against the background of the character of the God who wills and the content of that will. This perspective saves the serious inquirer from absorption in his or her own security and personal fulfillment. Yet this larger vision does not cancel God's will for individuals. The will of God for

---

47. Lloyd John Ogilvie, *Discovering God's Will in Your Life* (Eugene, OR: Harvest House, 1982), 10.

48. Gordon T. Smith, *Listening to God in Times of Choice: The Art of Discerning God's Will* (Downers Grove, IL: InterVarsity Press, 1997), 16.

the individual finds its home in the will of God for the whole of creation. An exclusive emphasis on either of these complementary poles distorts God's intention."[49] "The will of God," writes Gerald Sittser, "has to do with what we already know, not what we must figure out. It is contained in Jesus' command that we seek first God's kingdom and righteousness. The will of God, then, consists of one clear mandate—that we make God the absolute center of our lives."[50] Perhaps believers should be investing in their relationships with God and not in mere formulas for discovery or in principles for wisdom. As Philip Yancey puts it, "The Bible contains little specific advice on the techniques of guidance, but much on the proper way to maintain a love relationship with God."[51]

Our representative of the relationship view is Gordon T. Smith. Among his several books, Smith has authored three on the subject of decision making: *Listening to God in Times of Choice: The Art of Discerning God's Will; Courage and Calling: Embracing Your God-Given Potential;* and *The Voice of Jesus: Discernment, Prayer and the Witness of the Spirit.*[52] Against the wisdom view, Smith argues that Christian decision making is an ancient concern of Christians and not a recent invention of the specific-will school of thought. But, against the specific-will view, Smith is concerned with the over-abundance of "how-to" approaches that neglect the living relationship with God that is to characterize the life of a believer. Thus, in this volume, Smith will argue for the relationship view as the correct perspective on Christian decision making.

---

49. Ben Campbell Johnson, *Discerning God's Will* (Louisville: Westminster/John Knox, 1990), 31. Johnson writes further, "This model repudiates the notion that we must seek and seek to find God's will. The will of God comes to us; we need only receive it" (p. 49).

50. Gerald L. Sittser, *The Will of God as a Way of Life: How to Make Every Decision with Peace and Confidence*, rev. ed. (Grand Rapids: Zondervan, 2004), 52.

51. Philip Yancey, "Finding the Will of God: No Magic Formulas," *Christianity Today*, September 16, 1983, 27.

52. Smith, *Listening to God in Times of Choice*; idem, *Courage and Calling: Embracing Your God-Given Potential* (Downers Grove, IL: InterVarsity Press, 1999); and idem, *The Voice of Jesus: Discernment, Prayer and the Witness of the Spirit* (Downers Grove, IL: InterVarsity Press, 2003).

Clear Labeling

But I've learned by experience—and, oh, how I've learned by experience!—that metaphors are always risky. With a single metaphor, a pastor can communicate two messages that he/she **intended** *to communicate but six messages that he/she did not.*

—KYLE LAKE[53]

While the views represented by our three contributors are indeed substantially different from one another, we must admit that the labels used to identify them might be somewhat misleading if pressed. In particular, we encourage the reader to fight the temptation to assume that the label of one view means the other views lack the feature pictured by that label. Such assumptions would be harmful errors of the straw man kind. To be more explicit, the "specific-will" label represented by the Blackabys does not necessitate that the views of Friesen and Smith deny that God can make specific plans; the "wisdom" label for the view represented by Friesen does not necessitate that the views of the Blackabys and Smith are against wisdom; and the "relationship" label for the view represented by Smith does not necessitate a lack of relationship in the views of the Blackabys and Friesen. Rather than indicating anything negative about the other views, each of these labels is selected as a positive, representative feature of the view so identified.

We should note that, on the subject of God's will, many Christian thinkers and writers draw upon elements from more than one of these three schools of thought. Furthermore, the contributors to this volume each have their own nuance of the particular school of thought they represent. Nevertheless, we have selected these contributors as fair and balanced representatives from their respective viewpoints, not to represent every other writer in their own camp, but to encourage the discussion between camps on the topic of Christian decision making.

---

53. Kyle Lake, *Understanding God's Will: How to Hack the Equation Without Formulas* (Lake Mary, FL: Relevant Books, 2004), 16 (emphasis in original).

5. Decision Making and God's Will

Most of us handle . . . routine decisions with relative ease. But life often presents us with many larger decisions that confront and confuse us. These are the big, crucial decisions which, when we make them, turn around and make us.

—HADDON W. ROBINSON[54]

No matter what their preferences are on schools of thought regarding God's will, all believers have decisions to make every day. When Scripture gives clear guidance on an issue, believers can be assured that the direction is God's will (even if we find obedience to that clear direction uncomfortable!). But the debate over God's will actually rages in the area of big life decisions where there are no clear statements of Scripture. While some people may try to ascertain God's specific plans for trivial decisions, it is when facing the weightier choices in life—decisions that have life-changing impacts—that Christians particularly long for clear guidance from God. Whether or not I know with certainty God's will on a particular matter, I may still need to make a choice, a commitment, a decision. What direction do the three main schools of thought on searching for God's will have for us with regard to Christian decision making? How do their approaches differ? How are they similar? What would they have us do in facing our day-to-day decisions?

This volume is not primarily designed to be a mere critique of all the different approaches to decision making, and it is not a defense of any particular school of thought. Rather, we are attempting to bring together key representatives of the major positions in this discussion so that our readers can quickly assess for themselves the options. So, in order to make this more practical, we think it fitting to have each contributor apply his approach specifically to several classic realms of decision making in which Christians struggle to know God's will—namely, careers, relationships, and stewardship.

Career questions include: What "calling" or career should I pursue? Where should I go for education or training? Which job should

---

54. Robinson, *Decision Making by the Book*, 10.

I take? Relationship decisions include: Should I get married or stay single? Whom should I marry? Should we have children? Should we adopt children? How many children should we have? Stewardship choices include: What home should I purchase? How should I invest my money? How should I invest my time? With which local church and/or ministry should I be involved? In order to focus our discussion and sharpen our comparison of the three differing schools of thought on decision making and God's will, we have crafted three hypothetical—but very realistic—decision-making stories for our authors to examine through the lenses of their views on searching for God's will.

Case 1: A Career/College Decision

Susan, a prospective college student, wants to make the right choice regarding higher education. Higher education is very expensive, and she is determined that she will not attend any institution unless she knows for certain that it is God's will for her life. To what extent can she be guaranteed to know absolutely ahead of time which institution is God's will for her? Or is she better off making an informed and prayerful decision, trusting that God has granted her the information she needs to stay within God's plan, even if the decision must be made apart from certain knowledge of God's specific will?

Case 2: A Relationship Decision

Joe and Nancy have been dating for two years, have many shared interests, and enjoy one another's company. They are both finished with college and involved in careers, although it is uncertain where their separate careers may take them in the future. Indeed, both are feeling the need to make a decision about marriage and family. How do they make this decision? Is each of them "God's will" for the other? How can they know for sure?

Case 3: A Stewardship Decision

David and Rachel are new to the area and want to find the right local church in which to become involved. First Local Church is nearby and would afford them the opportunity to build into their local community, and it would be convenient for their busy schedules. But Second Large Church, while much farther away, offers many more opportunities for their young children and more ministry options for themselves. To complicate matters, they just heard about Third Church, a new start-up ministry that is so small that they do not yet have their own facility and meet in a school building. But the worship is fresh, and the people are less "churchy" than the other places they have visited. The preaching is passable at First and Third Churches but dynamic at Second Large Church. The opportunities for their children are best at Second Large Church, but it is far enough away to make David and Rachel wonder about making the most of those opportunities. The ministry of Third Church needs lots of effort from all its participants, and balancing competing time demands is an issue for David and Rachel. In which church should they invest themselves? How can they best decide?

In examining these three cases, we will see how the different schools of thought on decision making and God's will approach real-life situations. While these stories are specific, the decision-making processes outlined by each approach will be informative regarding the different views on God's will, and the demonstration of their principles will have broader instructional value.

Now, then, let us begin the discussion.

Chapter 1

DISCERNING GOD'S WILL

The Specific-Will View

HENRY AND RICHARD BLACKABY

1. Introduction

Perhaps the question most frequently raised by Christians today is: What is God's will for my life? We live in a complicated world with a bewildering array of opportunities and challenges. Christians in every age have needed and sought divine guidance. Life is too precious to squander with bad decisions. Therefore we must call upon the one Person who can infallibly guide us to the best choice every time. Believers also seek to know God's will so they can honor Him with their choices and so their lives can make positive contributions to God's kingdom. It is crucial that Christians clearly understand how to know God's will.

We will present here what has sometimes been labeled the traditional view of knowing God's will. The core belief of this perspective is that God not only has a specific will for individuals but also communicates that will to people so they can follow it. As pastors and teachers we have both spent many years helping Christians discern God's will. Our role was not to discover it for them but to help them through the process of finding it. In our experience, most of the time when people have come asking for help in knowing God's will, they already knew what it was. They just didn't know they knew. God had been speaking clearly to them; they were just not sure how to recognize His voice.

2. Foundational Truths for the
Specific-Will View

The following foundational truths are helpful when seeking to know God's will. The specific-will view leans heavily upon them.

The Nature of Scripture

The Bible declares, "All Scripture is God-breathed and is useful for teaching, rebuking, correcting and training in righteousness" (2 Tim. 3:16). God's commands, teachings, and principles found in Scripture are authoritative for Christians. Personal experience and Christian tradition are valid in our decision-making process only as they align with scriptural teaching. Moreover, the example of how God dealt with people in the past is provided in the Bible for the continuing benefit of every generation. The Bible is a God-centered book. It reveals God's nature and how He relates to people. If we want to know how God will relate to us today, the definitive place to learn this is the Bible. While the testimonies of those who have walked with God throughout two thousand years of church history are pertinent, they are supplemental to the Bible's teachings, and they do not possess the same authority. When people's experiences run contrary to Scripture's teachings, Christians must always take their instruction from God's Word.

From the beginning of the Bible to its end, God gives clear instructions to individuals and to people corporately, guiding them to know how to live and how to serve Him. One approach taken when interpreting Scripture, however, suggests that the personal experiences chronicled in the Bible do not provide the normative pattern for modern Christians because in biblical times God was still composing the Bible. The conclusion is that He was more active in people's lives during that time than He is today. Now that we have the written Word available to us, the argument says, we can go to it to find God's commands and teachings for our guidance. Therefore, we no longer need God's direct intervention in our lives. Included in this perspective is a caution against drawing out-of-context inferences from Bible passages.

This standpoint has weaknesses. Notably, nowhere in the Bible are readers cautioned that they should not expect their walk with God to be like that of believers in biblical times. Nowhere in Scripture are readers informed that biblical characters were given entirely unique treatment by God. Taking this line of argument, one could conclude that the lives of biblical characters are so unique that their examples have no relevance for any of us. To place biblical characters and their experiences with God in a category that completely contrasts with our lives would reduce much of the Bible to irrelevance for us. Either the stories of people recounted in Scripture are relevant to us and to how we walk with God, or they are not (see 1 Cor. 10:1–13).

Regarding context, every Bible passage certainly was written at a particular time and addressed a particular circumstance—hence the hesitation of many to draw inferences for our lives from passages written for situations far removed from the present day. Since the culture and worldview of the biblical era was different from ours, it is often argued that many of Scripture's instructions are no longer culturally relevant for contemporary situations. But, while it is important to know the context of Scripture passages, the Bible reveals truths about God that apply to any age.

For example, Jeremiah 29:11 declares, "'For I know the plans I have for you,' declares the Lord, 'plans to prosper you and not to harm you, plans to give you hope and a future.'" These words have greatly comforted countless believers who needed assurance that in the midst of their difficult circumstances, God had a plan for them and a purpose for their suffering. But is this comfort legitimately taken? The promise in this verse certainly was spoken in history to a specific group of people. Through Jeremiah, God sent this message to the Jewish exiles in captivity in Babylon, assuring them that He had not abandoned them despite the appearance of their present circumstances. God had positive intentions for them during their time of bondage. Some conclude that had these people been ordinary individuals (like you and me) instead of the ancestors of the Messiah, God would not have had any special plans for them. Rather, the exiles would have been forced to make the best of their situation, as you and I must do. The argument is that the unique situation of the Jewish people called for this divine involvement but that this is the exception to the pattern of life and not the rule.

We disagree with this conclusion. The fact that this passage, like every Scripture, was written within a particular setting does not negate the truth contained within it. The eternal God does not change (Mal. 3:6). Moreover, the God who related to Abraham, Moses, Isaiah, and the apostles is the same God who relates to us today. His ways and purposes in one age still have profound implications for people of every generation. Jeremiah 29:11, penned in response to a specific situation during the sixth century B.C., expresses a foundational truth about God that has enormous relevance for us today. At the time Jeremiah wrote this, God had recently punished His people severely. Their enemies had triumphed over them, and God had allowed devastating circumstances to envelop them. Throughout the centuries since that time, God's people have continued to undergo His discipline, to suffer at the hands of their enemies, and to face tribulation. And, like the Israelites, Christians have had to repeatedly turn to God in humility for His deliverance. Could God have a particular purpose for allowing you to undergo trials today? Certainly. Though Jeremiah's contemporaries had experienced humiliating defeat and destruction, they were encouraged to place their trust and hope in God. God was prepared to meet them at their lowest point and to bring good out of their situation.

This truth of God is also demonstrated in the New Testament. John the Baptist and Jesus both told the first-century Jews how to find their way back to God to receive His blessing, even in the midst of their subjugation to the Roman Empire. When Peter was arrested and facing execution, God's response brought him hope and freedom (Acts 12:7). Paul and Silas were imprisoned, yet God freed them from their bondage and brought salvation to their captor (Acts 16:26–40). At the close of the New Testament, as Christians were facing persecution for their faith, God had a message of hope for the churches that assured them of God's ultimate victory

(Rev. 1–3). Church history is likewise filled with examples of God's comfort and guidance during times of suffering and persecution. Today, this same God will take us from where we are, no matter what depths we have reached, and move us to a place of usefulness to Him once again.

Just as the Israelites needed God to help them find their way back to Him, so God is prepared to guide us back into a full relationship with Him when we stray from Him (James 4:8). Does God know how He could use our lives to impact His kingdom for good, regardless of how much we have previously failed Him? He does. The specifics will vary, depending on the people and the circumstances, but God's desire to address His people's sin and bondage remains constant in any age. There is no better place to see what God is like and how He relates to people than in Scripture. If the Bible does not present a picture of the normative Christian life, then there is no other place Christians can turn to see how they should relate to God today. Conversely, if Scripture can be summarily dismissed because it was originally written in a particular setting, then the Bible cannot be the authoritative guide for Christian living.

It is imperative to understand that Scripture is the authoritative source for knowing how we should live the Christian life; our personal experience is not. Some conclude that because they struggle to know God's will, this proves God does not have specific plans for them. They do not hear from Him, so they assume He must no longer speak to people. This line of argument is fallacious at best and dangerous at worst. The same reasoning could be applied to the claims of Christ: since many people today struggle to accept what Jesus said, His statements must therefore be exaggerated, misguided, and/or only applicable to a special few. But the reality is this: When people fail to grasp the clear teaching found throughout Scripture, their lack of understanding does not negate the truth of God's Word.

Likewise, some people abuse the process of knowing God's will and claim God has led them to do things that clearly violate the teachings of Scripture. Again, their fallacious claims do not invalidate the truth that God *does* guide people. Some pastors are reluctant to teach that God specifically leads believers because they fear the potential abuses. Perhaps church members will profess all manner of outrageous dreams and visions leading them to divorce spouses and marry others or to quit their jobs and camp out on their rooftops waiting for Jesus' imminent return. Sadly, history is replete with people who credited God for decisions that merely came from their own desires or delusions. However, their misguided actions do not eliminate the truth that God does give specific direction to His people. Some physicians have been grossly negligent in their duties, yet we must not discard the entire profession of medicine or stop receiving medical care. Rather, we seek the counsel of doctors who are ethical, competent, and successful. Just as there are people who do ungodly things in God's name, so, on the other hand, countless numbers of Christians have experienced clear, unmistakable guidance from God.

The Bible is not only the inspired, authoritative Word of God; it is also God's redemptive message in its totality. God's Word, including the Old and New Testaments, is complete. No further revelation is required for people to learn the nature of God or to know how they might be saved (1 John 5:13; Rev. 22:18–19). Everything people need to understand about God in order to successfully live the Christian life is found in the Bible. Where we need help is in the application. For example, Scripture clearly instructs us to love our enemies (Matt. 5:38–48). But what does this look like in our day? Does that dictate that we do not defend ourselves when a colleague slanders us in order to overtake our position in the company? Does it mean there should be no accountability for those who abuse us or harm those we love? It is the role of the Holy Spirit, living within us, to help us obey Scripture's instructions in the specific details of our lives. Therefore, when God speaks to people today, He is not providing new revelation or writing an addendum to Scripture; He is applying His Word to the particulars of our lives.

In summary, we must seek our understanding of God's will from our study of the Bible. Scripture alone is authoritative for the

Christian life. Christian tradition, as well as people's personal experiences, can affirm what Scripture teaches, but these cannot supersede or invalidate its instruction. While we will cite specific and personal illustrations in the coming pages to clarify our position, these are intended to be supplementary to the biblical view and not foundational to our argument.

The Nature of God

The better we understand what God is like, the easier it will be to recognize when He is leading us. If we are not familiar with Him, it will be difficult to recognize His voice. The prophet Isaiah was bewildered over his circumstances until he encountered God (Isa. 6:1–10). When Isaiah saw the true God, he not only was terrified but he also gained immediate meaning and direction for his life. Saul of Tarsus was aggressively striving to achieve highly ambitious career goals. Once he met the living Christ, however, his own plans appeared to him as worthless in light of what God wanted to do through him (Phil. 3:4–11).

If you have been taught to practice a self-centered Christianity, you will invariably become frustrated when God does not respond to your requests the way you expect Him to. God is not a cosmic recreation director, travel agent, or administrative assistant. He is not our servant. He is our Lord. God is the Creator of the universe. We are to yield our will to His. He intends to be glorified through His creation. We are to live in such a way that we bring honor to Him. God declared, "I am the LORD; that is my name! I will not give my glory to another" (Isa. 42:8). Some view God as a doting, heavenly Father who receives no greater delight than when His children are happy. This portrayal, however, wrongly exalts people to a level that is unbiblical. Moreover, it greatly diminishes the Bible's characterization of God.

God is not honored merely by our doing what we want or what makes sense to us. He is glorified when we willingly and joyfully surrender our will to His. He is pleased when we sincerely pray as Christ did, "Not my will, but yours be done" (Luke 22:42). Jesus taught us to submit ourselves to the Father, praying, "Your will be done on earth as it is in heaven" (Matt. 6:10). How do heavenly creatures carry out God's will in heaven? They perform it instantly and unquestioningly. Angelic beings do not wander around heaven trying to do what they sense would be best. Each heavenly creature accomplishes God's purposes exactly as He directs. Likewise, the Bible teaches that God's human creatures on earth are to live their lives in obedience to divine directives. Paul explained, "I no longer live, but Christ lives in me" (Gal. 2:20). Paul clearly understood that the Christian life is to be lived in complete surrender to every prompting and directive from the indwelling Christ.

We can safely conclude that God has given each of us a mind and He intends for us to use it. Certainly wisdom books such as Proverbs have been divinely inspired to give us sound, practical counsel. Scripture also promises that God will grant wisdom to those who ask for it (James 1:5). But the reality is, apart from the Spirit's guidance and enlightenment, we cannot think like God does. Our own reasoning may conclude that something makes sense or is reasonable to do, but that does not mean it will please God.

God's ways are not our ways (Isa. 55:8–9). Paul declared that people do not innately understand spiritual matters nor do they naturally pursue God's will (Rom. 3:9–12). Even though we are Christians, we live in bodies of flesh that continue to be susceptible to sin (Rom. 8:10). In fact, we are so inherently disoriented to God that we do not know how to do something as basic as pray unless the Holy Spirit enables us (Rom. 8:26–27). That is why the Christian life must be lived in absolute dependence upon the guiding and sustaining work of the Holy Spirit. It is imperative, therefore, that Christians continually abide in Christ, for apart from our daily communion and dependence upon Him, we can do nothing (John 15:5).

Furthermore, we do not know what lies in the future as God does. Jesus told His disciples, "But when he, the Spirit of truth, comes, he will guide you into all truth. He will not speak on his own; he will speak only what he hears, and he will tell you what is yet to come" (John 16:13). The Holy Spirit is privy to the counsel of the heavenly Father (1 Cor. 2:9–12). He knows what God has for us in the future. That same Holy Spirit resides within every believer. The Spirit therefore can guide us to meet what lies ahead in ways we could not possibly comprehend ourselves.

When Richard was a pastor, he would habitually pray over a list of church members on Monday mornings. One week, the Lord gave him a heavy burden for one particular young man, a newlywed. Richard took a moment to write him a brief note, assuring him that God loved him, had a tremendous future in store for him, and that the young man and his wife could trust the Lord and His will for their lives. Wednesday morning Richard received a phone call. "How did you know?" asked the young man. "How did I know what?" Richard responded. "How did you know that today I would be laid off of my job?" Due to serious government cutbacks, the hospital where this man worked had to make sudden, drastic cuts in their workforce. As this bewildered young fellow made his way home, he noticed the postman filling the apartment mailboxes. There was the note from his pastor, assuring him that God loved him, would guide him, and could be trusted. How did Richard know to write a note on Monday so this church member would receive encouragement on Wednesday only an hour after being laid off his job? He didn't. But the Holy Spirit, who knows the future, knew; so He guided Richard to take a specific action that day.

We do not always know what is best for us and for those we love, but God does. God's nature is perfect love (1 John 4:7–8). The way He relates to us will always be characterized by absolute, pure love. So, as God continually seeks to accomplish His divine, redemptive purposes, He is also constantly aware of what is best for us. Jesus declared that He came to give abundant life (John 10:10). He also explained that behind His teaching was the desire that His "joy may be in [us], and that [our] joy may be complete" (John 15:11). God wants His people to experience His unquenchable joy (John 17:13). Such joy, however, does not come from doing what we want but from fulfilling God's will and bringing Him glory. The very night Jesus told His disciples He wanted *His* joy to be in *them,* He was preparing to be arrested and brutally crucified by His enemies in order to accomplish His heavenly Father's will. The kind of joy Jesus wanted His disciples to experience would grow out of an absolute obedience to the Father's will. Our deepest joy comes from relating intimately with our heavenly Father and obeying Him wholeheartedly.

God knows far better than we do what will lead us to experience joy in our daily living. He has given us His clear commandments to safeguard us from harm and to help us experience abundant life. In life we face many important decisions and opportunities: Should I take this job offer or not? Should I marry that person or this one? These may not be choices between right and wrong, but the decisions we make can have long-standing consequences for the joy we experience in our life. Furthermore, the path we elect to follow can have profound ramifications for others as well.

God loves us enough to grant us free will. He did not create us as robots without autonomy to make decisions. To have done so would have robbed us of the joy we experience when we voluntarily choose to follow Christ's directions. Nevertheless, it would be unloving for an all-knowing God to remain silent while aware that one decision would lead to heartache and pain while a different decision would result in abundant life. How could a perfectly loving God allow us to proceed unwittingly toward disaster when His Spirit could easily guide us to a better option?

At one time Richard was a seminary president. The school was providing a needed ministry by training people for full-time Christian service, yet the seminary was small and had limited financial resources. Clearly, the current level of its endowment fund was not generating enough earnings to sustain the institution. A representative for the foundation of an affiliated organization met with Richard to tell him how much more money the seminary could earn by transferring its endowment fund to his foundation. Many other organizations and individuals Richard knew were investing with this company. Richard respected this representative and saw no compelling reason not to channel the seminary endowment fund from its current investor to this reputable company. It appeared the seminary was poised to dramatically increase its earnings if it made the switch. As Richard prayed, however, the Holy Spirit would not give him a sense of peace about the investment. Instead, a strong uneasiness persisted as Richard prayed about this seemingly sensible move. This was not a choice between right and wrong. Both options were upstanding, Christian organizations. Scripture did not provide any direct guidance to make this decision, but the choice would have important ramifications for the seminary's future. The seminary leadership did not want to regret their decision. Ultimately, trusting the prompting of the Holy Spirit, they declined to transfer their funds. The following year a major scandal unfolded in that financial institution. Eventually it was dissolved. Clients received back only a fraction of their original investments. Had Richard relied merely on a pros and cons list, he might reasonably have concluded he should invest his school's valuable assets with this organization, though it was destined to lose millions of dollars. Clearly the Spirit, who knew the future, had protected the seminary at a critical point of decision.

Some have suggested that the greatest good the Lord can do for us is to give us free will to make our own choices, even if those decisions lead to disappointment. The ability to choose for ourselves is presented as the ultimate sign of maturity. Certainly God would not be expressing perfect love if He took away our free will and forced us to always do exactly what He wanted. But the greatest good He can give us is the opportunity to willingly follow His will, not our own best thinking. God's love is demonstrated when He prompts us to do what is best but allows us the freedom to decide whether to accept His guidance.

God's will, like salvation, is always on God's terms, not ours. He does not force His way upon anyone but invites us to receive His direction and to submit to it. By choosing of our own volition to accept what God has prepared for us, we enter into His eternal joy. Taking into account that God is infinitely loving, all-knowing, and unchanging, we can better understand why, just as in biblical times,

God chooses to offer His people His wisdom in place of their own limited reasoning.

The Redemptive Purposes of God

Another aid to knowing God's will is to understand the way He works. God is the cosmic Creator. He lives and functions in eternity. God does not exist to help us achieve our goals and to accomplish our plans. He is always in the process of orchestrating His own universal purposes. "I am God, and there is no other; I am God, and there is none like me. I make known the end from the beginning, from ancient times, what is still to come. I say: My purpose will stand, and I will do all that I please. From the east I summon a bird of prey; from a far-off land, a man to fulfill my purpose. What I have said, that will I bring about; what I have planned, that will I do" (Isa. 46:9–11). The entire Bible presents God as actively at work carrying out His redemptive plans.

God knows the eternal destiny of every person, so He is constantly working to fulfill His saving purposes around the world. That is a priority with Him. God does not want anyone to perish (2 Peter 3:9; cf. John 3:16; 1 Tim. 2:3–4). His desire is that everyone should enjoy everlasting life. God is the only one who knows what eternity is like. Only He knows the full implications of what it means to "perish." Perishing for eternity must be horrendous if God was willing to sacrifice His own Son to save people from such a fate. Therefore, what God will guide us to do in our own lives will relate to His activity in saving those who are in danger of perishing.

Humanity in general, and particularly Western culture, is relentlessly self-absorbed. Our society ardently promotes a radical autonomy and license to pursue pleasure with abandon. God's purpose, however, is not to make us happy or to ensure that all our wishes come true. His focus is on redeeming the millions of people who do not know Him as Lord and Savior. God's love for the people of the world compelled Christ to leave the safety and glory of heaven to die an excruciating death on a cross. We should not be surprised, then, when God calls us to do things that make us uncomfortable in order to accomplish His will through us. God's priority for our lives is not that we be comfortable but that we think and act like Jesus (Rom. 8:28–30). This means more than merely asking ourselves, "What would Jesus do?" It implies that we live our lives in the same way Jesus did. Jesus did not take the initiative in making His own decisions. Rather, He testified, "I tell you the truth, the Son can do nothing by himself; he can only do what he sees his Father doing, because whatever the Father does the Son also does" (John 5:19). Jesus was sinless, and He knew God's Word better than anyone. Yet even He did not make decisions based merely on what He wanted to do or what made the most sense to Him. Rather, He constantly yielded His will to that of His Father.

Jesus set the standard for us to follow by His own example. Just as He relied on the Father for continual guidance, the clear biblical pattern is that the Father constantly approached people with specific instructions. God provided Noah with minute details on how to build the ark (Gen. 6:14–16). He guided Abraham to the land in which he should dwell (Gen. 12:1). He dictated exact dimensions for the construction of the tabernacle (Exod. 26–27). He gave the prophets precise words to declare (Ezek. 2). When God communicated with people in the Old Testament, they knew it was God speaking, and they knew what He was telling them.

The struggle for some people came at the point of their obedience to what they knew God had told them. For example, when Gideon set out a fleece, he was not trying to determine what God was telling him (Judg. 6:36–40). It was because he was afraid to accept and obey what God had already clearly told him. An angel had been sent to relay God's specific message to Gideon (Judg. 6:11–18). The angel had even shown Gideon a sign by miraculously burning up the sacrifice Gideon had offered (Judg. 6:19–24). Gideon put out a fleece, therefore, not to determine God's will or to demonstrate his faith, but because he lacked faith to believe what God had told him.

The New Testament makes it clear that the only way for us to have a relationship with Christ is for Him to be our Savior and Lord

(Luke 6:46). Jesus exercised His lordship over His followers by instructing them how they should live. In the Gospels when Jesus encountered people, He often told them what they should do. He gave the rich young ruler specific and unique instructions (Luke 18:18–22). When He went by the boats of the fishermen, He invited them, "Come, follow me, . . . and I will make you fishers of men" (Mark 1:17). When His disciples offered their own suggestions on how they thought Jesus should conduct His ministry, Jesus often countermanded them and gave His own directions (Mark 1:38; Luke 9:12–13, 49–50). Jesus never hesitated to tell His disciples what to do. Likewise, He gave direction to individuals He met along the way and to the multitudes when He preached.

When Jesus instructed people to do things, it was not always to do what seemed most logical to them. Rather, it was what Jesus knew would best advance God's kingdom. When a would-be disciple volunteered to follow Jesus as soon as he buried his father, Jesus gave him the unorthodox guidance to let the dead bury the dead (Luke 9:60). When another claimed he was ready to follow Jesus as soon as he bade his family farewell, Jesus gave the unusual advice that he should not look back when following Him (Luke 9:62). Jesus rejected what seemed to these people like logical, even noble things to do because He sought to align His followers with the accomplishment of His redemptive mission.

When we adjust our focus from our own interests to God's universal purpose, it becomes clear why God would lead us in the way He does. For example, was there anything inherently wrong with Abram continuing to live in Haran, or Isaac staying in Gerar, or Moses herding sheep on the back side of the desert, or Esther minding her own business, or Peter and Andrew expanding their fishing enterprise? Not really. All of these would have been reasonable pursuits. The issue was that God was seeking to accomplish His divine purposes in their day, and He intended to use these people to achieve them. As a result, all of these individuals had to surrender their own goals and comforts in order to become involved in God's activity. As they did, God called them to go to places, to perform feats, and to accomplish things that took them well beyond what they could ever have imagined they would do.

The world teaches modern Christians to be self-centered rather than God-centered. Our focus is on what God will do *for us* rather than on what God intends to do *in* and *through us*. If we are to grasp God's will, we must begin by seeking it in terms of God's redemptive purposes. Knowing God's Word and understanding His nature gives us the perspective we need to comprehend our role in God's plan.

One of the most ludicrous questions people ask is: "Should I seek God's will about *everything*? Must I pray and ask Him what brand of toothpaste I should buy and which breakfast cereal I should eat?" If you have a self-seeking approach to your walk with God, you may become immobilized as you worry about missing God's will in every minute detail of your life. If you believe God is carefully designing each breakfast menu for you down to whether your eggs should be poached or scrambled, you can become utterly self-focused. Clearly some mundane aspects of our lives are not life-and-death matters; nor will they influence eternity. They simply require wisdom in our decisions. God's Word does provide clear direction for the overall way we approach daily life. For example, the book of Proverbs has much to say about handling our finances wisely. It also addresses many other issues related to daily living. These do not require hours in a prayer closet. They merely call for obedience to godly principles. Some decisions in our lives, however, have far wider repercussions.

Some of our choices will have an enormous impact on our usefulness for God's kingdom. The person we choose to marry can either enhance or hinder what we do in God's service. Our career path has a major impact on what God will do through us to advance His purposes. Likewise, some of our daily decisions have implications for how God will carry out His Great Commission through us. Does it matter to God if we choose to spend our day shopping at the mall instead of visiting a friend? While neither may be a morally superior choice, God knows if our decision could have an impact that day for His kingdom. On some days it might not make any significant difference. On others, someone's eternal destiny could be involved. The general issue we must constantly be aware of as we make decisions is how God may choose to use our decision making to involve us in His redemptive activity in our world.

The fundamental question for every person, therefore, is not, "What is God's will for my life?" but, "What is God's will?" God's redemptive activity in my world gives perspective and purpose to my individual life. Understanding God's priorities for my workplace, my city, my neighborhood, my family, and my church will give me the proper perspective for how God wants to include my life specifically in His activity.

The Nature of Sin

A certain impediment to knowing and doing God's will is sin. By its nature, sin separates people from God and leads to death and judgment (Rom. 6:23). From its inception in the human experience, sin has been deceiving people to assume an exalted opinion of themselves. The serpent whispered to Eve, "You will not surely die. . . . For God knows that when you eat of [the fruit] your eyes will be opened, and you will be like God, knowing good and evil" (Gen. 3:4–5). Satan was stoking the initial human feelings of pride. Pride led Adam and Eve to believe they should make their own choices and become autonomous from God. Pride still convinces us that we are being restricted and subjugated by having to rely on God for His instructions and by having to do what He says. Adam and Eve ultimately chose to value their autonomy from God over obedience. The consequences were disastrous.

Pride, that ancient vice, has had plenty of modern manifestations through the ages. During the seventeenth and eighteenth centuries, a movement known as deism grew popular. Its followers became enamored with human reason, which was assumed to be sufficient to overcome any human dilemma. Deists claimed that God was like a cosmic clockmaker who designed the universe and its workings based on reason. Therefore, they concluded, its mysteries could be unlocked through human thinking. With His creation established,

God allowed it to function without His interference. People could rely solely on their intellect to figure out how to live with one another in harmony. They also could understand God and His works sufficiently through scientific inquiry and rational thought. The idea of God's direct intervention in the lives of His creation, including the miracles recounted in Scripture, was rejected.

In contemporary times some still maintain that since God has given us His commandments, teachings, and wisdom sayings in Scripture, Christians who use the minds God gave them are perfectly capable of making wise decisions apart from God's direct involvement. Furthermore, it is assumed that to seek God's guidance in decision making is a form of spiritual immaturity in which people abdicate their responsibility to make prudent decisions and ask God to do the thinking for them. This approach elevates human thinking far beyond the level God views it. It treats God like the deist's cosmic clockmaker, who provided His people with some commandments and principles and then abandoned them to work things out on their own.

The apostle Paul clearly recognized his own inability to effectively live the Christian life in his own strength. He confessed,

> I know that nothing good lives in me, that is, in my sinful nature. For I have the desire to do what is good, but I cannot carry it out. For what I do is not the good I want to do; no, the evil I do not want to do—this I keep on doing. Now if I do what I do not want to do, it is no longer I who do it, but it is sin living in me that does it. So I find this law at work: When I want to do good, evil is right there with me. For in my inner being I delight in God's law; but I see another law at work in the members of my body, waging war against the law of my mind and making me a prisoner of the law of sin at work within my members. (Rom. 7:18–23)

Despite Paul's best intentions, his sinful flesh stifled his desire to act righteously and constantly tempted him to do wrong instead.

Paul thanked God who, by His Spirit, bestowed on him the ability to overcome the selfish desires of his flesh and to follow the leading of the Holy Spirit.

The reality is that our ability to think and to act as we should has been radically marred by sin. Though we are Christians, we cannot assume our thinking is godly. We should not suppose that our best deductions will accomplish God's purposes. Sin appeals to our pride. Sin leads us to use our reason to rationalize our sin. As the deist Benjamin Franklin once quipped, "So convenient a thing it is to be a *reasonable creature*, since it enables one to find or make a reason for every thing one has a mind to do."[1] Sin makes us want to be self-reliant, autonomous from God and others. Pride tells us it is demeaning for us to serve or obey anyone.

There lies the fault in the teachings that say God's greatest desire for people is that they make their own choices using their own wisdom rather than seeking divine guidance. The assumption is that people are fully capable of knowing and doing what is best for them. This view also concludes that autonomy is a higher good than obedience to God's will, and it upholds the idea that the greatest joy people can experience is in making and living with their own decisions. Yet the call of Scripture from beginning to end is not a call for independence but for obedience.

God's Word declares that the Lord "is able to do immeasurably more than all we ask or imagine, according to his power that is at work within us" (Eph. 3:20). Christ is able to accomplish supremely more in and through us than we could ever imagine. If we try to speculate what our lives can become and what God can achieve through us, our human reasoning cannot begin to comprehend these things. How loving, then, would it be for God to set aside His glorious purposes in favor of allowing us to choose our own, obviously inferior plans? Pride can convince us we are better off living as paupers who make our own choices than as children of the king who seek the king's guidance. Jim Elliot, missionary to Ecuador, declared, "In my own experience I have found that the most extravagant dreams of

---

1. H. W. Brands, *The First American: The Life and Times of Benjamin Franklin* (New York: Anchor Books, 2002), 41.

boyhood have not surpassed the great experience of being in the will of God, and I believe that nothing could be better."[2] He would not trade his own goals and achievements, no matter how lofty, for the abiding joy of being in the center of God's will. For the one who truly knows God, the former pales in comparison to the latter.

The nature of sin is such that, on this side of eternity, we are still hampered by its deception and still tempted toward disobedience. The truth of the matter is that our sinfulness means we need God's guidance.

The Nature of Salvation

A fifth foundational reality to consider as we seek to understand God's will is what happens to us when we are converted. Before we became Christians, we defaulted to our selfish, sinful desires. Sin encouraged us to seek autonomy from authority and accountability and to be the masters of our own fate. But when we became followers of Christ, we repented of our sin and submitted to Christ's lordship. At the moment of our conversion, the Holy Spirit entered our life (Acts 2:38).

Jesus described what the Holy Spirit's presence would be like in the disciples' lives. He said, "And I will ask the Father, and he will give you another Counselor to be with you forever—the Spirit of truth. The world cannot accept him, because it neither sees him nor knows him. But you know him, for he lives with you and will be in you. I will not leave you as orphans; I will come to you" (John 14:16–18). Jesus told His disciples not to dread His departure because He would send them *another* (meaning, like the last one) counselor or helper. While the Holy Spirit would not be visible to the disciples as Jesus had been, He would perform the same function in their lives as Jesus did. Jesus had guided the disciples and told them what to do. He had directed where they went and taught them about the kingdom of God. He had determined when to send them out, and He told them what to preach. He decided when they would participate in a miracle. As Jesus prepared to depart, He

2. Elisabeth Elliot, *Shadow of the Almighty: The Life and Testament of Jim Elliot* (New York: Harper and Row, 1958), 196.

knew they would be lost without Him if not for the Holy Spirit's continual guidance.

After Jesus' ascension, the Holy Spirit would guide the disciples into all truth (John 16:13), tell them what He heard from the heavenly Father (John 16:13), prepare them for things to come (John 16:13), give them words to speak (Matt. 10:19–20), and reveal to them what the heavenly Father intended for them (1 Cor. 2:9–12). The Holy Spirit would even help them know what to pray (Rom. 8:26–27).

Because future disciples would be so dependent upon the Holy Spirit's guidance, the apostle Paul exhorted Christians, "Since we live by the Spirit, let us keep in step with the Spirit" (Gal. 5:25). Since the Holy Spirit is to function in us in the same way that Jesus led His disciples, it is critical that we come to recognize the Spirit's activity in our lives. If we want to know how the Holy Spirit will operate in our lives, we should observe how Jesus walked with His disciples. When the Twelve considered the huge, hungry crowd listening to Jesus, their reasonable plan was to send the ravenous crowd away. Jesus countered by instructing them instead to organize everyone into groups of fifty and to prepare to experience a miracle (Luke 9:12–15). When Jesus encountered misguided thinking among His followers, He corrected it. For example, Peter boldly declared that he loved Jesus too much to allow any harm to come to Him. But Jesus rebuked him (Matt. 16:23). Peter's loyalty was admirable and even flattering, but Jesus had surrendered His life to His Father's will, and He insisted that Peter likewise yield his will to Him.

After Christ's ascension, the book of Acts tells us that the Holy Spirit continued to work to accomplish God's purposes. The Holy Spirit led Philip to minister to the Ethiopian eunuch (8:29, 39). The Spirit instructed Peter to eat food he had been taught from his childhood to avoid (10:9–16). He was also directed to go to the house of a Gentile, although this would have been unthinkable to him before (10:17–20). The Holy Spirit forbade Paul from doing missionary work in Asia and Bithynia (16:6–7). Through the prophet Agabus, the same Spirit alerted Paul that he would be arrested by his enemies (21:10–14). Just as Jesus gave practical guidance and instruction to His disciples, so the Holy Spirit provided the early Christians with the directions they needed to spread the gospel throughout the known world (1:8). The nature of salvation is such that all followers of Jesus have this same Holy Spirit ready to give practical guidance.

3. Hearing God Speak His Specific Will

The key to knowing God's will is being able to recognize when He is speaking to you. Even a cursory examination of the Bible reveals that God communicates with individuals. From the first book, Genesis, where God spoke to Adam and Eve in the garden, to the close of the Bible in Revelation, where the risen Christ communicated with the apostle John, the testimony of the Scriptures is that God interacts with His people.

Throughout the biblical record, God did not adhere to one method of communication. In the Old Testament, God communicated through all of these means: creation (Ps. 19:1–2); angels (Gen. 19:1–13; Judg. 6:12; Dan. 9:21); prophets (Deut. 18:18–22; 2 Sam. 12:7; 1 Kings 12:22–24; 20:42; 21:20–23; 2 Kings 1:3–4); dreams (Gen. 37:5–11; Dan. 2:1–45); visions (Gen. 15:1; Isa. 6:1–13); casting lots (Lev. 16:8; Josh. 7:14); Urim and Thummin (Num. 27:21; Neh. 7:65); a gentle voice (1 Sam. 3:4; 1 Kings 19:11–14); fire (Exod. 40:38; Deut. 4:33, 36); a cloud (Exod. 40:38); a burning bush (Exod. 3:1–4); preaching (Jonah 3:4); judgments (Deut. 28:15–68; Amos 4:6–12); symbolic actions (Isa. 20; Jer. 32:6–15; Hos. 1:2); signs (Isa. 7:3, 14; 8:3–4; Hos. 1:4, 6, 9); miracles (Exod. 4:1–8); writing on the wall (Dan. 5); a donkey (Num. 22:21–35); a trumpet (Exod. 19:16, 19; Zeph. 1:16); thunder/lightning/smoke/storms (Exod. 19:16; 20:18; 1 Sam. 12:17–18; Job 40:6); a fleece (Judg. 6:36–40); the sound of marching in the treetops (2 Sam. 5:22–25; 1 Chron. 14:14–17); face-to-face conversation (Exod. 33:11); and personal heart conviction (Neh. 2:12; 7:5).

In the New Testament God also varied His ways of communicating. He spoke through the risen Christ (John 20:14–18; Rev. 1:9–16); nature (Rom. 1:18–20); angels (Matt. 1:20–24; John

20:12; Acts 27:23–25); dreams (Matt. 2:12–13); visions (Acts 9:10–12; 10:9–17; 16:9); prayer (Acts 22:17–21); prophets (Acts 11:28; 21:10–11); casting lots (Acts 1:23–26); signs and wonders (Matt. 24:3; John 20:30–31); preachers (1 Thess. 2:13); Scripture (Matt. 4:4, 7, 10; Luke 24:27, 45); an unbeliever (John 11:49–53); the church (Acts 11:1–18; 15:1–35); a direct word from God the Father (Matt. 16:17; Luke 3:22; 9:35); and the Holy Spirit (Acts 8:29; 13:2).

In addition, Scripture frequently indicates that God spoke to someone without divulging the specific manner in which He communicated (Gen. 8:15; 12:1; Exod. 24:12; Josh. 7:10; 1 Sam. 16:1; Isa. 38:4; Hos. 1:1). Evidently, the *means* God used to speak to people was secondary. *That* God spoke was crucial. God did not always communicate in an audible voice. Perhaps God varied His methods so that people would not trust in a method but in Him. God is infinite. His ways of communicating are innumerable. It is therefore incorrect to conclude that since we have never heard God's audible voice, He does not speak today. God's audible voice is only one of innumerable ways God can communicate with you. If we focus on just one means of God's communication, we may inadvertently miss several other ways He is presently making His will known to us. The key to hearing God's voice, then, is not to figure out a method, but to be spiritually open so that we recognize His voice however He chooses to communicate with us (Mark 8:18).

Those who struggle to hear God's voice might wrongly conclude that God no longer speaks to people as He did during biblical times. Jesus assured His disciples that the Holy Spirit would play an active role in their lives: teaching, convicting, reminding, and helping (John 14:26; 16:7–15). Nowhere in Scripture after the birth of the church in the book of Acts do we find God announcing that He will no longer be communicating directly with His people. Christianity is not merely a religion; it is a relationship. Someone who becomes a Christian does not simply agree to believe a set of doctrines, to adopt a moral lifestyle, or practice certain religious rituals; that person enters into a personal relationship with Jesus Christ (Acts

3:19–20, 26). The nature of any healthy relationship is communication. To assume we can maintain an intimate, growing relationship with the most important person in our life without ever hearing from that person appears untenable. Through our relationship with Christ, He will guide us as He did the twelve disciples. And, as in any relationship, the closer we grow to Him, the better able we are to recognize when He is speaking.

Since the Holy Spirit lives within us, God is always present in our lives. He will guide us by His Holy Spirit. When the twelve disciples walked with Jesus, they could see Him and hear His audible voice. Now we relate to the Holy Spirit, and He has four primary ways in which He speaks to us: through Scripture, prayer, circumstances, and other believers.

Scripture

The Bible is the primary way God communicates with His people. The Holy Spirit will take the words of Scripture and apply them directly to your life. While all of Scripture contains wisdom, the Holy Spirit will use particular passages to convict, encourage, rebuke, and guide you in specific ways (Eph. 6:17). The verses of Scripture are not merely ancient writings from which we can ascertain principles for living. God's Word is active and powerful and able to discern the thoughts and intentions of the heart (Heb. 4:12). When the Holy Spirit speaks to you, He is not creating more Scripture. Rather, He is applying His words directly to your life.

For example, Jesus declared that if we know of someone who has something against us, we should leave what we are doing, even if it is worshipping God, and quickly be reconciled (Matt. 5:23–24). This command is always applicable to all Christians. Yet one day the Holy Spirit might draw your focus directly to this verse with an unusual degree of intensity to help you realize that you have a relationship presently needing attention. You immediately recognize that the Spirit is telling you to go and make things right. In this way the Spirit brings the truth of God's Word directly to bear on your situation. While that verse has always been true for your life, the

Spirit opened your eyes so you could see its direct application to you in that moment.

The Bible does not specifically address every potential decision, such as where to live or which career path to take. However, the Spirit will take the Scriptures and apply them to your life to help you know what to do in these situations. It might be a quickening in your spirit as you read a particular passage. A single verse or entire passage might suddenly jump out at you as you are reading. A friend or your pastor might mention a verse that speaks directly to your situation. If you are sensitive to the Holy Spirit and diligent to spend time in God's Word, you will find clear direction there for your life.

Scripture also serves to authenticate what God is saying to you. God will never tell you to do something He has prohibited in Scripture. Therefore the Bible is the plumb line by which you should evaluate everything you sense the Holy Spirit might be telling you. It is also the standard by which you can measure what others claim God has told them. If someone advises you to do something that contradicts biblical teachings, that person is misleading you.

Prayer

A second way the Holy Spirit speaks to us is through prayer. Prayer is a conversation between us and God. It is not an exercise wherein we list our wishes and render formulaic recitations. It is a time for God to speak to us and to lay His heart and will upon our lives. In fact, we do not know what to pray unless the Holy Spirit guides us (Rom. 8:26–27). While we commune with God, the Holy Spirit may bring particular Scriptures to mind that let us know His thoughts on what we are praying about. As we pray, the Spirit may alert us about God's plan for a certain individual and give us a specific burden to intercede for that person. Again, we ought to confirm everything that we sense God might be saying to us by what the Bible says. Prayer provides a tremendous opportunity for God to speak to us if we enter our prayer times with the proper attitude. Our time with God should be characterized by a reverent spirit, a humble heart, and a willingness to listen to our Creator. The reason more people do not hear from God is that they do not take the time through prayer to listen for His voice.

Circumstances

God also speaks through the circumstances of life. For example, a young couple we know recently sensed God leading them to take a six-week break from their jobs to serve at a medical clinic in Africa. It was going to cost them several thousand dollars. This was a newlywed couple just starting out in their careers. They did not have the necessary funds, so they tried to sell a recreational vehicle to cover some of the expense. All winter they received no inquiries to their advertisement. Some of their friends began to question whether God had really told them to go on the mission trip, since the financial details were not coming together. They met with their church's missions committee and explained their situation. One committee member suggested that perhaps they were aiming too low. Maybe God wanted them to sell their vehicle for *more* than they had been asking. The day after they advertised it at the higher price, it sold. Still being $1,500 short, the couple prepared to borrow the remaining funds. Then their pastor told them their church had taken a collection for them and had raised $1,520.00. They now knew with certainty that God was guiding them to go on the mission trip, for He had used their circumstances to confirm the call. And, though this couple was unaware of it, a church member who was a former nurse approached a local medical clinic to ask for the donation of medical supplies for their mission trip. The clinic gave generously and included many expensive and specialized medicines. The donated supplies were exactly what the African clinic sorely needed. That couple, as you might imagine, experienced a marvelous, life-changing mission trip.

God often will use events in your life to guide you to know what you should do. Whether it is a job offer, an invitation from a mission agency, a surprise check in the mail, a visit from a friend, or a seeming coincidence, God can use any life event, good or bad, to communicate with you. The important factor is not the occurrence itself but how the Holy Spirit interprets your circumstance for you.

When the Spirit leads you through circumstances, His guidance will always be consistent with the clear teaching of Scripture. We do not use our circumstances to interpret Scripture; rather, Scripture helps us understand the events of life.

Fellow Believers

God sometimes sends us a message through other people. In the Old Testament God often spoke to people through the prophets. In the New Testament God also spoke through prophets such as Agabus (e.g., Acts 11:27–30; 21:10–11), but He also communicated through other believers apart from prophetic revelation (e.g., Acts 9:26–27; 15:1–35).

Today the Holy Spirit continues to work through the lives of believers to convey His message to other members of the church body. God designed the church as a body that consists of interdependent parts. Because believers are bound together in the body of Christ, the Holy Spirit can speak through each member of the body to other members. It could be through a phone call or an e-mail coming at just the right moment. It might be through the wise counsel of godly church members who recognize God's activity in your life and who share their observations. This is one reason why it is so crucial to be actively involved in a local church. It allows others the opportunity to walk alongside you and to help you interpret your life circumstances and God's activity around you. You still must evaluate what others tell you by the standard of God's Word, but today, as in biblical times, God chooses to communicate with us through the words and wisdom of other people.

Henry is a member of a large church with eight thousand members. One Sunday during a prayer time, worshippers were invited to kneel at the front of the auditorium to pray. Henry's attention was drawn to a young man who appeared to be earnestly praying. Henry did not know him but felt the Holy Spirit nudging him to leave his seat and go put his arm around the young man and pray for him. Henry began to pray out loud, "Lord, I sense You are speaking to this young man, I ask that You would give him the courage and determination to do whatever it is You are leading him to do."

Suddenly the young man cried out in tears, "It's you! It's you!" He explained that he had just graduated from law school much to the delight of his parents, but he sensed God leading him to not take on a law practice but instead to enroll in seminary to prepare for Christian ministry. He knew his parents would be disappointed, and he wanted to be absolutely certain he was doing the right thing. So during that prayer time, he had knelt and fervently sought confirmation. If the Lord did indeed want him to walk away from his legal career and enter Christian ministry, would God send someone to confirm that direction? "God sent Henry Blackaby" the young man exclaimed, "author of *Experiencing God: Knowing and Doing the Will of God*." Of course when Henry had suddenly felt the prompting of the Holy Spirit to join a stranger praying at the front of the church, he had no idea that by doing so he would be God's mouthpiece to someone desperately seeking a divine word.

Summary

Whether the Holy Spirit speaks through Scripture, prayer, circumstances, or other believers, your recognition of His voice depends upon the condition of your heart (Deut. 30:17–20). When you are insensitive to God's Word and disoriented to His activity, you can witness a miracle and yet not recognize what God is communicating (Mark 6:52). However, if your heart is eager to hear and to obey what God says, He will guide you. As you respond, He will accomplish His purposes through you. It is a matter of spiritual focus. When you pray and ask God to guide you, watch carefully for what happens next. According to Scripture, God *does* speak, but you must be prepared to recognize His voice.

4. The Existence of God's Specific Will

Does God have a specific will for your life? It is clear from Scripture that He does have particular intentions for people. God said to Jeremiah: "Before I formed you in the womb I knew you, before you were born I set you apart; I appointed you as a prophet to the nations" (Jer. 1:5). Clearly God had plans for Jeremiah's life.

Jeremiah could not have rejected those plans and remained in God's will. When the prophet's ministry became difficult, he longed to find another career, but God would not release him from his divine calling (Jer. 15:10–21; 20:7–12).

The psalmist declared,

> For you created my inmost being; you knit me together in my mother's womb. I praise you because I am fearfully and wonderfully made; your works are wonderful, I know that full well. My frame was not hidden from you when I was made in the secret place. When I was woven together in the depths of the earth, your eyes saw my unformed body. All the days ordained for me were written in your book before one of them came to be. How precious to me are your thoughts, O God! How vast is the sum of them! (Ps. 139:13–17)

While there is poetic imagery in these verses, the biblical truth is apparent: God knew the psalmist before he was born, and God had plans for his life. The apostle Paul declared of the psalmist David, "For when David had served God's purpose in his own generation, he fell asleep; he was buried with his fathers and his body decayed" (Acts 13:36). Likewise people such as Moses, Samson, Samuel, Mary, and John the Baptist were all born with a divine purpose for their lives as God worked to carry out His redemptive mission.

The Bible presents numerous examples of God announcing His will for the lives of people from every walk of life. Kings, government leaders, paupers, even harlots and thieves, all found that the Lord had specific plans for them. God told Abraham He intended to do a great work through his life to bless the families of the earth (Gen. 12:1–3). God also directed the lives of people such as Noah, Sarah, Joseph, David, Isaiah, Ezekiel, Jonah, and Elizabeth, the twelve disciples, Paul, and Lydia. In every case these individuals had their own plans for their lives, which God radically altered in order to accomplish His purposes through them. The risen Christ completely changed Paul's heart and commanded him to be His minister to the Gentiles (Acts 26:12–18). One cannot read Scripture without finding God intervening in His people's lives to achieve His purposes. The focus of God's activity was not to give these people a good life. In fact, God's intervention generally complicated their lives and led them to attempt things far beyond their comfort level, their perceived strengths, or their previous experience.

It has been argued that God speaks to people only when He plans an unusual divine event but not in the mundane aspects of our lives. As we said earlier, God does not need to provide a blinding light in the grocery store aisle to lead us to the correct toothpaste. However, He will guide us in matters that meet specific needs in our lives and the lives of others. God told Elijah what and when to eat (1 Kings 19:5–7). Jesus gave instructions to salvage a party (John 2:7). He told people where to fish (John 21:6) and when to fish (Matt. 17:27). These instances might not appear to have enormous significance for God's redemptive purposes, but God chose in these instances to give guidance to people's ordinary concerns.

There are some who take the extreme view that everything we do, right down to the smallest detail of our lives, is prescribed by God. They are like the fellow who stumbled and fell down an entire flight of stairs. As he painfully rose to his feet and brushed himself off, he muttered, "I'm sure glad to get *that* over with!" We are not suggesting that God is a heavenly puppeteer, orchestrating every act of every person. Nevertheless, the Bible does reveal that God had specific things He wanted people to do as part of His redemptive plan for humanity. To disobey Him—as Jonah, Achan, and numerous others mentioned in the Bible discovered—is to place one's life perilously in opposition to God and His will.

Some claim that God rarely speaks to people in our modern time. This view holds that while God may intervene in a life when He has unique, large-scale purposes for that person, most people are ordinary and should not expect God to speak directly to them. This perspective acknowledges that God did speak to men and women in biblical days but concludes that Abraham, Moses, Mary, Peter, and Paul were not ordinary people like you or me. This line of thinking assumes the way of walking with God that Scripture models is applicable only to those with divine assignments of "biblical" proportions. This view also minimizes the breadth of work God is currently accomplishing through countless believers around the world as He fulfills His Great Commission. The Bible is our only authoritative source to know how God will relate to us, so we must assume that the truths found in its pages also apply to us. While God no longer needs people to be in the lineage of the coming Messiah, or to walk along the Galilean roads with Jesus, or to write books of the Bible, He still continues to carry out His saving work in our world as He always has. There are currently more people populating the earth who need to hear the gospel message than ever before. God loves every one of those people and is seeking to bring salvation to them (Matt. 28:18–20). Just as He sent Jonah to evangelize the pagan city of Nineveh, so God continues to call out individuals to specific assignments in His global mission of world redemption. God still draws people to Himself. He is still building His church. As long as God still has work on earth to accomplish, He will continue to direct people's decisions and guide their lives so they can participate in achieving His divine purposes.

It is a grave misunderstanding to assume that God no longer has any significant work that would require Him to speak to us. It is also unrealistic to conclude that people will, on their own initiative, take on the tasks required to accomplish the Great Commission (Matt. 28:18–20). God wants to bring the gospel message to the most dangerous and violently anti-Christian regions in the world. Rarely will a list of pros and cons convince Christians living in the affluent comfort of North America to leave the safety and ease of their homeland. No line of logical reasoning would lead people to conclude they should endanger their lives to share the gospel in countries hostile to Christianity. Surely if every Christian in North America were seeking out and obeying God's will, there would not be so many Christian ministers and resources focused on one continent while countless other areas of the world go without any Christian witness. The salvation of humanity cannot hinge on believers merely doing what makes the most sense to them. God is going to encounter some of us, as He did Moses and Jonah, and send us to Egypt or Nineveh where we are unsure of the outcome or even of our own safety, but where God intends to accomplish a divine work through us.

Summary

Scripture is our guide for Christian living. It is clear from the Bible that God carries out His holy agenda on earth and He chooses to use His people to accomplish His plans. God does not leave us alone to figure out what we think would be best for our life or His kingdom. He loves us too much for that. He will actively communicate His will and implement His lordship in our lives. Church history testifies to numerous occasions when God orchestrated His purposes through His people.

As believers, we have a crucial role in God's kingdom that involves much more than merely avoiding sin. Our primary calling as Christians is to a relationship. Just as Jesus taught the task-oriented Martha that her sister Mary's enjoyment of His presence was preferable to Martha's service (Luke 10:38–42), so the main focus of our lives ought to be on developing a growing, intimate relationship with Christ (Phil. 3:8–10). The closer we walk with Him, the easier it becomes to recognize His voice. If we neglect our relationship with Christ, then we will have difficulty and find ourselves in desperate situations where we need immediate, divine guidance. However, if we live each day in close communion with God, we will not require a major soul searching to know what God wants us to do next. Rather, those decisions will become clear as a natural progression of what He has been doing in our lives to that point. A close relationship with God will compel us to submit to His will and to live in a way that accomplishes His purposes and glorifies Him. We do not know the future as God does; neither are our ways like God's. But as we surrender our will to His and seek to follow the leading of the Holy Spirit, He will guide us in the same manner Jesus led His disciples.

5. Case Studies

The truths of Scripture are not meant to be accepted merely intellectually. They are intended to be lived experientially (John 15:14). The application of biblical truths to our lives is critical when we seek to know God's will. The case studies in this volume are three examples of life situations in which people need to know God's clear direction.

Case 1: Susan and the Choice of a College

Susan's decision is significant for many reasons. The particular college she attends will have a huge impact on her future. Certain professors might challenge her to pursue a specific field of study. Some colleges might offer areas of specialization that others do not. The degree she earns will open various doors to her for future career opportunities and salary levels, or even further education. God knows what He intends to do through Susan's life and which college will best prepare her for that future.

Likewise, the college she chooses is important because God expects her to be on a mission with Him while she is a student. Her Christian witness on campus may result in certain college students coming to faith in Christ. Her service in a local church while she is a student may bring numerous blessings to her congregation. Her involvement in a Christian collegiate organization may allow Susan unique opportunities to go on international mission trips or to develop her leadership and evangelistic abilities. God may have certain people He intends for Susan's life to influence while she is a student. God knows which church and campus ministry will best suit her and allow her to be of maximum service for Him while she is in college.

The relationships Susan forms as a student could have both immediate and lasting effects on her life, helping her to grow as a Christian. She could enter into friendships that will last for years or even a lifetime. She might get to know prayer partners who will strengthen her devotional life. She may face personal hardships during her college years and receive great encouragement from her fellow students. God knows which school will best provide the kinds of friends and Christian support Susan will need during her college years.

God loves Susan with an infinite love. He knows how to maximize the effectiveness of her life. God also knows how to bring joy and peace to Susan. He knows which college will best prepare her for what He intends to do through her in the coming years. God knows if there is a particular collegiate minister or pastor who will leave a lasting impression on her. He knows if there is another college student who will become Susan's best friend and will encourage her during those pivotal years. Because God loves Susan, He will guide her to make the best decision possible. So, what should Susan do to ensure that she chooses the right college?

A Close Relationship

Susan must pray and spend time studying God's Word. Too many people wait until an immediate decision looms in front of them before they begin to search out the Lord's direction. The best way to hear from God is to spend time with Him regularly. As Susan daily seeks God's guidance, she will become familiar with His voice. When people neglect to ask for God's counsel, they can find themselves far from where God would have them. Then, when they finally seek God's will, major adjustments are required to align their lives back where God wants them to be. However, if Susan habitually does whatever God tells her, she will find the next step of obedience is not necessarily a dramatic leap. She will recognize it as the natural progression in the direction God has been clearly guiding her.

If Susan walked with God during high school, she will discover that God has already largely prepared her for her entrance into college. He may have led her to choose classes in high school that are now required for her college program. He certainly will have led her to work hard toward a GPA that satisfies the college entrance requirements. Issues such as scholarships, references, or other matters will fall into place for this new stage in her life because she listened to God during the years preceding this important decision.

Conversely, if Susan went her own way during secondary school, she may discover that important prerequisites for university admission are not in place. Her GPA may be too low for the program that would best suit her. She may have forfeited opportunities for financial support. Because she has not walked with God carefully in the years preceding this important step in her life, she will discover that life is more complicated for her and there are several loose ends she must now sort out. It is not that God is unwilling to guide her now. But had she sought His leading earlier, she would already be on the path He had for her.

Total Submission

To know God's will, Susan will need to surrender her own will to Him. There is a profound difference between genuinely seeking God's way and merely asking God to affirm what we want to do ourselves. Using her own wisdom, Susan might be distracted by a school's location or its prestige. She might be persuaded by the advice of her friends or parents. But if she makes herself totally open to God's leading, He might take her on an adventure she would otherwise have missed.

George Müller was diligent in pursuing the Lord's guidance and was keenly aware that he must hear from God in order to be effective in his pastoral ministry. He wrote,

> Rather than presuming to know what is best for the hearers, I ask the Lord to graciously teach me the subject I should speak about, or the portion of His word I should explain. Sometimes I will have a particular subject or passage on my mind before asking Him. If, after prayer, I feel persuaded that I should speak on that subject, I study it, but still leave myself open to the Lord to change it if He pleases. Frequently, however, I have no subject in my mind before I pray. In this case, I wait on my knees for an answer, trying to listen for the voice of the Spirit to direct me. Then, if a passage or subject is brought to mind, I again ask the Lord if that is His will. Sometimes I ask repeatedly, especially if the subject or text is a difficult one. If after prayer, my mind is

peaceful about it, I take this to be the text. But I still leave myself open to the Lord for direction, in case He decides to alter it, or if I have been mistaken.[3]

According to Müller, the Lord was always faithful to lead him. He stated, "I never remember . . . a period . . . that I ever sincerely and patiently sought to know the will of God by the teaching of the Holy Ghost, through the instrumentality of the Word of God, but I have always been directed rightly. But if honesty of heart and uprightness before God were lacking, or if I did not patiently wait upon God for instruction, or if I preferred the counsel of my fellow men to the declarations of the Word of the living God, I made great mistakes."[4]

Müller strongly believed the greatest single factor in finding God's will on a matter was the absolute surrender of his personal volition to God. Susan will need to set aside all of her biases, fears, and desires and genuinely seek to hear what God tells her about her college education. The testimony of Müller and countless other believers through the ages assures her that God is true to His word and He will reveal to her things she could not know on her own (Jer. 33:3).

Yielding ourselves to God does not mean we are doomed to misery. Some misguided Christians assume that God never gives us what we want or what will make us happy. We have heard people claim, "Don't say what you don't want to do. Sure enough, that is exactly what God will make you do!" That is unbiblical. God wants us to experience joy. The psalmist testified, "Delight yourself in the LORD and he will give you the desires of your heart" (Ps. 37:4). In yielding to the Lord, we do not sacrifice our happiness on the altar of God's will. Actually, our own preferences often rob us of the joy God knows we could experience. We become enticed by worldly attractions. We are enamored with temporal things and cannot see

---

3. George Müller, *The Autobiography of George Müller*, ed. Diana L. Matisko (New Kensington, PA: Whitaker House, 1985), 31.
4. Basil Miller, George Müller, *The Man of Faith: A Biography of One of the Greatest Prayer-Warriors of the Past Century* (Grand Rapids: Zondervan, 1941), 51.

the future. So we choose what seems good to us and we miss God's best. But when we surrender our will to the Lord so that our desires correspond to God's will, we are best prepared to experience true joy. God knows far better than we do which path will bring abundant life. We must trust our lives into His hands and believe His will is best. That is why Oswald Chambers concluded, "It is more and more impossible for me to have programmes and plans because God alone has the plan, and our plans are only apt to hinder Him, and make it necessary for Him to break them up."[5]

Our relationship with God is more important than the degree we earn or the career we choose. If God were to reveal all of His plans for our future at once, we might rush off in an attempt to accomplish God's assignments and in the process neglect our relationship with Him. God always gives enough guidance for us to take the next step. Then He waits for us to respond in obedience. In Susan's case, God might lead her to attend college, but He might not reveal to her what degree she will ultimately earn. Perhaps God has plans for Susan to earn a medical degree. However, she may lack the confidence at the outset of her college experience to attempt such a demanding program. God might lead Susan to enroll in a seemingly less ambitious bachelor of science degree for the present. Once she begins college, God knows she will excel in her studies and soon attract the attention of the medical school. Having obeyed God thus far, it will not be a large step to convert her program into a premed degree.

Spiritual Markers

To understand what God wants her to do next, Susan should review the spiritual markers of her life. These are the moments in her past when God clearly spoke and guided her in a particular direction. God does not act randomly. He is purposeful in His ways. Because God knows what He intends for your life when you are an adult, He will begin the process when you are young. Events and

---

5. David McCasland, *Oswald Chambers: Abandoned to God* (Grand Rapids: Discovery House, 1993), 109.

life experiences can seem random or independent from others and yet actually be the deliberate, progressive work of God preparing you for what He intends to do through you later. If you look back over your life and highlight the various spiritual markers, you will discover that God has systematically been preparing your life for what He knows is to come. Identifying the direction God has been leading you helps you to understand where He is guiding you now.

For example, a review of Susan's spiritual markers might include the following:

+ She gave her life to Christ at ten years old. Her Sunday school teacher explained that becoming a Christian meant Jesus was her Lord, and to follow Him she must do whatever He told her. Susan recalls that even as a young girl, she sincerely yielded her life to God and promised she would do anything and go anywhere God told her.

+ When Susan was twelve, she had a profound encounter with God during summer Bible school at her church. A missionary from Africa told of the tremendous suffering people endured because of their poverty. Susan was deeply moved and wept as she heard how many children died because they lacked the most rudimentary medical care. During a dedication time, Susan offered herself for whatever way God might want to use her life.

+ When Susan was fifteen, her high school science teacher took her aside and commended her aptitude for biology. He advised her to consider medical school. Susan still remembers the powerful way she sensed the Holy Spirit confirming what her teacher was saying.

+ Throughout the following year, Susan found herself especially drawn to incidents in the Scriptures where people were healed. As she wrote in her journal during her quiet times, she made numerous notes about God's care for the sick. It seemed as if every time she opened her Bible, Susan's attention was captured by the stories of those who were ill and suffering.

+ At seventeen, Susan went to youth camp. That summer the speaker gave a powerful challenge to young people to be willing to do whatever God told them. As she listened, Susan felt an overwhelming sense that God was calling her to medical missions. She knew that to do anything else would be to disobey God's clear call on her life. During the altar call, Susan sought out a counselor to pray with her as she yielded her life to this calling.

If these were some of Susan's spiritual markers, they would provide much guidance as she planned for university. A call to medical missions would obviously steer her toward medical schools. She would need to investigate programs and schools that could lead her into the medical field. She might focus on a Christian university with a special program for medical missions or a university that provides specialized training that would open doors for her on the mission field. While her spiritual markers can't make her decision for her, they will provide a clear sense of direction and make it much easier to measure her possibilities against all God has been saying to her thus far. Rather than merely choosing based on pros and cons, she will evaluate her options in light of God's activity throughout her life. This involves more than merely taking a survey of her life to see where her aptitudes lie. Rather, she is reviewing how God has led her through the various events of her life. The focus of spiritual markers is on God and His activity.

Confirmation

Susan should spend regular time reading her Bible and praying. Scripture reading and prayer are not simplistic approaches to decision making. God told Joshua the key to his success would be meditating upon and obeying God's Word (Josh. 1:7–8). As Susan studies it, the Holy Spirit will apply God's Word directly to her situation. The Spirit will use Scripture to convict her in areas where her life needs adjusting. Many respected Christian leaders such as George Müller, Hudson Taylor, and Oswald Chambers recounted that God used particular Scripture verses to guide them to take specific actions. Likewise, as Susan prays over the possibilities that lie before her, the Holy Spirit can give her a distinct peace about which university is the one God wants her to attend. As Susan asks the Lord to guide her, she must be spiritually alert so that she does not miss what the Lord does next. Opportunities that present themselves should be scrutinized against the backdrop of what God already has told her.

It is important for Susan to record in a journal what she is hearing God say each day. God may not give her the entire answer at once. He may lead her step-by-step as she daily reads the Scriptures. One reason God leads people in this manner is because He is more interested in their relationship with Him than in their activity (cf. Isa. 1:10–20). If God revealed His complete plan for all of Susan's life at the outset of her college years, she might be tempted to neglect her daily relationship with the Lord and instead focus on doing what God had told her. Susan might become frustrated and immobilized if she seeks to know God's complete plan for her life before she begins moving forward. By revealing His will to Susan step-by-step, God keeps her in a position of daily communion with Him, where she must keep her focus on Him rather than on His plan.

Perhaps Susan is intrigued one day as she reads Ephesians 6:1–2, "Children, obey your parents in the Lord, for this is right. 'Honor your father and mother'—which is the first commandment with a promise." Susan knows that her godly father has some strong feelings about where she should attend college. She understands that whatever decision she makes, she must do it in a way that honors her parents. On another day she reads 1 Corinthians 10:31, "So whether you eat or drink or whatever you do, do it all for the glory of God." Susan realizes that in choosing a school her motive should be to glorify God. In focusing on God rather than on her own preferences, she will view prospective schools in a different light. In 1 Corinthians 12:18 she reads that God is the one who adds members to the church body. In the process of leading her to a university, God also will be guiding her to become involved in a particular church, so even though more than one college may appeal to her, the proximity of a mission-minded church will influence her decision. As Susan identifies what God is saying to her each day through His Word and through prayer, a picture will begin to emerge of the school God wants her to attend.

The Holy Spirit often speaks through fellow believers. Certainly Susan should seek counsel from her godly parents as well as her pastor or youth minister. She should enlist others to pray for her as she makes this weighty decision. While she should never substitute advice from another believer for a word from God, Susan should be aware that God often chooses to speak through other believers. It may be that a physician who is a member of her church takes a special interest in Susan. The doctor might offer practical counsel that Susan recognizes as a word from God. God places people in a church body to be interdependent (1 Cor. 12). Fellow members may see things in us we do not recognize ourselves. When George Truett was a young man, he was preparing to be an attorney. But his fellow church members had observed God's hand on his life and were convinced God was calling him into Christian ministry. They actually called an ordination service for Truett without even telling him in advance! Truett would eventually serve as the revered pastor of First Baptist Church of Dallas for four decades.

God also speaks to people through circumstances. Susan should do her homework! She ought to search for the schools that can best train her for what she knows God has called her to do. She might correspond with the most promising schools to see what scholarships or assistance they can offer. Available housing can be an issue. Transportation and opportunities for part-time jobs are also considerations. The point is not that Susan simply makes a list and chooses the school that offers the most. Rather, by investigating various schools, she gives God the opportunity to speak to her through the circumstances. For example, Susan might find that a degree from one nationally renowned medical school would bring her extra status. But she may be impressed with a smaller, lesser-known school that will allow her more experience and time working closely with her professors. Or, as she visits various campuses, she might meet a collegiate minister who knows her father and who mentions he would love to have her work with his ministry. Again, the key is not to compile a list of pros and cons and choose the location with the longest pros list. That is how non-Christians make their choices. But, as Susan meets people and contacts various schools, God has new avenues to speak to her. It is what God says to Susan through her investigation of schools that is critical to her decision.

As Susan has sought God's will through reading her Bible and praying, as well as seeking the counsel of other believers and listening to God speak through her circumstances, she has been waiting on the Lord for the assurance that will tell her to proceed in a specific direction. This is ultimately how she will know she is right where she ought to be. At times everything can look like it is perfect. One school might offer everything she needs. It might provide the most generous scholarships and boast the most comfortable student housing. Yet, despite all the seeming advantages to attending the school, Susan might feel uneasy in her spirit about enrolling. Her friends might urge her to enroll where they are going, and yet the Holy Spirit may not release her to do so. It is always unwise to proceed with a decision if you are unsure of God's leading. It is better to keep praying and seeking until you are sure.

We know a man who was enjoying a successful career as an actuary. He lived a comfortable life on acreage in Arkansas with his growing family. But God began to give him a restless spirit. Through a series of events, he came to realize God was calling him to resign his job and to enroll in seminary. But which one? He investigated all the seminaries in his denomination but did not feel at peace about any of them. Then he learned of the seminary in Canada of which Richard was president. Enrolling there seemed ridiculous. As an American student studying in Canada, he would likely be unable to work. Uprooting his wife and four children and taking them to a foreign country certainly did not look like the logical thing to do. When he heard that Richard would be speaking at a church in Little

Rock, he and his wife decided to attend the Sunday service to hear him. As they drove to the church that morning, they practiced a song based on Philippians 1:6 that they were to sing at their church that evening. It talked of how God would complete the work He had begun in them. As they discussed this truth, they speculated about how God would bring to fruition all that He had been doing lately in their lives in calling them into ministry and instructing them to attend seminary. When it was time for Richard to preach, the first words out of his mouth were, "I am here today to tell you that what God begins, He always completes." Then he began his message based on Philippians 1:6. The couple immediately sensed they were in the middle of a divine appointment. They later met with Richard and through that conversation they recognized God was clearly leading them. The man moved his family to Canada to attend seminary. Then he remained in Canada and went on to earn a law degree. During all that time he and his family were strategically involved in several new church plants. Today he still serves as the director of the denomination's foundation.

As this man went through the process of seeking God's will, he sensed God leading in a direction he himself would not have considered. God spoke to him through His Word, through prayer, and through the wise counsel of others. The church service that Sunday was when God used circumstances to confirm His leading and to give the couple peace with their decision. The Holy Sprit assured them they were in the center of God's will. Events would prove that God had indeed guided them. Likewise, Susan can know the peace that God has guided her to a specific school if she will carefully follow His leading and then wait on the Holy Spirit to give her an assurance that she is in God's will.

Case 2: The Marriage Decision for Joe and Nancy

Apart from deciding to follow Christ, choosing a spouse is the most important issue we face. Our life partner exercises enormous influence on our future, our children, our career, our social relationships, and our usefulness to God. God intends to guide us in the decisions that have the most impact on our lives and on our effectiveness in His service. Because so much hinges on whom we marry, Joe and Nancy are wise to seek the mind of the Lord in this matter, and when they do, God will be pleased to guide them.

First, as in Susan's case, both Joe and Nancy should be maintaining a daily, intimate walk with their Lord. If they have been carefully following the Holy Spirit's leading over the two-year period of their courtship, they will be much better able to know if the Lord is leading them into marriage. Many couples are careless in the standards they uphold while they are dating. They do not keep their relationship God-centered; then when a pregnancy occurs or pressure from family and friends comes, they become confused and don't know what to do. But when a couple is seeking to hear from God and to honor Him throughout their relationship, it is far easier to recognize whether God is leading them into the next stage of their relationship or telling them to break up.

Second, God's Word gives wisdom and clear guidelines that can serve as a basis for their decision. For example, Scripture exhorts believers not to be joined with unbelievers (2 Cor. 6:14). If Joe is a Christian and Nancy is not, Joe need go no further in seeking God's leading. Light and darkness cannot be joined. The Bible also charges wives to respect their husbands (Eph. 5:33). Nancy may have affectionate and romantic feelings for Joe, but if she does not genuinely respect who he is, what he is doing, and where he is going, she should not marry him. Likewise, in Ephesians husbands are commanded to love their wives in such a way that they would lay their lives down for them (Eph. 5:25). While Joe may be attracted to Nancy, if he refuses to adjust his life to hers or to make allowances for her, then he is not prepared to marry her. These are some guiding principles the Bible provides that help to screen possible marriage partners. They tell us certain kinds of people *not* to marry or situations in which the marriage would go against scriptural teachings. But they fall short of identifying the one person God knows is best for us. However, God is ready and willing, through His communication with us, to take us further and bring us to that person.

Obviously, Joe and Nancy need to have feelings for one another. Some people claim that feelings have nothing to do with whom you marry. All that matters, they say, is that you determine the one God wants you to marry and then get married out of obedience to God, regardless of whether you are attracted to the person or not. This is dangerous counsel! Romantic love between a husband and wife is not only good; it is biblical (see Song of Solomon). There may be times when it seems obvious or inevitable that two people should marry but there are no romantic feelings between them. Perhaps Joe and Nancy are the only single young adults in their small church. Maybe they have been dating because, in their small community, the options are scarce. Marrying someone because he or she appeared to be the only option has been the foundation of countless divorces. God created romantic love, and He intends for it to be a part of the marriage relationship. If mutual attraction is not evident between Joe and Nancy, they ought to consider whether they are meant only to be friends.

Conversely, feelings of romantic love are insufficient on their own to justify marriage. The world today is obsessed with romance. Various media bombard us with images promoting lust and glorifying sex. Christians can easily be swept away by the same infatuation. Feeling strong chemistry toward someone does not indicate God is leading you to marry that individual. Feelings alone cannot dictate your marriage partner. Hollywood certainly is not the authority on romance, no matter how many "love stories" it churns out. Ephesians 5:33 exhorts women to nurture more than romantic feelings toward their spouse. Women are to demonstrate respect for their husbands. True love is not self-serving. True love lays its life down for another. If Joe and Nancy love each other romantically and are willing, even compelled, to put the other first, then they should confirm what they are feeling by comparing their spiritual markers.

In Susan's case we mentioned that spiritual markers can greatly help in decision making. Both Joe and Nancy should review the times in their lives where God clearly guided them in making decisions. When God unites two people in marriage, they become one flesh (Matt. 19:5–6). Therefore, whatever God has done in their lives separately now comes to bear on their union. The joining of two individuals does not nullify what God has done previously in each of their lives. Rather, marriage creates a synergy in which both partners are better able to experience and achieve all God has purposed for them.

As Joe and Nancy carefully examine their spiritual markers, they will see if marriage to each other is consistent with what God has been doing in their lives individually. They may discover numerous intersecting and merging threads in God's activity in their lives. For example, God may have been working strongly in Joe's life about personal holiness. He attended a men's conference, where he was deeply convicted that he should live a life of purity for the sake of his future wife and children. When Nancy was a child, her father was unfaithful to her mother and abandoned the family. Nancy felt the deep pain that the sin of adultery brings into a home. As a result, for years she has prayed earnestly that the man she marries will be a faithful man of integrity. Further, God may have led both Joe and Nancy to value their involvement in their local church. Perhaps they both experienced profound encounters with God through which He led them to undertake leadership roles in their congregation. Both of them know that whoever they marry must be committed to the church. Possibly both had a significant time in their lives when God placed a burden for missions on their heart, and both may have already been on short-term mission trips. As Joe and Nancy review what God has done in the past, they may discover that God has placed their lives on the same trajectory. It may be that He has been preparing them separately to match and complement one another. This would provide strong evidence that God is leading them to marry.

Unfortunately, some couples become infatuated with one another, or with the concept of being in love, and so they disregard everything God has been doing in their lives up to that point. Joe may have felt called into Christian ministry but then met Nancy, who may have come from a troubled, dysfunctional background.

Though professing to be a Christian, she is weak and unstable in her faith. They might marry with feelings of love for one another. But when Joe begins the process of preparing for his calling, he will discover his wife is reluctant to make the necessary sacrifices. Not feeling any sense of call to ministry herself, Nancy only wants her husband to get a job so they can afford to purchase their first house and start a family. When Joe becomes involved in ministry activities, Nancy grows jealous of the time he gives to the church. Ultimately Joe could end up surrendering his efforts to become a pastor and live the rest of his life wondering what might have been if he had been supported in his call to the ministry.

When two people marry, both must make adjustments if they are to live together successfully. However, marriage does not eliminate a person's dreams or God-given passions. Rather, marriage ought to enable those things to become a reality. If marrying someone means that a man or woman must set aside a calling from God, the couple ought to carefully consider whether God is leading them together in the first place. God is not haphazard with people's lives. He would not lay a burden on Nancy's heart for international missions for years and then lead her to marry someone who has no interest in missions at all. God does not call us toward one thing and simultaneously tell us to marry someone who will prevent us from following through with His leading. All too often we have seen young people seriously respond to God's clear calling to a certain vocation or ministry, only to abandon that calling because an opportunity for marriage presented itself. Some of the most unhappy and frustrated Christians we know now feel trapped in a relationship that prevents them from serving God as they know they were called to do. A wise couple will examine their individual spiritual pilgrimages to determine if marrying each other is the evident progression in God's activity in their lives.

Joe and Nancy would be astute to seek the counsel of godly friends, pastors, and mature couples in their church. People in love are notorious for ignoring the advice and cautions of others who "just don't understand" their situation. This closed mind-set has led to major marital problems. If a union is initiated by God, other

Christians will see the evidence. People will notice if Nancy's relationship with Joe brings her joy and confidence. If Joe is growing more serious about his faith and excited about his future, then other believers will affirm their relationship. However, if people notice that Joe and Nancy seem to be constantly experiencing conflict and strong disagreements or if Joe dominates Nancy or discounts her opinions and dreams, then friends may wisely suggest that Joe's influence on Nancy's life is not what God intends for it to be. At times people are blinded by infatuation, or they worry that this is their only opportunity to be married and have children. Many foolishly convince themselves that they can reform their spouse after the wedding. That's why it is good for every couple to listen to the sober counsel of loving, godly friends to help them see clearly and not through the distorted lenses of emotions.

A final means of determining if God is leading Joe and Nancy to marry is the test of joy and peace. Jesus intends for His followers to experience joy (John 15:11; 17:13) and peace (John 14:27; Phil. 4:7). The inevitable result of the Holy Spirit's work in a believer's life is joy and peace (Gal. 5:22). If doubts plague one or both members of a couple, something is wrong. A sense of deep peace and joy in your spirit is strong indication that you are aligned with God's will.

Two important questions regarding marriage and God's will are often asked: "Is there one and only one person out there God intends for me to marry? And if I miss that person, does that mean I will never be married?" The infinite God knows what is best for us. He is aware of every person inhabiting the earth, and He knows out of all those people which one is best suited to you. You should not be filled with fear that you might make a mistake. Nor should you roam the globe, making sure you have not missed the perfect bride or groom. Walking with God day by day is a natural process, and as you follow Him and trust Him, He will lead you to the life partner He has chosen for you.

It is true we can sometimes miss out on God's best. If God were not sovereign, we would all be without hope. In every area of our walk with God, He is always leading us from where we are to where He wants us to be. If we did not follow Him as we should have earlier in our lives, we might have missed those wonderful opportunities to meet and marry that someone who would have been God's special gift to us. However, that does not mean God will not grant us marriage and a fulfilled life. Failing to walk with God always carries a cost, but God's grace is far reaching. It can redeem us from any situation and bring us God's best for that stage of our lives. So you need not berate yourself or become obsessed with what might have been had you been trusting God at an earlier age. God always has a perfect will for your life as of this moment. As you wholly trust God right now and seek Him with all your heart, He will guide you into that will today.

Case 3: The Choice of a Local Church for David and Rachel

First, David and Rachel need to be assured that God is the One who adds members to a church body. First Corinthians 12:18 states, "But in fact God has arranged the parts in the body, every one of them, just as he wanted them to be." Scripture teaches that Christ is the head of the church (Col. 1:18). Likewise, Jesus claimed that He would build His church (Matt. 16:18). Through the church, Christ is actively working to redeem humanity. As a result, God fashions each congregation so that it is fully equipped to carry out the assignment given to it by its Head.

Christ has given every congregation the task of carrying out the Great Commission (Matt. 28:18–20; Acts 1:8). Included in that worldwide mandate are many specific responsibilities. Some churches are given a special burden to reach out to the local university, or to a nearby prison, or to immigrants who do not speak English, or to the inner city. Because each area of ministry requires specific equipping, Christ will add members to each body as necessary to carry out the congregation's commission.

Therefore, David and Rachel need to approach this decision with a God-focused perspective rather than a self-centered view. Each of the options described in their story is a fine church, and David and Rachel could grow and serve in each of them. While they do want to find a church home that will meet their family's needs, their larger concern is where God wants to place them in order to accomplish His purposes through that particular congregation. The question therefore is not merely, "What's in it for us?" but, "To which congregation is Christ adding us?" The church that offers the most ministries to them and their family is not necessarily the church where God would have them. God knows if David and Rachel's family would flourish in a smaller church that offered numerous opportunities to serve and in which they were able to become good friends with the pastor and his wife. They must trust that God knows things they are unaware of themselves. God knows if the oratorically gifted pastor of Second Church will be resigning in six months. God knows if First Church is about to undergo a painful church split. This does not mean God would never lead people to join a church that currently has no pastor or that will experience conflict. It does mean that in every decision we make, we cannot entirely trust what our own limited perception tells us. We must rely on God's wisdom instead and keep going back to the truth that He is the one who adds members to a church body.

Second, to discern God's will, it bears repeating that David and Rachel must be daily walking with their Lord so they are receptive to His leading. They must release their will to God and be prepared to become members of whatever church He leads them to join. It may be tempting to choose the church that is the most convenient or prestigious or entertaining; but if they are walking closely with God, their hearts will be open to what He has in store for them. God may want them to have a new experience that challenges and stretches their family. He knows their children's future. He has the right to place them in whatever church He chooses.

The safest way to know where God is leading them is to be daily reading His Word and praying. They will not stumble across a Bible verse one morning that says in red letters, "Thou shalt join First Church." However, the Holy Spirit can use the words of Scripture to clearly lead His people in making decisions. For example, David and Rachel may both be reading through the book of Acts and become deeply impacted by the way the Holy Spirit began churches in homes and places outside traditional church buildings. They might share with each other that although they have always been a part of traditional churches, they are both becoming intrigued with participating in a church plant. Or perhaps they have been studying the book of Judges. Over and over again they read how one generation of Israelites would follow God but their children would choose to reject His ways. As they discuss this sad truth, David and Rachel determine that God is guiding them to do whatever is necessary to ensure that their children grow up to love and serve Him the way they do. While this truth is relevant to all Christian parents, David and Rachel may sense God saying that this needs to be the prominent concern in their choice of a church family. So, they discern that God is pointing them to Second Church, where the children's programming is strong. Or, perhaps as they read their Bibles, God begins to show them Ephesians 5:15–17 and other verses that speak of being wise managers of their time. David and Rachel feel convicted over the way they have allowed their careers and commitments to create a harried and stressful life. They know their children are suffering the consequences of their frenetic lifestyle. They sense God leading them to make wiser use of their time. They also realize that because of the distance to Second Church, the commuting time would probably cause them to miss church activities and eventually to resent having to drive their children to their weekly church events. The distance also would make it difficult for them to invite their friends and neighbors to church. These considerations help direct them to join First Church, which is closest to them and requires the least travel time.

Each of the verses mentioned above were in David and Rachel's Bibles all along. God did not have to inspire additional Scriptures to guide them specifically. Likewise, all three Scripture passages are the divine Word of God and are therefore relevant to every believer. But without the discerning guidance of the Holy Spirit, David and Rachel could become confused and frustrated in trying to apply them all to their current situation. The Holy Spirit must take these biblical truths and help this family apply them to their particular situation at this time in their lives. If David and Rachel were making this same decision ten years later, these verses would still be meaningful and applicable, but the Spirit might use them to bring about an entirely different decision. Every verse of Scripture is true and ought to be followed. But the Holy Spirit can emphasize some verses for you and direct you to certain passages as a way of leading by God's Word for your current stage of life.

Third, God's people can be His messengers to David and Rachel. They would be wise to visit each church. They ought to attend a small-group Bible study in each congregation so that they have the opportunity to meet people and gain a better understanding of what each church is like. They might make an appointment to meet with each pastor. If a pastor is too busy to meet with them, that could be a message in itself. When talking with the pastors, David and Rachel ought to ask questions about the mission and direction of the church. They should find out what is on the pastor's heart. Churches tend to take on many of the values and priorities of their pastor. Praying with the pastor could tell them about the minister's concern for people in the church. Likewise, worshipping in each congregation provides a valuable opportunity for the Spirit to speak to David and Rachel. It might be that they feel refreshed in the worship at Third Church in a way they have never before experienced. Perhaps they are both deeply moved by the sermon at Second Church. The Spirit might impress on them that they need to be regularly attending a church where they can be fed and challenged spiritually each week, even if it means they must drive farther to get there.

Ultimately, the Spirit can grant David and Rachel a sense of peace to assure them which congregation they ought to join. The joy and peace of the Lord is far different from the religious enthusiasm that some churches work up among their members. It does not always come from the largest or most beautiful church. It might be the least likely congregation for their apparent and perceived needs, and yet the Spirit can produce a strong sense of peace whenever David and Rachel attend.

The church where Richard accepted a pastorate right out of seminary was small and struggling when he arrived as pastor. A church down the street of a similar denomination was one of the largest congregations in the nation. It had a spacious, attractive, high-tech building. The music was excellent in quality, and the church offered all the latest children's programming. Richard's church could not begin to compete with this megachurch for new members. Still, they saw several wonderful families join their smaller church after visiting the larger congregation. Often the new members would tell Richard that it didn't make sense to them. The other church had fine preaching, great music, and far more programs and opportunities for their children. Yet they could gain no peace about joining there. They would come to Richard's small congregation and sense a peace in their spirits that told them they had come home. Soon, they would become actively involved in serving and leading. The church members would reach out to their children and see them come to faith in Christ. Their families would experience the joy of being a part of a growing, loving church family, and they would realize that God had wisely guided them to the place where they could thrive. If these families had taken out a sheet of paper and listed the pros and cons of each church, they quickly would have concluded that the larger church had everything their family needed. Yet the Holy Spirit would not release them to join it.

The Holy Spirit seeks to guide people in the same way Jesus led His disciples. He knows where we can serve Him most effectively. He knows which church needs us most. He knows which congregation includes people who will take a genuine interest in our children and who will pray for and care for our families. Those who are willing to wait until the Holy Spirit grants them peace in their decision will find that the Spirit will accurately guide them to the congregation He wants them to join.

6. Conclusion

We have presented what some call the traditional view of God's will. Simply put, it holds that God does have a specific will for your life and He will guide you to find it. If the testimony of Scripture is our guide, then there is no shortage of examples of God doing exactly this. Church history also is filled with examples of God making His will clearly known to individuals.

The danger in seeking God's specific will for your life is that you can inadvertently concentrate more on God's will than on God. God ought to be your focus. You do not discover God's will. God reveals it to you out of the intimacy of your walk with Him. God chooses to do this because He wants to involve your life in accomplishing His redemptive purposes. Seeking God's will is not a self-centered exercise. We should not expect God to devise all kinds of wonderful plans that will make us happy, comfortable, and safe. Rather, God's will is to redeem humanity. We can only comprehend God's will for us when we understand God's purposes in our world.

To understand God's will, we must be able to recognize when He is speaking. God is a Person. Christianity involves a close relationship with that Person. It should not surprise us that a personal God would communicate with us. God does not merely give us doctrines or morals; He gives us Himself. Yet we are not equals in the relationship. God is infinite. He knows the future. He knows what is in the hearts and minds of every person. He also has His own intentions. Therefore, whenever we make a decision apart from God, we do so in the midst of ignorance and ambiguity. It is only as we seek God and His guidance that we can expect to be in the center of His will. Those who have sought to know God's will and who have experienced God working powerfully through their lives will testify that there is no greater way to live the one life God has granted to each of us.

A Wisdom View Response to the Specific-Will View

GARRY FRIESEN

Introduction

I was impressed with the biblical and effective argument for the specific-will view. The Blackabys' discussion on "Foundational Truths" would make a good introduction to what all of our presentations should be. They have a genuine faith commitment to

Scripture and see its authority above tradition, experience, and our faulty reason, which is demonstrated by dozens of passages used to support their view.

Their foundational truths include serving a God who deserves and requires obedience to His will in all things. They are captured by God's redemptive purposes and take sin seriously. They know that without God's guidance we will soon fall into a treacherous pit. They glory in God's salvation, which includes the new covenant promise of the indwelling, empowering Holy Spirit. Their essay reveals pastoral hearts and great wisdom.

I have described the *Experiencing God* book as "the traditional view with an edge," but in this essay I sensed their best presentation. Its care with Scripture and application made it more convincing and more formidable to critique. My response is an interaction with brothers in Christ on a debatable issue, one that does not involve a basic tenet of the Christian faith. Believers differ, but we must accept each other regardless of our varying opinions.

Concerns About a Specific Will of God

The Blackabys take a position that I have called the traditional view, but it is aptly named the specific-will view. This refers to a specific will of God for each individual that will guide him or her to the right decisions. This view uses the biblical term *God's will*, but not in its normal theological senses. Theologians recognize that the term can be used of God's moral will or His sovereign will. The Blackabys hold to these two definitions, but their viewpoint adds a third use of the term *will of God*. When they exhort us to seek, find, know, and obey the will of God, they mean a specific, detailed plan for each believer.

The specific-will view has dominated thinking on guidance in evangelical circles, but now it is being challenged. Rather than assume the validity of the specific will, we must ask, Where is a clear example in Scripture where the term *God's will* means a specific will for each believer? It is best to agree with the theologians through the ages that God's will in Scripture refers to His sovereign will or His moral will.

Mundane Decisions

The Blackabys try to sidestep a serious flaw in the normal definition of God's so-called specific will. Historically, the specific will has been described as applying to every decision, but the Blackabys say that the specific will covers only decisions that are not "mundane." The basis for this is not biblical definition but practical necessity. No one can follow the specific-will view for every decision. Which ones are "mundane"? What if some of those mundane decisions turn out to be crucial? For example, where you sit in a college classroom could be the key to meeting your future spouse! Inadvertently, the Blackabys default to a wisdom approach. Apparently, wisdom determines which decisions are mundane. Once "mundane" is determined, they say these decisions "simply require wisdom." The specific-will view will not work with life's many small decisions. The options in these decisions are often equally acceptable, but the specific-will view has no category for decisions with equally acceptable options.

The Blackabys also attempt to avoid the concept of a "second-best" will of God, which is common in this viewpoint. Second best is what you get if you miss God's specific plan. Is there one person in the world whom you should marry? They say, yes. What happens if you marry the wrong person? Well, you lose out on God's first choice, but you can still have a fulfilled marriage and "God always has a perfect will for your life as of this moment." Is this a second "perfect" will? Might there be a third or fourth? It is better to say that sin always brings loss, but we can fully please God today by obeying His moral will. There is no need for several "perfect" wills or the "second-best" will.

The advantage of a specific will is partly based on God's knowledge of the future. He knows what to choose and what to avoid. The illustration of Richard's uneasiness about a financial investment program was a powerful example; but if their viewpoint were literally true, it would need to explain why this seminary was struggling while making perfect financial decisions. Many other believers who hold the specific-will view did invest. Why did they feel a peace to do so? Certainly, God knows the future, but James teaches us to say, "If it is the Lord's will, we will live and do this or that" (James 4:15). We are not promised such insight into the future. The school I am affiliated with did not invest in this failed financial program either. When asked why not, the institution's chief financial officer replied that this company was violating some basic financial principles. This is better guidance than a feeling of a lack of peace. When we feel uneasy, we should ask why, not take the feeling as a message from God.

The Blackabys say, "We must call upon the one Person who can infallibly guide us to the best choice every time." The specific view makes a big promise! If the proponents of the specific-will view were literally making the best choice every time, we would not be writing this book. They would be making perfect decisions, and the rest of us would be mucking around in ministry mediocrity. One reason this book is being produced is that most believers following the specific-will view realize that they are not making perfect choices.

Concern About Examples

The Blackabys face a tension with the biblical examples they use. They do have clear examples where God spoke, the recipients knew exactly what He said, and they knew what to do. Moses is listed in the essay and emphasized in *Experiencing God*. Is he the norm for the Christian life? No, Moses was a "prophet" and a unique one at that (Num. 12:6–8; Deut. 34:10). They list guidance examples from both testaments: Noah (Gen. 6:14–16), Abraham (Gen 12:1), the tabernacle instructions (Exod. 26–27), Jesus' instructions to the disciples (Mark 1:38; Luke 9:12–13, 49–50), Philip (Acts 8:29, 39), Peter (Acts 10:17–20), Paul (Acts 16:6–7), Agabus (Acts 21:10–14), and others. They say, "God who related to Abraham, Moses, Isaiah, and the apostles is the same God who relates to us." Yes, it is the same God, but that is not the issue. The question is whether this same God is giving all believers *the same direct revelation* that He did to Abraham, Moses, Isaiah, and the apostles. The specific view wants to take the apples of direct revelation (e.g., the Moses example) and prove the oranges of subjective guidance. This subjective guidance includes a particular application of Scripture, reading circumstances, impressions in prayer, and non-inspired comments from fellow believers. The authors don't claim to have prophetic or apostolic apples, only subjective oranges. After the list of biblical examples, we expect them to claim that they have prophets or apostles in their church, but they do not. We expect stories of miraculous revelation, burning bushes, and angelic visits, but there are none.

Let me oversimplify the specific-will argument. God spoke to prophets by direct revelation, and this proves that He "speaks" to every believer through circumstances. God spoke directly to His apostles with His authoritative message, and this proves that He "speaks" through some of the advice of believers. An angel told Philip to go into the desert to witness to one man, and this proves that God will impress your heart to give witness to one person rather than another.

They wisely say that guidance will not add to the canon and that it is not "new revelation." At the same time, they want all the results of revelation: God told me; it was clear; I must obey. But they do not claim miraculous revelation. Their examples are nonmiraculous, subjective, and usually harmonize with a "wise" decision. A more charismatic version of the specific-will position argues these examples more consistently. They claim to have the same direct revelation, regular miracles, angelic visitations, prophets, and sometimes even apostles. The Blackabys, however, give miraculous examples as proof of nonmiraculous guidance.

Their case would be more convincing if they presented biblical examples of people being guided in the nonmiraculous subjective means they expect. The wisdom view takes the miraculous examples of guidance seriously. It is possible for God to give specific guidance by miraculous revelation. And, if He does this, it will be a miraculous angel, not a stirring impression; it will be through a voice out of the fire, not a feeling in the heart.

One of the reasons people have looked closely at other models of guidance is that the complete clarity promised by the specific-will view is not the experience of God's people. It is true that when God gave direct revelation to Moses, Moses knew it was God. He knew what God told him, and he knew what to do. That is the nature of direct revelation, but it is not the nature of subjective guidance. It will not bring certainty of God's speaking. It can be helpful, but it is not revelation. Such guidance does not have authority, and it will always be subjective, not God's "clear" speaking.

The Blackabys say, "To understand God's will, we must be able to recognize when He is speaking." This was not a problem for a prophet or an apostle. Once you define God's "speaking" as reading subjective impulses, however, then you are left with trying to pick the divine impressions from all the other impressions. Rest assured, if God actually "speaks" revelation to you, you could not miss it even if you wanted to.

Concern About "God Speaks"

Normally, when we say God spoke, we are referring to direct revelation to a prophet or apostle or to the words of Scripture. To use the same language and apply it to God "speaking" through circumstances—or through a friend—is misleading at best. A subjective reading of circumstances may be helpful, but when you call it God "speaking" and then use the same wording for a revelation to Isaiah, confusion will arise. They are not the same.

A summary of the logic might be outlined in three sentences:

1. God spoke to prophets and apostles.
2. These examples show that God speaks to His people.
3. God speaks today through circumstances and other means.

The meaning of "speaks" in the third sentence is dramatically different from its meaning in the first sentence. The result is that either the first statement is watered down or the third is given disproportionate significance. The Blackabys are arguing that things have not changed and God is still "speaking" to His people. The reality is that they have changed the meaning of the word *speaks*.

When they describe the Holy Spirit impressing a certain understanding of a Bible verse, they are describing illumination, not God's "speaking" a specific application. When they sense God speaking in prayer, they are reading their inward impressions during prayer. When they are sensing the Spirit interpreting circumstances, they are evaluating the context in which the sovereign God has put them. When they receive advice from another believer and are impressed in their spirit, they are sensing the wisdom or rightness of the advice. All of the above factors are helpful in making a decision, but the Blackabys have added a subjective impression to the process and called it God "speaking." Don't ignore these helpful means, but don't transform a holy hunch into "God said."

Variety of Means in Which God Speaks

The Blackabys list an impressive variety of ways that God communicated: through creation, angels, prophets, dreams, visions, casting lots, Urim and Thummim, a gentle voice, fire, a pillar of cloud, a burning bush, and other means. A few on their list might be debated, but most of them are clearly means of direct, miraculous communication. However, they are not claiming that God speaks to us through these same means. They conclude, "The *means* God used to speak to people was secondary. *That* God spoke was crucial." True, but that does not solve the problem. If you have not received a prophetic dream, then using the prophetic example for support is not convincing.

Sovereignty and Guidance

The Blackabys believe in a sovereign God who works all things together for good, but their confidence that God is guiding us in everything does not emphasize His sovereignty. The specific-will view believes that God guides in everything—which sounds like an appeal to God's sovereign will—but theologically it looks to a specific will. Biblically, the sovereign will is a more appropriate place to know that God is guiding down to the details rather than a postulated specific will.

What About "Freedom" and "Wisdom" Verses?

I have questioned the specific-will view on the interpretation of its biblical support. They should return the favor and critique mine. They should give better exegesis on the passages that the wisdom view uses for support. In particular, Scripture uses "freedom" concepts. If there is only one right person to marry, what does Scripture mean when it says a widow is "free to marry" any believer (1 Cor. 7:39)? What does the Bible mean by "free"?

The wisdom view bases its theology on many examples of Paul and others describing their decisions in wisdom terms. Paul claims direct revelation (e.g., the Macedonian vision in Acts 16:9–10) or says, "we thought it best" (1 Thess. 3:1). Such wisdom verses are the biblical foundation of the wisdom view. Why call a decision "good," "better," and "wise" if that is not the issue? Have we misinterpreted these verses supporting freedom and wisdom? If so, what is a better interpretation?

Application of the Specific-Will View

The foundation of the Blackabys' application section is simple: God tells us the choice, and we "become familiar with His voice." Those who are close to God will recognize His voice from all the other voices. By recognizing His "voice," they do not mean understanding direct revelation but reading impressions.

Now God did "speak" to Moses while he was alone in the wilderness, but the Blackabys connect their understanding of God's "speaking" to the process of evaluative research. They encourage research on schools that fit your gifting, believing that God will give you specific impressions during the process. In reality, this allows wisdom to narrow down choices, so it is not really just an impression telling you what to do.

Their use of spiritual markers is helpful. These markers are usually events that reveal the passion, the gifting, and the aptitudes of the person. In reality, wisdom is being applied, using important spiritual information from the past; but if you view past markers as an authoritative "call," you will cut yourself off from God's future wisdom. The Blackabys contrast these "markers" with a "pros-and-cons" list. But are these markers not a great source for listing the content of the spiritual "pros and cons" more clearly?

How can one resist such a good story as the man who chose Richard's seminary using Philippians 1:6 as a sign? Let me resist a bit. God used the sovereign "coincidence" to connect the man and

Richard, but that does not constitute a guidance command. What matters was their conversation, which God sovereignly brought about. My guess is that the man saw Richard's heart, wisdom, and pastoral care and grew interested in a seminary led by such a president. My guess is that he also heard good spiritual wisdom from Richard on how God could use this seminary in his life.

Should Joe and Nancy marry? I do not believe there is only one correct person to marry. On the other hand, I encourage Joe and Nancy to listen to everything else the Blackabys wrote about their marriage decision. These were the words of gifted and insightful pastors. I would tell Joe and Nancy, "If you follow their practical pastoral advice, you will make a good and godly decision no matter what view of guidance you hold. So I advise you to remember Paul's words, that you are free to marry whomever you wish, and then let your 'wishing' be guided by the Blackabys' advice."

In the choice of a church, there was an emphasis on listening to wisdom when you felt an impression about it. The factors in choosing a church should be looked into but followed only when God impresses them to you. The example of a family not choosing the big full-service church is used to refute a "pro-and-con" mentality. The implication is that no one would choose the small church on the basis of wisdom. God had to use a feeling of "peace" to seal the small church deal. I've worshipped in churches of all sizes, and it is not that simple. I left a large wonderful church during seminary days to minister in a poor struggling minority church. I can understand why wisdom might choose the small church that most needed workers, that had more authentic community, and that received direct care from the pastor.

In conclusion, I have always seen many biblical strengths in the specific-will view of decision making. Its strongest point is that it always teaches us to obey the moral will of God. Furthermore, this view often includes a process that involves research, evaluation, and application of wisdom in order to narrow choices down. The Blackabys are especially strong at adding pastoral wisdom and insight into the process. I believe that the way of wisdom is more biblical, but if you choose the specific-will view of guidance, I recommend that you follow the Blackabys' version of it. You will have so much godly wisdom infused into the view that it is unlikely that you will be misguided by a foolish or sinful impression.

A Relationship View Response to the Specific-Will View

GORDON T. SMITH

Foundational Questions

The Blackabys identify a primary longing of contemporary Christians—to know the specifics of God's will or God's call for the circumstances of their lives. I am not sure I see their point that, as often as not, people already know God's will before they come looking for assistance. To the contrary, it has been my experience that Christians often face genuine bewilderment and uncertainty about their circumstances, sometimes because those situations are complex. But their main observation is an apt one: God has a specific will for His children and one of the most vital needs Christians have is to learn how to recognize God's voice and then live in response to the call of Christ.

The Blackabys also affirm that God speaks directly to believers, that He is an immediate witness in the life of the contemporary Christian. Yet, when they describe it, He is not an *immediate* witness per se. Rather they contend that God—that is, the Spirit—speaks "through" four media or means. God "speaks" through (1) the Scriptures, (2) prayer, (3) circumstances, and (4) other believers. Later they also speak of "peace" as a means of the Spirit's directing, which might suggest a more immediate experience of the Spirit. But the focus is on these four means, particularly the first: the Scriptures.

Further, they approach this topic on the basis of "foundational truths" that merit affirmation. They rightly assume the authority and life-giving quality of the Scriptures. And it is appropriate to suggest that the dynamic of God's relationship with people described in the Scriptures provides us with insight into how God might relate to Christians today. When Jesus speaks to His disciples and says those immortal words, "I no longer call you servants [but] . . . I have called you friends" (John 15:15), the Christian today should see this as directly relevant for her or his life.

Having said this, it is equally important that we respect the particular historical circumstances of the Scriptures; only then can we truly apply the ancient text. We should not assume that a promise given to a biblical character is necessarily applicable to all Christians at all times. The promises have personal meaning only if they are truly universal in application. Nevertheless, the Blackabys are right to insist that the normative character of the Scriptures is then complemented by the work of the Spirit, who guides Christians in the application of ancient principles.

Additionally, the Blackabys appropriately speak of the character of God—a fundamental point of reference—and rightly they affirm that the critical reference in this regard is the glory of God. The heart of the Christian calling is always to seek the glory of God and the in-breaking of the reign of Christ and to live in radical dependence on Christ and in response to the guidance of the Spirit. And in this orientation—to the glory of God and to the guidance of the Spirit—the Christian can always trust in the fundamental goodness of God. But what strikes one is this: while God's constancy is an appropriate reference, for the Blackabys the will of God is static and thus God Himself comes across as static. There is a lack of energy, genuine spiritual energy, when our primary orientation is toward a fixed, static plan that God has for a person's life, laid out indefinitely into the future. Furthermore, this is reflected in the almost obsessive focus on the fact that God knows the future. In reading the specific-will view, we get a sense that the focus of faith for the Christian is in the omniscience of God with respect to this "future." While the Christian certainly rests in the confidence of God's providential knowledge, this seems to be distinct from the focus of the Scriptures, where the confidence of the Christian is on the goodness and power of God.

Further, while rightly affirming the honor and glory of God, the Blackabys unnecessarily pit the will, honor, and glory of God over against human longings and purposes. It seems a false distinction to say that the fundamental question for every person is not, "What is God's will for my life?" but, "What is God's will?" To the contrary, we must insist that the first question is an essential question: each person is called to seek the specifics of God's intention for her life as a steward of her gifts, opportunities, and responsibilities. Each person seeks the will of God; but he seeks it specifically for the life he is called to live. We do not need to polarize between "God's will" and "God's will for my life"; there is no other context in which to live out the calling and will of God than precisely in our lives.

Then also, the Blackabys suggest that our lives are best lived when we spend time in what they call "redemptive activity in the world" rather than in leisure activities. The problem with this idea is that it so often leaves people driven to do religious activities without actually living in the light of God's redemptive work. Sometimes it is God's will that we relax in the work of God rather than always assume that we need to be active for God. The approach of the Blackabys provides no perspective that would free us to discern what we are being called to do and not called to do. Can we never affirm that God is calling us to relax, to rest in the work of God? The Blackabys appropriately seek to locate this discussion about divine guidance in the overall work of God in the lives of Christians—our experience of the salvation of God needs to include an appropriation of the grace of God's guidance in our lives. But they seem to have a rather narrow conception of the nature of God's salvation.

But with these caveats, I affirm the aptness of identifying the foundational questions the Blackabys identify: the authority of Scripture, the glory and purposes of God, and the call to the Christian to identify with the redemptive purposes of God in the world.

Responses to the Specific-Will View

A response to the specific-will view needs to consider the four "means" that the Blackabys identify as the ways in which God speaks: Scripture, prayer, circumstances, and the counsel of others. What soon strikes one in reading this is that these four "means" are selected rather arbitrarily, and it is not clear what relation there is between them—though, as will be noted, they insist that the "primary" way is through the Scriptures. The Blackabys insist that their approach is scriptural and does not depend on either tradition or experience, but it is not clear that there is a biblical basis (or any basis!) on which these four "means" are selected. One wonders if this is a case of insisting on the sole authority of the Scriptures while actually depending on tradition and experience. Better it seems to me, as I will do in my own essay, to appeal unapologetically to both tradition and experience and then affirm how these are vital criteria and means for discerning the guidance of God.

But the primary concern is that, while the Blackabys speak of these four means, there are no clear criteria for discerning what God is saying "through" these means. Just as the selection of these four seems arbitrary, it also follows that how God speaks through them is seemingly rather arbitrary. How does one know what text of Scripture, what impression in prayer, what specific circumstance, or what word from a fellow believer means anything? When they speak of the capacity of the Christian to know the will of God for their circumstances, they seemingly appeal to nothing more than sincerity and good intentions. One could easily conclude that all that matters is the right disposition: if you are open and willing, then you will be able—through Scripture, prayer, circumstances, and others—to know the purposes of God.

Disposition is hugely important. If we are not disposed to the call of Christ, we will not likely recognize it. The Blackabys are right to affirm the need for radical openness and, indeed, an eagerness to know the call of Christ. But good intentions are not good enough; there must be clear criteria for discernment, or there is no true capacity to discern. This becomes most evident when we consider how the Blackabys respond to the case studies that have been presented.

They rightly insist on the importance of time with God—the value of prayer and personal communion with Christ. Indeed, they belabor this point in their case studies, such as in the case of Susan, where they write that she should "genuinely seek to hear what God tells her about her college education" and spend much time in the Scriptures and in prayer. But with no criteria for discernment, this radical openness and sincerity will only lead to frustration. Or, worse, it will lead to choices based on good intentions and little more. They urge Susan, if she feels "uneasy in her spirit," to wait. This is appropriate; but they do not give her a basis for critical thinking about this uneasy feeling and for knowing, if and when she does have peace, that this peace comes from God. One gets the sense that if she feels good about it, it must be from God, as long as her intentions are oriented toward God's purposes for her life.

Further, the Blackabys are right to affirm the reality of continuity. God's new work in our lives is always in continuity with what God has already been doing. And on this assumption, they provide the imaginative creation of a potential series of events in Susan's life. The significant problem with this, however, is that it does not sufficiently account for the discontinuities and the surprises of God. God often leads people into new avenues of work and relationships that, while in some continuity with past experience, in actual fact represent new opportunities that defy conventional wisdom. Often the continuities are seen only in retrospect, such as why Moses might be chosen to confront Pharaoh or why Saul should be called to lead the mission to the Gentiles. But for both Moses and Saul, God's direction came as a dramatic redirection of their lives.

In other words, the overall tenor of the Blackabys' specific-will perspective is safety and stability, without much space for discerning the points of discontinuity when God calls us to something that can only be attributed to the intervention of God. Thus, one wonders if God is really not so significant a factor after all, for He seems to be replaced by a series of relatively arbitrary guidelines for decision making. While the intent is there to affirm the priority and initiative of God, there is no real basis for discerning this divine initiative.

The lack of a basis or criteria for discerning God's will is particularly evident in their use of Scripture. They write, "The Bible is the primary way God communicates with His people. The Holy Spirit will take the words of Scripture and apply them directly to your life." While affirming that the Scriptures provide a basic framework for life, they also insist that verses in Scripture can provide specific guidance for the Christian. For example, with respect to the example of Susan and the question of a college choice, they write that Susan might be struck by the words of Ephesians 6:1–2 and the need to honor her parents, noting that perhaps her father has a particular preference for where she should study. This would then lead her, it is suggested, to lean toward attending that particular school. The same approach to Scripture appears in the counsel given to the couple seeking to discern which church they should join. The Blackabys note that the couple might be impressed by a particular passage of Scripture that might help them determine the intent of God for them.

Two things, however, are often unnoticed in this regard. First, this kind of decision-making method is entirely arbitrary. Susan might just as easily remember the text that indicates that a person is to leave father and mother (Gen. 2:24; cf. Matt. 19:5; Eph. 5:31) or, more pointedly, the text that actually says, "If anyone comes to me and does not hate his father and mother, . . . he cannot be my disciple" (Luke 14:26). Using this approach, this might suggest that she should actually *not* do what her parents want her to do! But second, and of greater concern, overall the Blackaby perspective does not sufficiently account for the efforts of the Evil One, specifically with respect to Scripture. We must recognize that the Evil One may well use Scripture to mislead us. Witness the Devil's use of Scripture that Jesus encountered during His temptations in the wilderness (Matt. 4:5–7; Luke 4:9–12). The fact that Scripture is quoted or comes to mind does not in itself indicate divine guidance.

The same principle and concern applies to the other "means" by which the Blackabys claim that God guides Christians. There is no criterion or basis for discernment—whether it is the use of Scriptures, the impressions received in prayer, the circumstances around us, or the counsel of others. How is one to know if something is from God? The authors affirm that one would feel peace, that the "result of the Holy Spirit's work in a believer's life is joy and peace." And they go on to affirm that a "sense of deep peace and joy" is an indication that a particular choice is "aligned with God's will." This is spoken of as a "means" of guidance, seemingly adding another means to the four already identified. But how is one to know whether or not this peace—presumably a feeling of serenity—comes from God? In other words, this approach to divine guidance seems arbitrary, evident particularly in its questionable use of Scripture.

A helpful vantage point for this discussion emerges in 1 Thessalonians 5, where we read Paul's exhortation, "Do not quench the Spirit" (v. 19 ESV). Paul's readers are called to a radical vulnerability and openness to the Spirit's initiative. But right on the tail of this call, the follow-up is given: test everything to see if it is good (v. 21). The Blackabys aptly profile the first half of this twofold call: the deep openness to God, the willingness to do what God is calling one to do, the affirmation of the priority of God's call, and the need to be immersed in Scripture and consistent in the practice of prayer. All this is most appropriate. But then one is perplexed by their lack of true criteria for discerning what Scriptures are used and how, what the experience of prayer would provide one who is seeking guidance, what circumstances mean or do not mean, and what the counsel of others reflects about the intentions of God.

Radical openness to God without discernment is naive and dangerous. Jesus recognized the words in the wilderness, even though Scripture was quoted, as coming from the Devil. Even the peace that the Blackabys mention may, in the end, be nothing but a pleasant feeling. And without a basis for discernment, one could conclude that if one has "peace," then this confirms that it is the will of God. But feelings are illusive and rightly need to be challenged and discerned. Again, without a basis for discernment—for testing impressions that arise from Scripture or any other source—this approach to guidance is not one that can truly aid the Christian facing a critical life choice.

Chapter 2

WALKING IN WISDOM

The Wisdom View

GARRY FRIESEN

1. Introduction

This book is long overdue. I am honored to join respected Christian leaders and authors in a discussion of God's guidance. I have great respect for both Henry and Richard Blackaby and for Gordon T. Smith. Their books are examples of speaking the truth in love, and their genuine faith and heart for God are an encouragement to me. Their ministry in touching others for the gospel exceeds what God has allowed me to accomplish, and I approach them as respected and highly esteemed brothers in the body of Christ.

Before partnering with them in this volume, I had not met them personally. But I had spent many hours reading their books. I pray that this publication will have the same constructive influence on your life as theirs have had in enriching my spiritual walk.

Though the issue of God's guidance is very significant to the well-being of believers in Christ, it is not a core doctrine of the faith—such as salvation by faith or the deity of Christ. As Douglas S. Huffman put it in the introduction, the nature of divine guidance belongs to the category of debatable issues, or "disputable matters" that lie in the "gray area" of doctrinal understanding. This is the sort of subject, then, that by its nature elicits a variety of viewpoints.

As we expound the strengths of our respective positions, I believe that we all share two goals. The first goal is understanding. We intend to offer a lively and enlightening interaction that will allow the reader to quickly grasp the viable evangelical positions concerning guidance. The apostle Paul counseled that in such matters, each believer must become "fully convinced in his own mind" (Rom. 14:5). We seek to help you accomplish that goal by presenting our views (and critiquing the others) as clearly as possible.

Our second goal is to model an attitude of humility and love. We begin by affirming that our unity in faith, grace, truth, and in our Lord Jesus is greater than our differences on this topic. When it comes to debating the merits of our respective positions on guidance, we know that we are fallible human beings—none of us has a corner on the truth. Our goal is to sharpen our own understandings, and that of the reader, so that we can better conduct our lives to the glory of God.

The last two chapters of my book, *Decision Making and the Will of God*, expound the theology and practice appropriate to debatable issues. I now seek to live out that theology. As I labor to show you the strengths of the wisdom view, I hope to provide an example of dealing with a debatable issue with clarity *and* charity.

So, with great appreciation for my fellow contributors, I turn to the matter of demonstrating why the way of wisdom is the best explanation of the Bible's teaching on God's guidance for believers.

Overview of the Wisdom View

The way of wisdom is summarized in four principles:

1. Where God commands, we must obey.
2. Where there is no command, God gives us freedom (and responsibility) to choose.
3. Where there is no command, God gives us wisdom to choose.
4. When we have chosen what is moral and wise, we must trust the sovereign God to work all the details together for good.

The first principle—*where God commands, we must obey*—is non-controversial. All the contributors to this volume agree that God's *moral* will (all of which is revealed in the Bible) is to be obeyed.

But how are believers to approach the myriad of choices that are not directly addressed by God's moral will? How are we to decide on those matters where the biblical text does not tell us what to do? That very practical question is answered by the second and third principles. And it is with these principles that we part company with the traditional view. From my study of the Scriptures, I have become convinced that God expects the believer to act freely and responsibly in choosing the option he or she believes to be a reflection of wisdom.

The second principle, which advocates freedom and responsibility in making non-commanded decisions, has been the most controversial. In my experience, there have been two reactions to it. Some who are accustomed to the traditional paradigm for discerning God's will have reacted negatively. It has seemed to them that I am really suggesting an *absence* of guidance—a form of Christian deism. But, as I shall demonstrate, that is not the case. God does care about our choices, and His guidance is abundant. On the other hand, many have responded to this principle with an overwhelming sense of relief and excitement—relief that they are not "missing God's specific will" and excitement over being entrusted with the responsibility of making choices that are honoring to God.

The third principle—*where there is no command, God gives us wisdom to choose*—explains the basis for making non-commanded decisions. This is actually an extension of the first principle, for the moral will of God commands wisdom in decision making (Eph. 5:15–16). All three views presented in this book agree on the importance of wisdom, but in this model it is determinative in making decisions that please God.

The fourth principle integrates the *sovereign* will of God into the process of decision making. It assures us that we can trust God to be at work in accomplishing His purposes as we seek to make choices according to His instructions. However, since God's sovereign will is secret, we cannot know it in advance of our decision making. So, any attempt to "discover" what is divinely hidden will inevitably be an exercise in futility.

These four principles comprise the heart of the way of wisdom.

Overview of the Traditional View

My discovery of the principles of the way of wisdom was precipitated by my previous indoctrination in, and subsequent frustration with, the traditional view of guidance. While this volume uses the label "specific-will view" (see chapter 1), I have called the perspective that seeks for God's individual will the "traditional view" because in my youth it was virtually the only approach being taught. As a teenager, I soaked up these steps to guidance so that I could apply them to my life.

Here are the key points of the traditional view:[1]

Premise. For each of our decisions, God has an ideal plan that He will make known to the attentive believer.

Definition. The expression "will of God" is used in three ways in the Bible: God has a sovereign will and a moral will, but He also has an individual (specific or ideal) will, which is a detailed life-plan specifically designed for each believer.

Proof. Support for the existence of an ideal plan for each person comes from four sources. (1) Reason—God knows all, makes perfect plans, and is our guide. (2) Experience—historical examples like John Wesley, William Carey, and George Müller testify to God's individual will. (3) Biblical examples—Jesus (Heb. 10:7–9), Paul (Acts 13:1–2), and Philip (Acts 8:26–29) are some who were guided by God specifically into His perfect will. (4) Biblical teaching—Scripture shows that God has an individual will for each believer (Gen. 24:1–67; Ps. 32:8; Prov. 3:5–6; Isa. 30:21; Rom. 12:1–2; Eph. 2:10; Col. 1:9–10).

Process. I can find God's individual will for my life through His road signs, which include the Bible, circumstances, the inner witness of the Spirit, mature counsel, personal desires, common sense, and supernatural guidance.

---

1. My understanding of the traditional view is presented in a fifty-page fictional seminar in the first edition of my *Decision Making and the Will of God* (Portland, OR: Multnomah, 1980), and it is outlined in the second edition (Sisters, OR: Multnomah, 2004). Both are available on my Web site: gfriesen.net. The scholarly evidence for this viewpoint is in my dissertation, "God's Will as It Relates to Decision Making" (ThD diss., Dallas Theological Seminary, 1978), 7–148.

Certainty. I can be sure of knowing God's will by the agreement of God's road signs, through prayer, communion with God, and the results of the decision, which will include a sense of peace in my heart.

Only later did I discover that what had become "traditional" for my generation is actually a historical novelty. The obsession for certain guidance guaranteeing foolproof decisions appears to be a preoccupation peculiar to modern Christianity in the last 150 years. Prior to the writings of George Müller, there was virtually no discussion of "how to discover God's will for your life" in the literature of the church. What I call the traditional view of guidance was an integral part of the theological culture of the Keswick Movement, which was very influential in England and America. As Keswick-trained missionaries spread across the globe, this view of guidance became part of the evangelical tradition through their teaching. I was among the recipients of that heritage.

Critique of the Traditional View

My initial problem with the traditional view was that I couldn't get it to work in the practical process of decision making. I encountered numerous frustrations, but chief among them was my inability to acquire certain knowledge of God's will for major decisions. The problem came to a head in my effort to obtain guidance for my choice of a college. I applied the steps to discovering God's will, and no clear answer materialized. When the deadline arrived, I resorted to a "fleece" methodology, which I would never recommend today (and is seldom recommended even by proponents of the traditional view). But in my desperation, it was the only way I could come to a decision.

As I later reflected on that experience, I didn't believe that the problem was God's inability to communicate; and even in retrospect, I don't know how I could have been more sincere in my application of the principles. That left only one other explanation for my difficulty: there was something wrong with my understanding of the biblical teaching on God's will. And so I embarked on a fifteen-year study that brought me to the view that I teach today.[2]

In the process of that study, I uncovered a variety of problems with the traditional view. In this essay I will discuss five.

1. The Problem of Exegesis

In the course of my exploration, I eventually read the entire Bible, paying attention to passages that talk about the will of God on the one hand and decision making on the other. When I came to the proof texts for the then-current explanation of guidance, I made a shocking discovery. Examined in context, the passages did not teach what my previous instruction had maintained. This discovery was initially disconcerting, but it gave hope that correction of my understanding could bring a sense of confidence in my practice of decision making.

What eventually became clear is that the explanation of God's will taught by the traditional view is incorrect. To the classic categories of "moral will" and "sovereign will," the traditional view has added a third concept of "individual will," which lacks valid biblical and theological support. Older theologians do not discuss God's individual (specific, ideal, or perfect) will because they do not see it as a bona fide biblical category. Many contemporary believers have merely assumed the validity of this third concept, having picked it up from the evangelical culture. It shows up in the prayers of godly people, who say things like: "Dear Lord, reveal Your perfect individual will for our church so we will know which candidate You have selected to be our pastor." That short prayer includes most of the distinctive elements of the traditional view and uses the term *will* in the third sense described above.

But this idea of an *individual will* of God that the believer *must discover* is based on faulty interpretation of the key biblical passages used to support it. God does have a specific, detailed plan (which includes individuals), but that is encompassed in His *sovereign* will

---

2. Over the years, I have written critiques of books on God's will as they have been published. Fifteen of these were printed in the appendix of the revised edition of *Decision Making and the Will of God*. These and twenty additional reviews are also available online at http://www.gfriesen.net/sections/book_reviews_overview.php.

(Eph. 1:11). God does have an ideal will for individual believers, but that is His *moral* will fully revealed in the Bible. There are unusual instances in the Bible where God announced a specific plan for an individual believer (e.g., Exod. 3–4), but it was always communicated by special revelation (not inner impressions), and the initiative always came from God (it was not "discovered" by the recipient). But the passages commonly cited in support of a specific, detailed plan that each individual must find are better interpreted as referring to God's moral will or His sovereign will. This is the foundational fallacy of the traditional view; all other problems flow from it.

A detailed analysis of the scriptural passages used to support the "individual will" is given in *Decision Making and the Will of God*.[3] For the purposes of this essay, a few examples will have to suffice.

In my youth, a favorite verse was the King James Version's translation of Proverbs 3:6: "In all thy ways acknowledge him, and he shall direct thy paths." "Direct" sounds like specific guidance, and "paths" could be a way of describing God's detailed, individual will. But modern translations have corrected this inaccurate translation to read, "He will make your paths straight" (NIV, NASB).[4] In Psalms and Proverbs, "paths" are understood as the general course of life (see Prov. 4:18–19). God promises successful living for those who follow His truth and commands (Prov. 11:5). This is a great promise of general guidance, but it is not talking about the traditional view's concept of an individual will.

Proverbs 16:9 says, "The mind of man plans his way, but the LORD directs his steps" (NASB). This passage is not a warning against

---

3. In the first edition, see pp. 97–115. In the second edition (25th anniversary edition), see pp. 54–78.

4. Frances Brown, S. R. Driver, and Charles A. Briggs, *A Hebrew and English Lexicon of the Old Testament* (Oxford: Oxford University Press, 1907), s.v. יָשַׁר (*yāšar*). See also Franz Delitzsch, *Proverbs, Ecclesiastes, Song of Solomon*, trans. M. G. Easton, vol. 6, *Biblical Commentary on the Old Testament*, by C. F. Keil and F. Delitzsch, trans. J. Martin et al. (Edinburgh: T & T Clark, 1857–1878; repr., Peabody, MA: Hendrickson, 1996), 232; Crawford H. Toy, *A Critical and Exegetical Commentary on the Book of Proverbs*, The International Critical Commentary (Edinburgh: T & T Clark, 1899), 222; and Otto Zöckler, *Proverbs, Ecclesiastes, Song of Solomon*, vol. 10, *A Commentary on the Holy Scriptures*, ed. John Peter Lange, trans. Philip Schaff (Grand Rapids: Zondervan, n.d.), 58.

failing to seek God's direction, as some have taken it. It is a straight-forward description of God's sovereignty at work. Man proposes, but the sovereign God disposes (see also Prov. 16:1)![5]

Romans 12:2 says, "And do not be conformed to this world, but be transformed by the renewing of your mind, so that you may prove what the will of God is, that which is good and acceptable and perfect" (NASB). This famous verse uses the expression "will of God," and the reader must determine what Paul means by it. Is it the sovereign will, the moral will, or the individual will proposed by the traditional view? Clearly, Paul does not mean God's sovereign will, for that cannot be discovered in advance. But both the moral will and the individual will of God could make sense in this verse. The traditional view argues that one must find or "prove" what this will is and notes that it is called the "perfect" will of God.

But there are good reasons why most commentators understand God's will here to be His moral will. Romans 12–16 is the practical section of Romans and lists many commands from God's moral will that are required for believers who put their lives on God's altar as a sacrifice (Rom. 12:1). The context is not discussing decisions like choosing a vocation or a mate. Romans 12:1 is followed by commands about using our gifts, love, devotion to believers, diligence, rejoicing, hospitality, and the like (vv. 6–14).

Furthermore, the moral will better fits the contrast between worldly conformity and transformation of the mind, for in other passages it is God's moral will, Scripture, which produces transformation (e.g., 2 Cor. 3:18). Most commentators agree that the will of God in this passage is better understood as moral rather than a so-called individual will of God.[6]

A related category of faulty exegesis is the penchant for reading texts about the leading of the Holy Spirit through the interpretive

---

5. Derek Kidner sees Proverbs 16:1 teaching the same truth as 16:9. "The meaning is . . . that for all his freedom to plan, man only . . . advances God's designs" (Derek Kidner, *The Proverbs: An Introduction and Commentary* [London: InterVarsity Press, 1964], 118).

6. That the moral sense of God's will is intended is supported by John Murray, *The Epistle to the Romans*, NICNT (Grand Rapids: Eerdmans, 1965), 2:115–16; C. K. Barrett, *A Commentary on the Epistle to the Romans*, Harper's New Testament Commentaries, ed. Henry Chadwick (New York: Harper and Bros., 1957), 233.

grid of the traditional view. Such passages are cited as support for guidance by means of the inward voice of the indwelling Spirit. But in context, they describe the Spirit's leading into righteous living, that is, the moral will of God.

The first case in point is Romans 8:14: "For all who are being led by the Spirit of God, these are sons of God" (NASB). A superficial reading of this statement could support the traditional view. "Led" certainly looks like guidance, and the Spirit is the agent. The context, however, is not dealing with daily decisions in non-commanded areas. Further, there is no indication that inward impressions are the means of the leading and no hint of the concept of an individual will. The word "led" is a nontechnical term and in itself does not indicate either the goal or the means of the leading.[7]

The extended passage of Romans 8:1–17 is about righteous living[8] and supplies Paul's answers to the problem of slavery to sin (Rom. 7:7–25). So Romans 8:14 is about experiential conformity to the moral will of God. It is not about making choices in non-commanded areas.

"Being led by the Spirit" equals living "according to the Spirit," where the believer is "putting to death the deeds of the body" (Rom. 8:13 NASB).[9] Paul is describing obedience to God and His moral will, which cannot be accomplished without the Spirit's aid in understanding the moral will of God (7:12, 14, 22; 8:3–4) and providing the empowerment to do it (8:6, 13). This is powerful guidance. Sons of God are those who are led by the Holy Spirit to put to death the deeds of the flesh and accomplish the moral will of God. This is a description of *all* true "sons of God," not just some believers who are sensitive to God's guidance for daily decisions.[10]

---

7. Walter Bauer, William F. Arndt, F. Wilbur Gingrich, and Frederick W. Danker, *A Greek-English Lexicon of the New Testament and Other Early Christian Literature*, 2nd ed. (Chicago: University of Chicago Press, 1979), s.v. ἄγω (*agō*).

8. John R. W. Stott, *Men Made New* (Downers Grove, IL: InterVarsity Press, 1966), 93.

9. Ibid., 92–93.

10. Very similar to Romans 8:14 is Galatians 5:18: "But if you are led by the Spirit, you are not under the Law" (NASB). The context is even clearer here. The conflict in the passage is between the believer's flesh and the Holy Spirit. The key to overcoming the flesh is to walk by the Spirit (5:16), and be led by Spirit (5:18). Failure to do this will

Romans 8:15–16 states, "For you have not received a spirit of slavery leading to fear again, but you have received a spirit of adoption as sons by which we cry out, 'Abba! Father!' The Spirit Himself testifies with our spirit that we are children of God" (NASB). The last sentence in this passage is sometimes cited to show that God uses impressions to speak to our inner person. The argument of the traditional view is that this passage indicates that God is leading us (cf. 8:14) by speaking to our human spirits directly.

C. E. B. Cranfield outlines two possible interpretations for these verses and neither supports the traditional view.[11] One understanding is that the Spirit uses the gospel to assure believers that they are children of God. I prefer Cranfield's second option, that both the believer's human spirit and the Holy Spirit witness together to assure the Christian that he or she is a child of God. On this reading, there would be two witnesses to my salvation: God's Spirit and my own human spirit. Each believer's own faith confession of salvation is significant ("Abba! Father!"), but it is partnered by that of the "Spirit Himself" who confirms the Word of God. Thus, as Moffatt's translation clarifies, "It is this Spirit testifying along with our own spirit that we are children of God."[12] Moule captures this beautifully: "'Doubtless thou art His own child,' says the Spirit. 'Doubtless He is my Father,' says our wondering, believing, seeing spirit in response."[13] This is an example of what the Spirit does when the Word of God is spoken. The objective truth of God's Word is inwardly confirmed as true to the heart of the listener. But this passage says nothing about the Spirit's "leading" in daily decision making by means of impressions on one's human spirit.

---

result in immorality (5:19–22), but being led by the Spirit produces growth in traits like love and joy (5:22–23). Again, the Spirit is leading the believer into God's perfect moral will.

11. C. E. B. Cranfield, *Romans: A Shorter Commentary* (Grand Rapids: Eerdmans, 1985), 189–90.

12. Romans 8:16. *The Bible: James Moffat Translation* by James A. R. Moffatt. Copyright © 1922, 1924, 1925, 1926, 1935 by Harper Collins San Francisco. Copyright 1950, 1952, 1953, 1954 by James A. R. Moffatt.

13. Handley C. G. Moule, *The Epistle of St. Paul to the Romans* (New York: A. C. Armstrong and Son, 1894), 224.

I think that many people schooled in the traditional view simply assume the existence of a Spirit-revealed, individual will that must be discovered, and they read that meaning into these key texts. In addition, some employ another category of exegetical fallacy when they use biblical examples of special revelation to illustrate the quest for God's individual will. For instance, they will point to God's encounter with Moses at the burning bush as a paradigm for the guidance God provides to believers today. But this, again, involves faulty hermeneutics.

To clarify this problem, we need to review the nature of special revelation. Throughout biblical history, God has broken in with specific messages to particular individuals. Some prime examples are Moses at the burning bush (Exod. 3–4), the choosing of the church's first missionaries (Acts 13:1–4), and Paul's Macedonian vision (Acts 16:10). In each case, God gave guidance to believers beyond His written moral will.

God's meeting with Moses at the burning bush is instructive (Exod. 3–4). Moses saw a bush aflame with fire that did not consume its branches. He heard an audible voice. Both the flame and the voice were sensory phenomena miraculously produced. The declaration of God's will for Moses was crystal clear: Moses was to lead the Israelites out of Egypt. This initial revelation raised several questions for Moses, chief among them, How would the Israelites know that God had sent him? None of them had seen the fiery shrub or heard the Angel of the Lord. God provided Moses with a trio of divine signs-on-command so that the Israelites would know the message had divine authority: the rod-to-serpent effect, the leprous-hand demonstration, and the water-to-blood phenomenon. These signs proved to be persuasive, and the people believed Moses' message (Exod. 4:31).

This encounter appears to be a prototype for subsequent transmissions of prophetic revelation (just as Moses prefigures all future prophets, cf. Deut. 18:15–19). In Deuteronomy Moses established three tests for claims of prophetic revelation: the prophet must come in the name of the Lord, his message must not contradict previous revelations, and it must be confirmed by accurate short-term prediction or other miraculous signs (13:1–5; 18:20–22). Miraculous confirmation alone was not conclusive (Exod. 7:11–12), but it was a minimum requirement for a true prophet.

We must carefully note the characteristics of special revelation. It is sporadic (rare), clear, strategic, initiated by God, supernaturally imparted, and miraculously confirmed. When it came, it intruded into the life of the recipient. It was not normative experience in any sense. Special revelation is not promised to every believer, so it is not to be expected.

For the most part, proponents of the traditional view agree with these observations about special revelation. When they instruct believers to seek God's guidance, they do not usually mean the kind of special revelation received by prophets and apostles. And yet, they will say, "Just as God provided guidance for His people in the Bible, so you can count on Him to lead you." *And every biblical illustration they use will be an instance of special revelation!* This is the exegetical fallacy I am talking about.

There are two reasons why traditionalists use such illustrations. The first is that both the biblical examples and the quest of the contemporary Christian concern divine guidance for decisions not directly addressed by Scripture. The believer wants God to tell him or her what to do; in the Bible God told the prophet what to do. But the characteristics of the guidance sought by the traditionalist differ *in every particular* from the specific guidance received by prophets. Revelation was sporadic; but moderns are taught that God's guidance is available for every decision. Revelation was clear in that the recipient knew that it was from God and knew the specific content of the message; the present-day traditionalist is trying to decipher inner impressions and clarify road signs that are inherently imprecise. Revelation was strategic, that is, it was imparted in order to advance God's program of redemption; traditionalist guidance concerns matters that are personal and mundane. Revelation was initiated by God; the contemporary search for God's individual will originates with the believer. Confirmation of revelation was miraculous; confirmation of inner leading is determined by "the eye of the beholder." For me, the contrast is striking. When I tried to apply the steps of the traditional view, I was *never* certain that I had found God's perfect will. The prophets of God were *always* certain and never in doubt.

The second reason such illustrations are used is that *there are no biblical examples of individuals discovering God's will following the methodology of the traditional view.* In fact, as we shall see, the actual instructions given in the Bible for making choices in non-commanded decisions point in an entirely different direction. And the examples of those instructions illustrate it perfectly. But it is not valid to use biblical examples of special revelation to support the traditional approach to finding God's individual will. Such an approach uses "apples" that do exist to illustrate "oranges" that do not.

What I have been laboring to demonstrate is that the biblical basis for the traditional view of guidance in non-commanded decisions is faulty. So it's no wonder I encountered problems when I tried to implement the recommended steps in discerning God's will. One day I had an epiphany: the search for something that does not exist will inevitably produce anxiety and frustration! The problems that result represent the practical consequences of flawed theology.

2. The Problem of Ordinary Decisions

Every day we make thousands of decisions, but most of them are so insignificant that we hardly notice them. Which seat in class? Which pair of socks? Beverage at lunch? The traditional view asserts that God cares for every detail, and so His individual will for you is very specific. But in practice no one can search out God's will for every decision; most don't even try. Instead, they reserve the discovery process for relatively "important" decisions. While the wisdom view can be consistently applied to small decisions as well as large ones, followers of the traditional view must abandon their theology for ordinary, less important decisions.

3. The Problem of Equal Options

The traditional view paints itself into a corner by claiming that for every decision there is only one choice that is God's individual will. If the traditionalist encounters two options that appear to be equal, that person's theology generates anxiety because he or she believes one option is God's perfect will and the other is outside of God's will. Making the wrong choice would be disobedience. The wisdom view recognizes that often several options are equally pleasing to God, so believers can freely choose with confidence.

4. The Problem of Immaturity

According to the traditional view, one must not act until one has discerned God's leading. But sometimes it is hard to get to the required level of certainty within the given time frame. So, when push comes to shove, even the traditionalist must decide. When a deadline approaches, one must find a way to have God speak quickly. In this common scenario, an immature believer will often resort to desperate (and unwise) measures to narrow the choices to one.

A common immature practice is called "putting out a fleece." This approach is based (inappropriately) on the precedent of Gideon (Judg. 6). When the decision maker doesn't know God's individual will, he or she establishes a circumstantial test by which, it is hoped, God will make the choice clear. As I related earlier, I chose my college through this method, and thankfully God protected me from my foolishness. With two weeks to go before the opening college class bell rang, I still had two schools open to me. I decided to put out a fleece to determine God's choice. I would ask my father a question about which of two jobs I should take for the last fortnight of the summer. If Dad said "Christian camp," I would interpret it as God's saying, "Go to the Bible college." If Dad said "radiator shop," I would take it as God's saying, "Go to John Brown University in Arkansas." Dad said "radiator shop," and I said, "Thank You, Lord, for telling me where to spend my next four years." I was sincere, but my theology was faulty. The "signs" I chose were irrational rather than wise, for there was no direct connection between this college and my uncle's radiator shop. The more foolish the fleece, the greater the likelihood one will end up making a foolish decision.

5. The Problem of Subjectivity

These problems are significant, but they cannot match the greatest practical problem of the traditional view—subjectivity. (I do not mean subjective in the sense of "personal" and in contrast to nonpersonal. I mean subjective in the technical sense of an opinion that cannot be substantiated by an objective source of truth.) This problem arises from the expectation created by the traditional view that the believer can and must have *certain* knowledge of God's individual will prior to committing to a decision. Practitioners of this approach frequently ask, "How can I know for sure what God wants me to do?" (see the first case study at the end of this chapter). The explanation, as we have noted, is that the seeker must attend to the inner "voice" of the Spirit (variously described as "the still, small voice," "inward pressure, urging, or prompting," "guiding impulse," "inner impression," and so on). Since such leading does not come with the clarity of revelation (either written or special), it must be verified and "tested" by other "road signs": circumstances, mature counsel, personal desires, and common sense. The problem, of course, is that none of these sources of guidance is objective. And if the source of knowledge is subjective, then the conclusion also will be subjective and hence uncertain.

Every honest seeker after divine guidance has experienced this dilemma. We all get inward impressions that prompt us to carry out a particular action. When that happens, what's the first question we ask? "Where did that impression come from?" And why do we ask that? It is because we know that there are any number of potential sources for these inner impulses: God, Satan, emotions (such as joy or fear), hormonal imbalance, insomnia, medication, the pizza we had for lunch, or any combination of these plus other potential contributors. But when it comes to non-commanded decisions, we are given no criteria in Scripture for distinguishing the inner impression of the Spirit from the impression of the self or from any other potential "voice." So how are we supposed to identify the source of an impression? I know of no useful answer.

Now our problems multiply because we also have no instruction on how to interpret the *meaning* of this "guidance." That's why the impressions have to be "tested" by the other indicators of divine direction. But is that really helpful? Can one's circumstances, for instance, point to God's direction? Perhaps they could if they were properly interpreted. Does the Bible encourage us to "read providence"? What sort of hermeneutics does one employ to exegete circumstances?

Job's "comforters" were emphatic about the meaning of Job's great misfortune, and they were painfully wrong. When Paul was bitten by a viper, the natives on the island of Malta were sure he must be a murderer. When Paul remained unaffected by the venom, they changed their minds and decided he must be a god (Acts 28). Wrong and wrong again. The only time that circumstances convey a divine message is when they are accompanied by explanatory revelation—as when a famine was declared to be judgment from God (Joel 2). Apart from divine revelation, one explanation is as poor as another.

In my judgment, the subjective nature of inner impressions rules them out as reliable indicators of God's individual will for several reasons. (1) There is no indication in *Scripture* that the Holy Spirit leads believers in non-commanded decisions by means of inner impressions. (2) It is impossible to determine with certainty the *source* of the impressions. (3) It is impossible to interpret with certainty the *message* of the impressions. (4) The need for *clarification* from the other signs calls into question the origin of the inner voice. And (5) since inner impressions are not revelation from God, they lack the necessary *authority* to compel obedience.

That last point is the bottom line. When God speaks, He communicates specific words that are clearly understood. His revelation is objectively true, and it must be followed. *Anything less than revelation does not have authority in decision making*; it is not the pure voice of God. That does not mean that impressions in the heart should be ignored or that they cannot be helpful. (More on that later.) It just means that subjective "voices" are not authoritative in the sense of commanding obedience.

It is my contention that the traditional view is looking for the wrong thing (certain advance knowledge of God's individual will) and asking the wrong questions ("How can I know God's will for sure?" and "Where does this inner impression come from?"). There is a better approach—the one taught in the Bible.

2. The Wisdom View Explained

The subtitle to the first edition of my full-length book on this subject is "A Biblical Alternative to the Traditional View." To say it caused a stir when it came out in 1980 would be euphemistic. The traditional view was so strongly entrenched at the time that most evangelicals were not even aware of an alternative to their understanding. I labeled the alternative the "wisdom view," but critics called it deistic, impersonal, and unbiblical. The book was branded as "the Russian Roulette view of guidance" and "the most dangerous book on the Christian market." It was banned by some Christian institutions, and one prominent evangelical leader called me a "heretic" for several years. During the past twenty-eight years, over a thousand people have written letters responding to the book—and most were positive. But I'll never forget the one that ended, "P.S. Everything you know is wrong." If the critics are right, you must be very careful as you read this chapter.

I didn't set out to be a troublemaker or disturber of the peace. As I indicated above, the study that led to my conclusions was prompted by the dissonance between my experience and traditional teaching. On the other hand, the harmony between the theology of the way of wisdom and its practice has brought peace and joy, not only to myself, but also to many others. That result doesn't prove that it is true. But it may indicate that it's worth careful consideration. What I ask of the reader is the attitude and approach of the Bereans, who "with great eagerness ... examined the Scriptures every day to see if what [he] said was true" (Acts 17:11).

Principle 1: God's Moral Will

As I studied the Scriptures to understand God's guidance, one important principle I had believed was reinforced. It is the first principle in the way of wisdom: *Where God commands, we must obey.*

This first principle has more depth than is evident at first glance. The moral will of God does not determine every decision, but it influences and affects every decision. This is because the moral will of God not only prescribes outward behavior but also governs our attitudes and motivations. The moral will of God demands that every choice be made for the glory of God and denies the validity of selfish choices.

I will not dwell long on this first principle.[14] While it is important, it is not distinctive to the wisdom view. Here's what we need to know about God's moral will:

> *Its Origin.* It is the expression, in behavioral terms, of God's character.
>
> *Its Communication.* It is fully revealed in the Bible.
>
> *Its Scope.* It touches every aspect and moment of life, including goals, attitudes, means, and perspectives (why, how, and what).
>
> *Its Impact.* It is able to equip believers for every good work.

Obviously, this principle is not new. What is new for some readers is that the wisdom view sees God's moral will as determinative. The moral will of God is the *only* will that must be sought, learned, believed, and obeyed. This is true since God's moral will includes the command to be wise (principle 3 on pages 124–31). The wisdom view believes that the search to "find" God's will is over. The traditional view thinks that it has just begun.

Principle 2: God-Given Freedom

"Love God and do whatever you please." Augustine got it right centuries before the traditional view was invented. Principle 2 is distinctive to the wisdom view and rather controversial: *Where there is no command, God gives us freedom (and responsibility) to choose.* Obviously, Augustine can be misunderstood. "Do whatever you please" cannot be divorced from "Love God." And "Love God" must be understood in the Johannine sense that one who loves God also keeps God's commands (John 14:15–23; 1 John 2:5; 5:2–3; 2 John 6). Figure 2.1 distinguishes the traditional view from the wisdom view.

---

14. For details see "Thy Word Is Truth," in Friesen, *Decision Making and the Will of God*, rev. ed. (chap. 8).

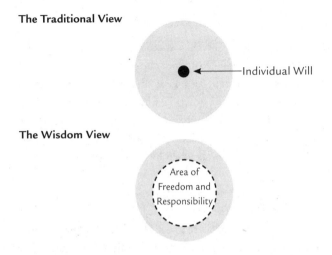

FIGURE 2.1. TRADITIONAL AND WISDOM VIEWS COMPARED

The Traditional View

The Wisdom View

This principle of freedom comes straight from God's gracious nature, but some advocates of the traditional view find it undesirable. They reason, "Who wants freedom of choice when God will make perfect decisions for you?" But this freedom was part of God's design for humanity from the very beginning.

Freedom from the Beginning

Consider the following imaginative rendition of . . .

"THE FIRST SUPPER"

(With Apologies to Moses Ben Amram[15])

Adam was hungry. He had had a long, challenging day naming animals. His afternoon nap had been refreshing, and his post-siesta introduction to Eve was exhilarating, to say the least. But as the sun began to set on their first day, Adam discovered that he had worked up an appetite.

"I think we should eat," he said to Eve. "Let's call the evening meal 'supper.'"

---

15. Assuming the Mosaic authorship of Genesis, Moses son of Amram (see Exod. 6:20) would have been the author of the original narrative.

"Oh, you're so decisive, Adam," replied Eve. "I like that in a man. I guess all the excitement of being created has made me hungry too."

As they discussed how they should proceed, they decided that Adam would gather fruit from the garden, and Eve would prepare it for their meal. Adam set about his task and soon returned with a basketful of ripe fruit. He gave it to Eve and went to soak his feet in the soothing current of the Pishon River until supper was ready. He had been reviewing the animals' names for about five minutes when he heard his wife's troubled voice.

"Adam, could you help me for a moment?"

"What seems to be the problem, dear?" he replied.

"I'm not sure which of these lovely fruits I should prepare for supper. I've prayed for guidance from the Lord, but I'm not really sure what He wants me to do. I certainly don't want to miss His will on my very first decision. Would you go to the Lord and ask Him what I should do about supper?"

Adam's hunger was intensifying, but he understood Eve's dilemma. So he left her to go speak with the Lord. Shortly, he returned. He appeared perplexed.

"Well?" probed Eve.

"He didn't really answer your question," he replied.

"What do you mean? Didn't He say anything?"

"Not much," Adam answered. "He just repeated what He said earlier today during the garden tour: 'You are free to eat from any tree in the garden; but you must not eat from the tree of the knowledge of good and evil.' I assure you, Eve, I steered clear of the forbidden tree."

"I appreciate that, but that doesn't solve my problem," said Eve. "What fruit should I prepare for tonight?"

From the rumbling in his stomach, Adam was discovering that lions and tigers were not the only things that growl. So he said, "I've never seen such crisp, juicy apples. I feel a sense of peace about them. Why don't you prepare them for supper?"

"All right, Adam," she agreed. "I guess you've had more experience at making decisions than I have. I appreciate your leadership. I'll call you when supper is ready."

Adam was only halfway back to the river when he heard Eve's call. He was so hungry that he jogged back to the clearing where she was working. But his anticipation evaporated when he saw her face full of consternation. "More problems?" he asked.

"Adam, I just can't decide how I should fix these apples. I could slice them, dice them, mash them, bake them in a pie, a cobbler, fritters, or dumplings. I really want to be your helper, but I also want to be certain of the Lord's will on this decision. Would you be a dear and go just one more time to the Lord with my problem?"

Adam was not keen on bothering the Lord again, but after Eve said some very nice things about him, he agreed to go. When he returned, he said, "I got the same answer as before: 'You are free to eat from any tree in the garden; but you must not eat from the tree of the knowledge of good and evil.'"

Adam and Eve were both silent for a moment. Then with light in his eye, Adam said, "You know, Eve, the Lord made that statement as though it fully answered my question. I'm sure He could have told us what to eat and how to eat it, but I think He has given us freedom to make those decisions. It was the same way with the animals today. He told me to name the animals, but He didn't whisper any names in my ear. Assigning those names was my responsibility."

Eve was incredulous. "Do you mean that we could have any of these fruits for supper? Are you telling me that I can't miss God's will in this decision?"

Adam explained, "The only way you could do that is to pick some fruit from the forbidden tree. But none of these fruits are from that tree. Why, I suppose," he continued, "we are free to eat a little from each one of them." Adam snapped his fingers and exclaimed, "Say, that's a great idea! Let's have fruit salad for supper!"

And so they did.

Needless to say, this parable was made up. The tongue-in-cheek tone is meant to force us to take Genesis 2:16–17 seriously. Right from the start, God gives a pattern of obeying the moral will ("you must not eat") and freedom where there is no command ("any tree," "free to eat").

Freedom Taught Throughout Scripture

The same pattern persists throughout the Scriptures. Old Testament food laws were strict (Lev. 11; Deut. 14), but they illustrate freedom within the regulations. From the specified menu of clean animals, the Israelite could make his choice (Lev. 11:2). The direction for one of the feasts was to purchase "whatever you desire" (Deut. 14:26 ESV).

God required certain sacrifices and prohibited others. In contrast, the "freewill offering" was a voluntary act to display devotion (Lev. 22:18; Num. 15:3). Even in the sacrifices required by God, there was the freedom of choosing which animal was used (Lev. 22:18–25).

The voluntary vow is another example of freedom (Num. 30:2; Deut. 23:21–23; Ps. 50:14; Eccl. 5:4–5; Nah. 1:15); it was neither commanded nor prohibited. Likewise, a former slave was invited to settle "wherever he likes and in whatever town he chooses" (Deut. 23:15–16).

The subject of food selection, so important in Eden and Israel, reappears in the New Testament, where God expanded the freedom related to the menu. "But food does not bring us near to God; we are no worse if we do not eat, and no better if we do" (1 Cor. 8:8). In the choice of food, the believer needed to avoid eating meat sacrificed to idols when it would cause a "weaker brother" to stumble into sin. Otherwise, Paul called one's choice a "liberty," a "right," a "lawful" thing, and a "freedom" (1 Cor. 8:9; 9:4; 10:23, 29; 1 Tim. 4:3–5). Most simply stated, "Eat anything" (1 Cor. 10:25). It is hard to conceive how Paul could have made it any clearer.

We know Paul valued a blameless conscience (Acts 23:1). And yet he said, "Eat anything . . . without raising questions of conscience"

(1 Cor. 10:25; cf. v. 27)! In context, Paul had shown that the meat in question was lawful. God had declared that eating such meat was not a moral issue and, so, not an issue of conscience. Thus, faith will believe God by *not* asking a moral question for the sake of conscience. This is a dramatic way of expressing the area of freedom.

Finish this verse (1 Cor. 7:19 nasb): "Circumcision is nothing, and uncircumcision is nothing, but what matters is _____." What matters? Circumcision was still debated in the early church, but Paul made it clear that it was not the sign of the new covenant. It was neither required nor prohibited. So, the verse ends, "but what matters is the keeping of the commandments of God." Since circumcision was not commanded of Christians, it was now *elective* surgery. Circumcision versus uncircumcision equals "nothing" (1 Cor. 7:19; Gal. 5:6; 6:15). Whatever is commanded (the moral will of God) "matters." If it's not commanded, it doesn't matter. That's freedom.

How is the believer to decide how much to give when the opportunity is presented? Should the Christian seek to discern God's leading? Here's Paul's answer: "Each one must give as he has made up his mind, not reluctantly or under compulsion, for God loves a cheerful giver" (2 Cor. 9:7 esv).

The choice of whether and whom to marry is certainly important, but it is viewed as a secondary issue by Paul. The primary question is how a believer can best serve God. Marriage is a subpoint of the greater question. Still, 1 Corinthians 7:39 is an eye-opener. "A woman is bound to her husband as long as he lives. But if her husband dies, she is *free* to marry anyone she *wishes*, but he must belong to the Lord" (emphasis added). The traditional view often applies its theology to marriage, but 1 Corinthians 7 is rarely emphasized (despite Paul dedicating forty verses to the subject!). In that chapter Paul never teaches that God will tell you whether to marry or whom to marry. Believers must marry only believers (the moral will of God), but we are free to be unmarried or married to whomever we wish (freedom).

Here is a fact that cannot be evaded: in every passage that discusses non-commanded decisions, at the very point where one might expect the biblical author to direct us to seek God's individual will, that never happens. Never. The area of freedom is God-given. He has chosen not to micromanage our choices within His moral will. Accepting that freedom and acting on it responsibly is not an exercise in selfishness, disobedience, or indifference. It is a principle stated by God, and He expects us to both believe it and enjoy it. To be blunt, if these verses about freedom don't mean freedom, what do they mean? What does "free" mean? Is there a better biblical interpretation?

Principle 3: God-Given Wisdom

Principle 3 answers the question, How do you make a God-pleasing decision within the area of freedom? *Where there is no command, God gives us wisdom to choose.*

Neither the traditional nor the relationship views are against wisdom. Proponents of those other views often will say that wisdom should not be ignored or that we should not expect God's individual will to be foolish or outlandish. The wisdom view, however, goes further and says that where God gives no command, wisdom is determinative for making God-honoring decisions.

This theology can be unsettling, for if we have freedom to decide, we also have responsibility to decide. But God's freedom should give us relief. And God's wisdom should give us confidence that we can make decisions pleasing to Him. So, as believers, we should be looking for wisdom promised by God (Prov. 8:17), not searching for a needle in the haystack of life (a.k.a. the dot "in the center of God's will"). God's promise of wisdom is given because God has commanded us to be wise people.

Old Testament Wisdom

The pursuit of wisdom in decision making permeates the entire Bible. The Old Testament Wisdom Literature (Job through Song of Solomon) is a good starting point. Why have this whole section in God's sacred library if He is going to reveal every right decision to us? But if the goal in decision making is wisdom, we need wisdom books and wisdom examples.

In Exodus 18, a dedicated Moses became a wise Moses. Jethro watched Moses judge the people all day long and, like a true relative, he butted in. But humble Moses listened. Jethro warned Moses that he would wear himself out, as well as all those in the long lines (Exod. 18:18). Jethro recognized that the judging must be done, but he had a wise suggestion on how Moses could shorten the queue (and survive!). Jethro advised Moses to select qualified leaders and train them in God's truth. Then they would judge most of the matters for Moses, and Moses would accept only the most difficult cases (Exod. 18:19–22). Moses agreed and followed the way of wisdom.

A beautiful slice of David's life is recorded in 2 Samuel 18. There we watch the courageous warrior put down his weapon and arm himself with wisdom. After Absolom usurped the kingdom, David and his soldiers ran for their lives. David wisely organized his troops and then unwisely said, "I myself will surely march out with you" (v. 2). Those risking their lives for the rightful king feared a stray arrow could kill David. They protested, "You must not go out . . . you are worth ten thousand of us" (v. 3). It was "better" for David to be protected and come out only if the need was desperate. David's sword was sheathed as he humbly and wisely said, "I will do whatever seems best to you" (v. 4).

The book of Ecclesiastes has one of the simplest proverbial advertisements for wisdom: "If the axe is dull and he does not sharpen its edge, then he must exert more strength. Wisdom has the advantage of giving success" (Eccl. 10:10 NASB).

These Old Testament books and examples are not commending wisdom as a nice accessory to life but as required equipment. The person who ignores wisdom is called naive, a fool, or a scoffer (Prov. 1:22). Since wise counsel is a readily available source of wisdom, it comes highly recommended (Prov. 11:14; 15:22; 20:18; 24:6). The Old Testament teaches wise decision making by its Wisdom Books and examples of wise men.

New Testament Wisdom

Jesus continued teaching on the role of wisdom. Some of His parables are built on the wisdom principle. Jesus taught that whether building a house or deciding a destiny, the wise man builds on a foundation of rock rather than sand (Matt. 7:24–27). Two parables about "counting the cost" show the kind of wisdom necessary for succeeding in difficult endeavors (Luke 14:28–32). The parable of the ten virgins describes the wisdom that is necessary for social invitations and, even more, God's invitation into His kingdom (Matt. 25:1–13). In His instructions to His disciples, Jesus commanded His servants to be wise, saying, "Therefore be as shrewd as snakes and as innocent as doves" (Matt. 10:16). This is the moral will of God ("innocent as doves") plus wisdom ("shrewd as snakes").

The witness of the Old Testament and of the teaching of Jesus to the significance of wisdom for decision making is impressive—and ought to be decisive. But the biblical teaching that most convinced me of the validity of the way of wisdom was the example and instruction of the apostles. As I studied the book of Acts and the Epistles, the questions I asked were these: How did the apostles make decisions when they were not being directed by special revelation? What procedures did they apply to "normal" (non-commanded) decisions? And what instructions did they give on how to make such decisions? As I began, I wondered how often they would direct believers to "discover God's individual will" or "listen to the inner voice of the Spirit." I was stunned to discover that they never, ever gave that counsel—not once. Instead, they modeled and expounded what I have been calling the way of wisdom.

One of Paul's most helpful phrases is found in the context of a missionary journey. "So when we could stand it no longer, *we thought it best* to be left by ourselves in Athens. We sent Timothy, . . . to strengthen and encourage you in your faith" (1 Thess. 3:1–2, emphasis added; cf. 1 Thess. 3:3–10; Acts 17:1–15). Here is an important decision made in the unfolding execution of ministry on the basis of wisdom—"we thought it best."

Elsewhere, Paul prepared for the sending of a gift with these words: "When I arrive, whomever you may approve, I will send them with letters to carry your gift to Jerusalem; and *if it is fitting* for me to go also, they will go with me" (1 Cor. 16:3–4 NASB, emphasis added). "If it is fitting" is an expression of wisdom. We are not sure what would make it fitting, but it was probably the size of the gift. Paul would act in wisdom, he said, when he saw the final context (see also David in 1 Sam. 22:3).

A charge of discrimination in the food service is the context for our next apostolic example. "So the twelve summoned the congregation of the disciples and said, '*It is not desirable* for us to neglect the word of God in order to serve tables. Therefore, brethren, select from among you seven men of good reputation, *full of the Spirit and of wisdom*, whom we may put in charge of this task. But we will devote ourselves to prayer and to the ministry of the word'" (Acts 6:2–4 NASB, emphasis added). The apostles perceived a ministry arrangement that was "not desirable" and, after review, came up with a wise and practical plan to meet the needs. The solution involved the selection of individuals to care for the widows. The required qualifications (Acts 6:3) were directly related to the moral will of God ("full of the Spirit") and being wise (full "of wisdom"). They did not assume there was an individual will of God whereby He had already made the choice. Rather, the qualifications related to finding godly and wise candidates.

Paul's later instructions for the selection of elders/overseers are comparable. Most of the qualifications are moral in nature (1 Tim. 3:1–7; Titus 1:5–9) summarized as "blameless" or "above reproach" (1 Tim. 3:2). Coupled with this moral dimension is the quality of demonstrated wisdom (1 Tim. 3:2, 4; Titus 1:8).

As I read of other apostolic decisions, I encountered similar terminology: "I think it is necessary"; "it seemed good"; or simply, "I have decided" (e.g., Phil. 2:25–26; Acts 6:2–4; 15:28–29; Titus 3:12). Luke even explained one of Paul's travel plans with the words, "for he was in a hurry" (Acts 20:16)!

By way of summary, then, the believer's goal in non-commanded decisions is to make wise choices on the basis of spiritual usefulness. The apostles, as well as the Old Testament saints and Jesus, model the use of wisdom in decision making. Furthermore, as we shall see, the apostles also directly commanded the use of wisdom as part of keeping the moral will of God.

Paul told the Corinthians, "I say this to shame you. Is it possible that there is nobody among you wise enough to judge a dispute between believers? But instead, one brother goes to law against another—and this in front of unbelievers!" (1 Cor. 6:5–6). Paul expected believers to settle their disputes with the help of the church. The church is capable and will some day judge the world and fallen angels (1 Cor. 6:2–3). Why ask for a wise person? Because it takes wisdom to sort out complex issues, determine an equitable settlement, and lead wounded brothers toward reconciliation.

First Corinthians 7 is one of the best passages for developing a theology of decision making. We saw earlier that it incorporates the principle of freedom with respect to the Christian widow ("she is free to marry anyone she wishes, but he must belong to the Lord," v. 39). This chapter also is filled with wisdom terminology that will guide the process of choosing. This is amazing. If Paul had held the traditional view, this chapter might be two verses long, not forty. He could have said, "God will tell you whether you are to marry and, if you should marry, He will reveal His individual will for whom you should marry."

Instead, Paul places the decision about one's marital status within the context of a higher and prior commitment—namely, service to God. He shifted the question from "Should I get married?" to "In what state can I best serve the Lord?" Then he discussed the pros and cons of each condition. Moral issues impinge on one's decisions, including sexual purity and conjugal responsibility (1 Cor. 7:2–5, 10–11). As he compared singleness to marriage, the terms he used for assessment are "good" (in the sense of "advantageous," not as the opposite of evil)[16] and "better" (vv. 1, 8–9, 26). The advantages of the single life included avoidance of pressures that their current situation brought upon them (vv. 26, 28) and freedom to

---

16. The word for "good" is the Greek καλός (*kalos*). For cross-references where this term has the idea of "beneficial," see Matthew 17:4; 18:8–9; 1 Corinthians 9:15. See Charles A. Hodge, *An Exposition of the First Epistle to the Corinthians* (Grand Rapids: Eerdmans, 1959), 108–9.

serve the Lord without the constant distraction of family commitments (vv. 7, 32–35). The advantages of marriage included help with sexual temptation (v. 2) and the passion that can consume someone who does not possess great self-control (v. 9).

These exhortations to apply wisdom in decision making are made even more explicit in other passages. "Be very careful, then, how you live—not as unwise but as wise, making the most of every opportunity, because the days are evil" (Eph. 5:15–16). "Conduct yourselves with wisdom toward outsiders, making the most of the opportunity" (Col. 4:5 NASB). In context, this wisdom encompasses practical wisdom as well as the moral will of God (cf. Eph. 5:17).

Finding Wisdom

If wisdom is the determinative issue for non-commanded decisions, how does the believer get such wisdom? The answer comes in several parts, but the core truth is that *wisdom is received from God by those who seek for it.* "I [wisdom] love those who love me, and those who seek me find me" (Prov. 8:17). No man is naturally wise (Prov. 3:7). Ultimately, this wisdom comes from God, who is wise in His very essence (Job 9:14; 12:13; Isa. 40:28; Dan. 2:20).

God sets the prerequisites for finding wisdom. He grants wisdom to those who manifest certain spiritual characteristics: reverence of God (Prov. 9:10), humility (Prov. 11:2; 15:33), teachableness (Prov. 9:9; 15:31; 19:20), diligence (Prov. 2:4–5; 8:17), and uprightness (Prov. 2:7). Finally, James says that the believer must have faith. "If any of you lacks wisdom, he should ask God, who gives generously to all without finding fault, and it will be given to him. But when he asks, he must believe and not doubt" (James 1:5–6).

In the pursuit of wisdom, the believer's approach is clear and God's supply is ample. First, the believer must ask God for it (James 1:5; Col. 1:9–10). Seeking wisdom is a faith endeavor, not an impersonal search. Research, study, inquiry, and reflection are required, but it is never merely academic when prayer is at its heart. God gives this wisdom through His Word, but He also gives it through a variety of channels such as counselors, personal research, and the experiences of life.

James's counsel includes a gracious promise: God will generously give wisdom to those who ask in faith. This is not a guarantee of human omniscience, instant answers, or injected wisdom apart from the walk of faith nourished by Scripture. Gaining wisdom is like the full Christian life. It entails progressive growth with the goal of being full of wisdom (cf. Acts 6:3).

After prayer, the second source of wisdom is Scripture. Psalm 119 is a feast of wisdom from A to Z. "Oh, how I love your law! I meditate on it all day long. Your commands make me wiser than my enemies, for they are ever with me. I have more insight than all my teachers, for I meditate on your statutes" (Ps. 119:97–99; cf. Ps. 19:7; 2 Tim. 3:15–17).

The third avenue God provides to find wisdom is outside research. Nehemiah's covert inspection of Jerusalem's shattered walls provided information he needed to begin rebuilding them (Neh. 2:11–16). Joshua dispatched two agents to gather battle information to enhance his military intelligence (Josh. 2). Luke "carefully investigated everything" before writing his gospel and Acts (Luke 1:3). Making a list of pros and cons for a selected option is in harmony with the spirit of Scripture (cf. Luke 14:28–32).

A fourth source of wisdom is wise counselors. "Plans fail for lack of counsel, but with many advisers they succeed" (Prov. 15:22). In general, we should seek two types of wisdom from counselors: biblical wisdom and experiential wisdom that applies to the decision at hand.

A fifth instructor is life itself. Agur, author of Proverbs 30, urges us to learn from "extremely wise" animals including ants, badgers, locusts, and lizards (Prov. 30:24–28; cf. Prov. 6:6–11).

Finally, we must note that God sometimes gave wisdom by direct revelation, though He has not promised it. An angel directed Philip to a seeker in the desert (Acts 8:29). Peter was told the counterintuitive fishing guidance that he should "cast the net on the right-hand side of the boat" (John 21:6 NASB). Paul's missionary itinerary was changed by the Macedonian vision (Acts 16:9). Although this is the exception, God did reveal wisdom directly to prophets and others.

FIGURE 2.2. WISDOM FOR DECISION MAKING

1. The Old Testament teaches wise decision making through its Wisdom Books and examples of wise men—"Wisdom has the advantage of giving success" (Eccl. 10:10 NASB).

2. Jesus commanded His servants to be wise—"Be as shrewd as snakes" (Matt. 10:16).

3. The apostles modeled wisdom in their decision making—"We thought it best" (1 Thess. 3:1).

4. The apostles commanded believers to use wisdom in decision making—"Conduct yourselves with wisdom" (Col. 4:5 NASB).

5. God has promised wisdom through the Bible, prayer, counselors, research, and experience—"If any of you lacks wisdom, he should ask God" (James 1:5).

So God provides wisdom and we must use it. Figure 2.2 summarizes the Bible's instruction to use wisdom for making decisions.

A word of caution is in order. Wrongly applied, the wisdom view can be as frustrating as the traditional view. In place of the elusive "dot" of God's individual will, one could substitute the impossibility of finding the "dot" of omniscient wisdom. The believer is required to make a wise decision, not be God. One could search for more wisdom forever, but of course that would be unwise! Wisdom must be sought in proportion to the magnitude of the decision, which also should determine the length of the search.

Principle 4: God's Sovereign Will

The fourth principle is the most difficult to understand, but it is also the one that gives the believer an inward confidence that God is our guide, even in the smallest of life's details: *When we have chosen what is moral and wise, we must trust the sovereign God to work all the details together for good.*

Revelation concerning God's sovereignty was meant to comfort us, but it is more common for us to argue about it. We don't know how to reconcile God's sovereignty with evangelism. But Paul was the greatest teacher of God's sovereignty while being the greatest evangelist in the early church. We cannot harmonize prayer and

God's sovereignty, but Paul's life and letters are full of prayers. In a similar way, while acknowledging the mystery inherent in God's sovereignty, I have come to appreciate the impact of God's sovereign will on decision making.

I define God's sovereign will as His predetermined plan for everything that happens in the universe. God is indeed "the blessed and only Sovereign, the King of kings and Lord of lords" (1 Tim. 6:15 NASB). God's sovereign will has specific characteristics that are worth noting.

First, God's sovereign will is *certain*. It will be fulfilled. It will not be frustrated by humans, angels, or anything else (Dan. 4:35). God determines how many times a sinner will shake his fist at the heavens and whether he will shake it tomorrow (James 4:15). Satan's machismo is limited by God (Job 1:12). To Paul's piercing question, "Who resists his will?" (Rom. 9:19), we must humbly answer, "No one!"

God's sovereignty is most amazing where it intersects with Calvary. The crucifixion of God's Son was the most horrendous act of evil ever perpetrated; but it was also a fulfillment of God's sovereign plan (Acts 2:23; 4:27–28). If the worst thing that ever happened could be the best thing that ever happened (by providing God's salvation), everything else is child's play.

A Redeemer was foreknown before the foundation of the world (1 Peter 1:20) and promised before Adam tossed away the core of the forbidden fruit (Gen. 3:15). The crucifixion was predicted in detail (Ps. 22), and the death of Messiah was interpreted as a guilt offering some seven hundred years before the event (Isa. 53:3–12). Judas's betrayal was prophesied (Matt. 26:24; Acts 1:16) and foretold by Jesus at the Last Supper (Luke 22:21). The time when the Messiah would be "cut off" was predicted by Daniel (Dan. 9:26). Whatever God ordains comes to pass.

Second, God's sovereign will is *detailed*—it includes all things. It ultimately determines which of our plans come to pass (James 4:13–15), the creation of all things (Rev. 4:11), the prince's personal plans (Prov. 21:1), the result of the rolling dice (Prov. 16:33), the believer's suffering (1 Peter 3:17), and our gracious salvation (Rom.

8:29–30; 2 Thess. 2:13–14). In a word, the sovereign God "works out *everything* in conformity with the purpose of his will" (Eph. 1:11, emphasis added).

The third characteristic of God's sovereign will is that it is *hidden*. Older theologians called it the "secret will" (Deut. 29:29). Only God knows in advance what is going to happen, and He is not telling (Ps. 115:3; Rom. 11:33–34; James 4:15). There are two exceptions to this secrecy. God uncovers His sovereign plan in predictive prophecy (Amos 3:7) and in revealing the ultimate destiny of believers and unbelievers (John 3:16; Rev. 20:11–15).

Sovereignty Questions

The thinking reader must sooner or later ask, "Does not God's sovereignty mean that He is responsible for sin?" We know that God is righteous in all His ways (Ps. 145:17). He is sovereign, even over the sinful acts of people (Acts 2:23), but He is not Himself a sinner (James 1:13). No full explanation of this paradox is given in Scripture (Hab. 1:3), but Paul ruled out of court any challenges to God's justice (Rom. 3:4–6). If we hold firmly to God's justice, an illustration suggested by Jonathan Edwards may help. Imagine a planet that is frigid by nature, but it is heated by the sun. The sun decided to move and the planet turned to frozen desolation. Did the sun make the planet cold? Well, yes and no. The sun did determine the temperature of the planet by removing its rays, but it did not produce winter conditions.

God's sovereignty raises the question of whether we make meaningful decisions. It might seem that fatalism is the logical conclusion to God's absolute sovereignty, yet Scripture holds to both God's sovereignty and human responsibility and sometimes in the same breath (e.g., Matt. 26:24; Luke 22:22). Judas acted freely and according to his nature, but God determined how his evil heart would respond. Apparently, God brings about the end without coercing the means. It was certain that Judas would betray Christ, but Judas was certainly responsible. If used carefully, the idea of "permitting" is a way of describing God's relation to evil events in contrast to God doing them directly (e.g., Mark 5:13; Acts 14:16).

If God determines something as certain, it seems as though He must manipulate the people and events leading to the outcome. But is this so? A biblical illustration is suggested by the paradoxical statement, "If you seek Him, He will let you find Him" (1 Chron. 28:9; 2 Chron. 15:2; cf. vv. 4, 15 NASB). I have played hide-and-seek with children like my nieces Brittany and Erica. I begin the game with adult knowledge of how capable young girls are at ferreting out a hidden uncle. I could pick a hiding place too difficult for them, but I'm a good uncle. I hide at the back of a closet. They diligently search and then notice legs coming down from a coat in the guest-room closet. "We found you, Uncle G.!" Did they find me, or did I determine to be found? In a sense they are both true. I did not control them, but I determined how the game would end.

Causality is more complex than a whodunit. Who was the cause of Job's misfortunes? Satan moved against Job with evil intent (Job 1:12). But then again, the Sabeans and Chaldeans actually were the ones who attacked his servants (Job 1:15–17). Then Job expands the choices when he rightly proclaims, "The LORD gave and the LORD has taken away" (Job 1:21). All three are correct, for causality is complex. God is the ultimate determiner, but He acts without taking away the causal roles of either humans or Satan. These considerations lead us to the fourth characteristic of God's sovereign will: it is *supreme*—without violating human responsibility or making God the author of sin.

Finally, God's sovereign will is *perfect*, for it works all things together for God's glory and our good. We all quote Romans 8:28 when the need arises: "God causes all things to work together for good to those who love God" (NASB). Underpinning this great truth is God's sovereignty. He does only good and then works the rest together for good. God's plan is perfect because God is perfect. All of our "why" questions ultimately must have the same answer: our loving God in His sovereign wisdom willed it so. As Os Guinness observed, "We cannot always know why, but *we can always know why we trust God who knows why*, and this makes all the difference."[17]

---

17. Os Guinness, *In Two Minds: The Dilemma of Doubt and How to Resolve It* (Downers Grove, IL: InterVarsity Press, 1976), 255 (emphasis in original).

FIGURE 2.3. GOD'S SOVEREIGN WILL IS . . .

Certain—it will be fulfilled.

Detailed—it includes all things.

Hidden—except when revealed by prophecy.

Supreme—without violating human responsibility or making God the author of sin.

Perfect—it works all things together for God's glory and our good.

According to Paul, you are starting to appreciate sovereignty when you stand in awe of God and then fall before Him in worship (Rom. 11:33–36). Wrestling with the concept of God's sovereignty should expand our view of God and deepen our worship as Lucy illustrates in C. S. Lewis's *Prince Caspian*. When she finally sees Aslan, the great Lion (and symbol of Christ), Lucy gazes up into the large, wise face.

"Welcome, child," he said.

"Aslan," said Lucy, "you're bigger."

"That is because you are older, little one," answered he.

"Not because you are?"

"I am not. But every year you grow, you will find me bigger."[18]

Sovereignty and Decision Making

Now that we have surveyed the biblical terrain of God's sovereign will (summarized in figure 2.3), we must inquire what relation it has to our decision-making process, particularly with regard to planning, circumstances, open doors, and fleeces (summarized in figure 2.4 on page 140).

One of the ways Christians get into trouble with applying the theology of God's sovereignty to daily life is by making faulty inferences from biblical doctrine. Some reason, "If God controls everything that happens, what point is there in making any plans?" But the biblical writers do not follow that "logic."

James provides the biblical perspective on planning. "Now listen, you who say, 'Today or tomorrow we will go to this or that city,

---

18. C. S. Lewis, *Prince Caspian* (New York: MacMillan, 1951), 117; see chapter 10 "The Return of the Lion."

spend a year there, carry on business and make money.' Why, you do not even know what will happen tomorrow. What is your life? You are a mist that appears for a little while and then vanishes. Instead, you ought to say, '*If it is the Lord's will*, we will live and do this or that.' As it is, you boast and brag. All such boasting is evil" (James 4:13–16, emphasis added).

In this sarcastic but sober illustration, James rips the self-sufficient merchants who do not recognize God or His sovereignty. Like the rich fool (Luke 12:16–21), their omission of God from their plans highlights their self-trust. Their boast is absurd, for life is like a vapor (James 4:14). James rebukes their arrogance, but not their planning; for, like Proverbs (21:5), he approves of planning. His corrective calls for humility that recognizes God's sovereignty through one small word: "if." There is nothing wrong with saying, "We will . . . do this or that" so long as it is prefaced by "If the Lord wills" as an expression of humility. God's sovereignty does not exclude the need for planning; it does require humble submission to His will.

A second inferential error moves in the opposite direction. Here the line of reasoning runs like this: "If God controls all things, I ought to be able to discern what He wants me to do by detecting His direction of my circumstances." Some proponents of the traditional view teach that we should "read providence" as a means of determining God's so-called individual will. It is not uncommon to hear believers say, "The Lord led me to do this." When asked what they mean, they will list a series of uncommon circumstances that convinced them that God was telling them to do this or that. However, nothing in Scripture authorizes us to interpret circumstances in that way. People can read almost any meaning into any circumstance.

Lightning strikes the steeple of your church. Why? Brother Bob says, "God is telling us to relocate to the suburbs." Sister Sue fears, "God is saying 'no' to our plans to expand the building." And Pastor Paul is sure that there must be an "Achan" in the camp prompting God's judgment. Solomon made it clear that such speculation is futile (Eccl. 1:1–11). We seek a message from a circumstance and, like the ancients, are wrong when we do so (Luke 13:1–3; John 9:2–3). We do better to speak as Paul did about Onesimus when he said only, "*Perhaps* the reason he was separated from you for a little while . . ." (Philem. 15–16, emphasis added). Or we should emulate Mordecai, who said, "And *who knows* but that you [Esther] have come to royal position for such a time as this?" (Esther 4:14, emphasis added). God did explain the meaning of a plague of locusts in Joel 2:11–17, but without such divine explanation, locusts are just locusts, and circumstances are just circumstances.

These cautions do not mean that circumstances are meaningless. They form the context in which we make choices. Don't try to read circumstances. Instead, look them carefully in the face, because wisdom must take them into account to make a good decision for this time and this place. Some decisions are wise because of the current context, yet they would be foolish under different circumstances. Do you lack the money for college? You probably should not register just now. But better yet, why not pray for God to change your financial situation, which would make it wise to enroll this year—maybe at Multnomah? (I'll save you a seat.)

"Open Doors" and "Fleeces"

There are two biblically related metaphors that could appear to challenge the prohibition against interpreting circumstances. Some have thought of the references to "open doors" in the New Testament as instances of God indicating a particular direction to take. Others think that Gideon provided the precedent for "putting out a fleece" as a means of seeking guidance through a circumstantial sign.

The concept of "open doors" appears primarily in the epistles of the apostle Paul. On one occasion, he explained his current ministry operations in this way: "But I will stay on at Ephesus until Pentecost, because *a great door* for effective work has *opened* to me, and there are many who oppose me" (1 Cor. 16:8–9, emphasis added). In another of his letters, he requested, "Pray for us, too, that God may *open a door* for our message, so that we may proclaim the mystery of Christ, for which I am in chains" (Col. 4:3, emphasis added).

It is clear that Paul is using the word picture of an "open door" to describe an opportunity for ministry. It is equally clear that such opportunities are provided by the sovereign will of God. The presence of such a "door" requires a decision: Should I walk through the door? Should I take this opportunity? What is not so obvious is whether an "open door" constitutes a virtual command from God.

Thankfully, there is one other passage where the matter is settled: "Now when I went to Troas to preach the gospel of Christ and found that *the Lord had opened a door* for me, I still had no peace of mind, because I did not find my brother Titus there. So I said good-by to them and went on to Macedonia" (2 Cor. 2:12–13, emphasis added). Behold, here is an "open door" the apostle walked away from. Why? Because in his judgment, there were other ministry concerns that took priority.

It should be evident that open doors are not divine commands but God-given opportunities to be evaluated by wisdom. Doors are opened or closed by the sovereign God. We normally walk through open doors, but like Paul we may pass one up for more pressing ministry (cf. Acts 16:27–28, 35–37). Doors facilitate entrance. It is foolhardy to climb in a window or tear down a wall when the front door is open. On the other hand a so-called "closed door" is not a command from God to abandon a ministry idea. When faced with such blocked opportunities, Paul would often wait, knock, and try again (e.g., Rom. 1:9–13). Sometimes it's just a matter of timing.

So what about the practice of "putting out a fleece"? A "fleece" differs from an "open door" in that the sign that is chosen as the means of God's guidance is selected by the one seeking guidance, not by God. This practice is based on the experience of Gideon recorded in Judges 6:36–38: "Gideon said to God, 'If you will save Israel by my hand as you have promised—look, I will place a wool fleece on the threshing floor. If there is dew only on the fleece and all the ground is dry, then I will know that you will save Israel by my hand, as you said.' And that is what happened."

Following Gideon's example, many believers seek to determine God's individual will by means of a circumstantial sign: "In essence, when you put out a fleece you say to God, 'If you really want me to carry out plan A, then please make the telephone ring at 9:10 PM, then I will know that plan A is what you want.' (You can make the 'fleece' anything you wish, just so long as it can serve as a 'sign' to you.)"[19]

Within the logic of the traditional view, this method makes some sense. It correctly recognizes God's control of providence. It is a clear and quick way to have God narrow your choices to one. This practice, however, is not supported by this passage. First, Gideon's "fleece" was a miraculous sign, not a circumstantial one. Second, Gideon already had clear guidance. He was asking for a confirmation of guidance already given, which is indicated by the phrase "as you said" (Judg. 6:37). Third, Gideon's demand for an initial sign and then a further sign (v. 39) was an expression of doubt, not a model of decision making. And fourth, in the case of Gideon, God chose to address his fear (which was the real problem) by graciously agreeing to his requests. But we have no biblical warrant for our assumption that God is agreeing to our terms when we put out a fleece.

So, if putting out a fleece is improper, why does it sometimes seem to work? The answer is that on some occasions the fleece that is chosen is really wisdom in disguise (or, dare I say it, wisdom in sheep's clothing). Consider a church board saying, "We will put out a fleece about the potential building program. If 90% of our people favor the project and are willing to sacrifice, we will know God wants us to move ahead." This "fleece" is more like wisdom in the disguise of a fleece, for church unity and willingness to sacrifice are keys to any church building project. I suspect that many use fleeces, not because they are theologically compelling, but because they need to have God reduce their options to one very quickly. But, neither Gideon nor the New Testament promotes the concept of fleeces.

All of us yearn to know that God really cares for the smallest details in our lives. The traditional view meets this need by postulating an individual will where God tells the believer every decision to

---

19. John White, *The Fight* (Downers Grove, IL: InterVarsity Press, 1976), 165. White does not advocate putting out a fleece. His very next statement is, "Forget about fleeces. If you've never used them, don't start. If you have, then quit."

make. But this is a misplaced confidence. Biblically, our confidence should be directed to God's sovereign will, which works every detail together for good. For example, if two options are equally moral and equally wise, the believer can confidently choose either. But the believer also can be certain that God is sovereign over that choice and providentially caring for every detail that it involves.

FIGURE 2.4. GOD'S SOVEREIGN WILL AND DECISION MAKING

1. God's sovereignty does not exclude the need for *planning*, but it does require humble submission to His will.

2. *Circumstances* define the context of the decision and must be weighed by wisdom, not "read" to find God's individual will.

3. *Open doors* are to be evaluated by wisdom as God-given opportunities, not divine commands.

4. "Putting out a *fleece*" is an invalid practice, but it occasionally works out well if it is really wisdom in disguise.

5. God's sovereignty should fill the believer with *confidence* that God cares and guides in the smallest details.

Applying the Principles

All of the views presented in this book are convinced that God is our guide (Ps. 48:14). Each, however, explains this reality differently. The wisdom view summarizes God's guidance under the four headings given in figure 2.5.

FIGURE 2.5. FOUR DISTINCTIVE WAYS GOD GUIDES

Moral Guidance: In moral areas, God guides by scriptural commands.

Wisdom Guidance: Where there is no command, God gives freedom and wisdom sufficient for every decision.

Sovereign Guidance: God secretly guides by working all details together for the believer's good.

Special Guidance: In rare cases God may supernaturally reveal (by voice, angel, or dream) a divine command to a specific person.

The response of faith to God's abundant guidance is both active and passive. Seeking, learning, and memorizing God's moral will must be very active. On the other hand, trusting God to be sovereign and to give special guidance when needed is passive. We humbly leave it in His hands.

God shows His personal care by guiding in every detail, but He guides us differently than the traditional view expects. God does not promise to tell us all the perfect decisions. He guides us as sons and daughters, not robots.

Moral, wisdom, and sovereign guidance are God's promised norms to be believed and expected, but special guidance is a possibility, not a promise. When no special guidance is given, we can trust that it is not needed and move confidently ahead.

A New Testament Case Study: Paul's Model Example

One of the reasons I am convinced that the wisdom view is correct is that it is both internally consistent (in its biblical theology) and practically useful (it works in the real world). This congruence is put on display in a surprisingly complete case study from the life of the apostle Paul—the explanation of his plans to visit Rome at the beginning and end of his epistle to the Romans. The first part is recorded in Romans 1:8–13:

> First, I thank my God through Jesus Christ for all of you, because your faith is being reported all over the world. God, whom I serve with my whole heart in preaching the gospel of his Son, is my witness how constantly I remember you in my prayers at all times; and I pray that now at last by God's will the way may be opened for me to come to you.
>
> I long to see you so that I may impart to you some spiritual gift to make you strong—that is, that you and I may be mutually encouraged by each other's faith. I do not want you to be unaware, brothers, that I planned many times to come to you (but have been prevented from doing so until now) in order that I might have a harvest among you, just as I have had among the other Gentiles.

This passage explains to the Romans Paul's plan to visit them, which immediately confirms the appropriateness of making plans.

He did not consider it improper to say, "I *planned* many times to come to you" (v. 13). There is no hint that he was looking for an individual will of God to determine his decision, and he did not view the hindrance to be a coded message from God. Several times he had prayed and planned to visit them. Now, he was trying again.

Paul prayed about his plans (vv. 8–10), asking the sovereign God to bring them to pass. He had been "prevented" thus far (v. 13). Through his prayers, he submitted himself and his plans to God's sovereign will and believed that if he made it to Rome, it would be "by God's will" (v. 10).

As the Romans read along, they might recognize that Paul's plans were based on previously established spiritual goals:

1. To provide spiritual ministry to the Roman believers (v. 11)
2. To further establish and encourage the church in Rome (vv. 11–12)
3. To receive encouragement from them (v. 12)
4. To win unbelievers to Christ (vv. 13–15)

Such goals could be accomplished in many places besides Rome, so why did the apostle choose Rome? This is not revealed until the end of the epistle (Rom. 15:20–29), where Paul writes,

> It has always been my ambition to preach the gospel where Christ was not known, so that I would not be building on someone else's foundation. Rather, as it is written: "Those who were not told about him will see, and those who have not heard will understand." This is why I have often been hindered from coming to you.
>
> But now that there is no more place for me to work in these regions, and since I have been longing for many years to see you, I plan to do so when I go to Spain. I hope to visit you while passing through and to have you assist me on my journey there, after I have enjoyed your company for a while. Now, however, I am on my way to Jerusalem in the service of the saints there. For Macedonia and Achaia were pleased to make a contribution for the

poor among the saints in Jerusalem. They were pleased to do it, and indeed they owe it to them. For if the Gentiles have shared in the Jews' spiritual blessings, they owe it to the Jews to share with them their material blessings. So after I have completed this task and have made sure that they have received this fruit, I will go to Spain and visit you on the way. I know that when I come to you, I will come in the full measure of the blessing of Christ.

If Paul's opening remarks generated anticipation of an apostolic visit, his final remarks may have reversed that effect. The Romans learned that they were not at the top of Paul's priority list—or second, or third, but fourth. Paul's plan to visit Rome was just one aspect of a much larger project. Paul revealed that his decision making process included the arrangement of his spiritual goals according to his priorities. Unlike many Christian leaders (who hide the reasons for plans behind a spiritual-sounding explanation like, "God told me"), he actually spelled out these priorities and reasons for his plan.

Paul's first priority was evangelizing Greece. This "apostle to the Gentiles" (Rom. 11:13) had a policy of preaching where Christ had not been named (Rom. 15:20–21). The hindrance that he again mentioned (Rom. 15:22) was likely the unfinished work in Greece. By this time Paul was ready to move on to his second priority, which was a trip to Jerusalem. The Romans knew geography well enough to realize that this would take him in the opposite direction. Paul desired to accompany the financial gift that was being sent to the saints in Judea (Rom. 15:26–28). This gift was highly significant since it was a tangible picture of the unity of the body of Christ, demonstrated by Gentile believers giving a gift to Jewish believers (Eph. 2:11–22). Some burly deacons could accomplish the delivery, but Paul's apostolic presence would highlight this symbol of unity.

Once the financial transaction was complete, Paul planned to head back west. To Rome? Actually, his ultimate destination was Spain, and he was hoping that, on the way, the Roman believers would help him complete that trip (Rom. 15:24). Spain was more important for Paul because Rome had the gospel, but Spain did not.

God did not direct Paul to Spain specifically. But He did tell Paul his primary ministry would be to Gentiles (Acts 9:15; 26:17) and that He would send Paul "far away" to reach the lost (Acts 22:21). Paul wanted to reach "all the Gentiles" (Rom. 1:5; 2 Tim. 4:17). In harmony with God's revealed commands, Paul wanted to reach the world in his lifetime.

That was the plan: Greece, Jerusalem, Spain, and, in passing, Rome. With his transparency about his plans, Paul ran the risk of offending some folks in Rome. But he valued mature believers and so modeled decision making for them.

Figure 2.6. STEPS IN PAUL'S DECISION-MAKING PROCESS

1. *Purposes*: Paul adopted spiritual goals that were based on divine revelation.
2. *Priorities*: He arranged his goals into wise priorities, determining what should be done first, second, third, etc.
3. *Plans*: Next, he devised plans that gave him a strategy for accomplishing his objectives.
4. *Prayer*: Through prayer, he submitted himself and his plans to the sovereign will of God. (No doubt, he also prayed for wisdom in the formulation of his plans, though not mentioned in this context.)
5. *Perseverance*: When providentially hindered from accomplishing his plans, he assumed that the delay was God's sovereign will. This conviction freed him from discouragement. Since his plans were sound, the only thing he adjusted was the timetable.
6. *Presentation*: Paul explained his decisions on the basis of God's moral will and his own personal application of wisdom.

History provides the postscript to this narrative. Paul eventually did make it to Jerusalem, Rome, and possibly even Spain. He did not anticipate two years of jail time in Caesarea. On the other hand, his transportation to Rome (with full military escort) was provided by Caesar. Paul's case history exemplifies the balance between engaging in long-range planning and seizing short-term opportunities. We can lay out Paul's decision-making process in six steps as summarized in figure 2.6. This is normative decision making according to the way of wisdom.

3. The Relationship View and the Voice of God

I have already narrated how my understanding of the way of wisdom came from personal study provoked by frustration with the traditional view. In a similar way, it would appear that the relationship view seeks to correct perceived problems with the wisdom view. Proponents of the relationship view agree for the most part with my critique of the traditional view, but they share an important point in common with it: the belief that, in important decisions, God will reveal the best choice by means of His inward voice.

The label for this view indicates a laudatory concern—that Christians engage in decision making within the context of, and informed by, their ongoing relationship with God. The biggest concern that advocates have about the wisdom view is that it appears to promote autonomous decision making.[20] Because it "loses touch with the classic mystical tradition,"[21] the wisdom view, it is said, does not look for God's direct participation in our decision making. The relationship view cannot imagine a scenario in which God is not intimately involved in our major decisions.

My first response to this emphasis is to applaud the insistence on the cultivation of one's relationship with God. The wisdom view advocates prayer for wisdom, but this must not be reduced to a pragmatic extraction of insight from God solely for one's own purposes. Prayer is to be *relational* before it is *petitionary*.

Having said that, I must again counter the notion that the wisdom view somehow excludes God's direct involvement in our decision making. As I indicated above, God's moral, wisdom, and sovereign guidance is abundant. The wisdom view disagrees with the traditional and relationship views in their shared belief that, in a given non-commanded decision, God will actually "tell" the believer what to do. But that does not mean that the practitioner of the wisdom view is leaning exclusively on his or her "own understanding"

---

20. "The 'wisdom' people essentially trust their own capacities to make choices" (Gordon T. Smith, *Listening to God in Times of Choice* [Downers Grove, IL: InterVarsity Press, 1997], 16).

21. Ibid., 102.

(Prov. 3:5) apart from God's involvement. I am not convinced that the perceived defect in the wisdom view is real.

The relationship view agrees with the wisdom view in reject- ing the traditional view's notion of a "blueprint": an ideal, detailed life plan uniquely designed for each person. It recognizes that the process employed by the traditional view is unworkable at the level of mundane decisions. But when it comes to strategic ("basic") de- cisions, this view maintains that one should listen for God's in- ner leading to discern the "best" choice—the one He wants you to make. In other words, while God does not have a specific will for every decision, He does have a specific will for isolated, life-shaping decisions.

Proponents of the relationship view make virtually no effort to establish a biblical basis for such a distinction in approach between minor and major decisions. And again, the proffered biblical illus- trations are instances of special revelation, not inward impulses. The primary sources of authority for this view are the individuals who hold it—notably luminaries of the mystical tradition such as Igna- tius Loyola and John Wesley. Such historical masters offer valuable insight, but their observations are not universally accepted; they do not rise to the level of apostolic authority.

In concert with the traditional view, the relationship view turns to the inner voice of the Spirit for guidance into the best choices. It acknowledges the difficulties in discerning the Spirit's voice amid competing alternatives, and it wisely counsels the believer to bal- ance the subjective witness of the Spirit by the objective witness provided through Scripture and the church. The relationship view affirms that God is eager for us to know and do what is best. Yet un- like the traditional view (as well as the biblical recipients of special revelation), this view cautions that there will always be an element of uncertainty in our decisions. Certainty that one has received di- vine guidance is not a realistic expectation.[22]

Followers of both the traditional and relationship views agonize over how to discern the true voice of the Spirit. For all the reasons I

22. Ibid., 34, 47, 65.

enumerated earlier (see "The Problem of Subjectivity" above), such angst is inevitable so long as the focus is on receiving direction from an inner voice.

Followers of the way of wisdom do not share this anxiety. This is not because we ignore inner impressions but because we regard them differently. Properly evaluated, impressions can be an excellent source of wisdom.

First, wisdom recognizes that the origins of impressions are multiple and mixed rather than single and simple. When others get a strong impression, the first question they may ask is, "Was it from God or from Satan?" But that is the wrong question. One may be able to discern a dominant source, but given the complexities of the interactions of body, soul, and mind, it is likely that a particular impression arises from multiple sources that are each influenced by factors or agents that are good and evil to varying degrees. Most impressions will stem from this mixture of influences, with none being perfectly good or perfectly evil. So wisdom doesn't waste time wondering about the source.

Second, we understand that impressions are not authoritative sources of divine direction. This means we are free to evaluate them for whatever help they might be to us.

Third, the standard for this evaluation is to be the moral will of God and wisdom. There are numerous occasions when an idea pops into a person's head apparently out of thin air. Subsequent reflection confirms that that impression is a first-rate idea for it promotes the achievement of godly goals in an effective way. Such an impulse ought to be followed, not as a gauge of God's ideal will, but as a wise way to serve God. On the other hand, those impressions that are either sinful or foolish ought to be ignored. If they violate common sense, distract one from accomplishing more important tasks, or otherwise result in a waste of time, they should be confidently rejected.

When I was in college, I decided to run for the office of student body president. I prayed that God would help me come up with some creative ideas for a campaign. I also sought advice from friends. One night I woke up at 3 AM with all sorts of ideas ricocheting around my groggy brain. I grabbed a pen and wrote down many of those ideas and then went back to sleep.

What was I to make of those nocturnal impressions? Were they from the Holy Spirit? I didn't have to ask that question. Was God responding to my prayer for help with my campaign? Yes, but those ideas were not revelation. They didn't have authority. God wasn't telling me what to do. He would help me to evaluate them on the basis of morality and wisdom to find the most effective ones. Fortunately, none of them were immoral. Some were downright goofy, and others were unworkable. Of twenty ideas, five formed the basis for my campaign. The rest were discarded. The "logo" for my campaign was the number 32 followed by the degree mark. It was a creative way to convey "Freezin" (which sounds the same as "Friesen"). It caught the attention of the student body, and it communicated well.

God was involved in that intangible, indescribable process called creativity. I don't know how the thoughts were formed during my sleep, and I didn't need to. I did need the wisdom to separate any ideas that were morally acceptable from any that were dubious, and the workable concepts from the foolish ones. Was God involved with me in that process? I have no doubt. When He answers prayer and imparts wisdom, such guidance should be appreciated as a fulfillment of His promise and bring joy to the heart of the recipient.

Working within his framework, I admire the way Gordon Smith builds safeguards into his evaluation of inner impressions. He echoes Paul's admonition to "test everything" (1 Thess. 5:21). To the previously described evaluation by Scripture, he adds three dimensions to the process of discernment: "(1) rational consideration of the options and obstacles, (2) extended time in prayer and reflection, and (3) accountability and discussion with others."[23] Surely any believer following this protocol would arrive at a decision that reflects wisdom and is pleasing to God—regardless of the theological construct he uses to describe the process. (There is a considerable overlap between what Smith calls "discernment" and what I call "wisdom.")

---

23. Ibid., 85.

My only caution is this: Do not give any impression the same authority as divine revelation. The testimony of Scripture is uniform. We are expected to make wise decisions; the requisite wisdom to obey this imperative will be granted to the believer who seeks for it from the right source, by the approved means, and with a godly attitude.

4. Case Studies

There are two aspects that must be addressed for each of the assigned case studies (see this volume's introduction for the case studies). The first is the *nature* of the decision in question: Can the decision makers have assurance that they are making the right choice? The second aspect concerns the *approach* to be taken: How should the individuals go about making their respective decisions?

If you have read my essay, you know that I would address the *nature* of each decision by framing the question differently. The appropriate quest in all three cases is not the "right" decision (in the sense of discerning and following God's individual will) but a *godly and wise* decision. If any of the decision makers in the case studies are bent on discovering God's (individual) will for their decisions, I can't help them.

So how would I respond if any of them came to me for guidance in finding God's specific will? It would depend on how time sensitive their decisions are. If time were of the essence, I would encourage them to find someone (perhaps a pastor) who holds to the traditional view of guidance. My attempt to "correct" their "theology of guidance" in the midst of a decision would create more problems than it would solve. I would encourage them to apply their current understanding of the decision-making process and trust God to guide them.

If the decision makers had the luxury of time and were open to exploring "a biblical alternative to the traditional view," I would suggest that they read the revised edition of *Decision Making and the Will of God*. If they had less time, they could read my essay in this book. An even shorter explanation of the wisdom view may be found on my Web site: www.gfriesen.net. If one of these exposures convinced them of the validity of the way of wisdom, then I could constructively engage with them in the process.

As I address the respective case studies, then, I will say no more about the nature of the objective. What I can offer are my suggestions on the steps to take in order to make wise decisions.

Case 1: Susan and the Choice of a College

As the reader may recall, I have some expertise in the *wrong* approach to choosing a college! Happily, subsequent educational decisions provided fresh opportunities to apply the principles of wisdom I have been espousing. Here are my recommendations for Susan.

1. Place this decision in the category of "very important" and deserving of much time, prayer, and wisdom. It isn't the most important decision a person will make, but it may well be in the top five. And apart from the decision to trust in Christ for salvation, it will likely be the first major life-shaping decision a person makes. People should give it the same time, attention, and energy they would give to a college course.

I don't know Susan's age, but if she is planning to attend college upon graduating from high school, she needs to begin serious preparations by the beginning of her junior year. Articles and books on "how to choose a college" offer checklists of things to do starting in one's *freshman* year.

2. The first order of business is prayer. It is also the second, third, fourth, and last order of business. Susan will need wisdom; wisdom comes from God. He gives to those who ask for it and who seek it from the right (secondary) sources. This most important step may be the one most easily overlooked.

3. Does the moral will of God address this decision? Not directly. There are no biblical passages on college choice. But the Bible does say a good deal about stewardship, which is involved in a large decision like this. So one of the key evaluative questions used in any decision making is: "Which choice represents the best stewardship of my resources (time, money, talents, academic aptitude, etc.) for the kingdom of God?"

4. I am a professor, so it comes naturally to me to make assignments. This decision will require a great deal of *research* on Susan's part. Computer proficiency will get her access to helpful articles on the Internet. She should start with general essays that help her see the component parts of her decision.[24] Other articles will help her analyze the "trees" that make up the "forest" she is navigating.

5. As she begins to explore the options, she may feel overwhelmed by the sheer volume she encounters. After all, there are some 4,200 post–high school educational institutions in the U.S. alone. She will have to develop a system for determining which schools she is even going to consider. The key to doing this is *knowing herself.* Her goal should be to find a school that will meet her particular needs and objectives. Does she want her school to train her for a specific vocation? Does she need a place where she can gain a broad education that will equip her for life, regardless of her ultimate career? Would she like to be trained for Christian ministry? Her answers to questions like these will help her to establish her goals and priorities, which in turn will shape her choice of a school.

She should identify her preferences for each of these factors: type of school, geographical region, setting (urban, suburban, rural), size, distance from home, and cost. She should weigh her preferences as to their importance. Her specifications in these areas will winnow down the field considerably.

6. Susan should not try to do all this by herself. The Bible tells us to consult with counselors. At the head of the list for most students will be parents. By virtue of their investment, parents will likely be the primary consultants on financial decisions. One resource to consult together is a book by Thomas A. Shaw: *College Bound: What Christian Parents Need to Know About Helping Their Kids Choose a College* (Chicago: Moody, 2005).

---

24. For example, see "Choosing Your College: The Basics" at www.petersons.com/ugchannel/file.asp?id=929&path=ug.gs.overview. Another is "25 Common Myths About College" by George Dehne at www.nrccua.org/resource/myth.asp. Other helpful sites: www.collegeview.com, www.collegeview.com/christian_college_directory.html, www.christiancollegementor.com, and www.christiancollegeguide.net.

The high school guidance counselors have the most experience and greatest expertise in navigating the terrain that leads to college. They can be especially helpful in establishing a schedule and identifying what steps to take in what order. They know what college entrance tests need to be taken, when, and where. They also have resources for scholarship applications, and they can help parents fill out FAFSA forms (the standard forms to apply for federal financial aid for college attendance).

7. Susan should give specific attention to her spiritual needs and goals. There are several considerations here. The first is that the college experience is not just about academic instruction. This is the place where adult life will be shaped. This is probably the first place a student will be free from parental direction. Susan will be choosing her values, cultivating her habits, and making decisions about her own beliefs. The environment in which she does this will be very important, for it will have a profound influence on the choices she makes.

The second consideration is this: secular institutions are often antagonistic to Christian faith, while Christian schools tend to promote advancement in one's spiritual life. Some Christian students attend universities where they maintain a vibrant testimony and influence others as "salt and light." Many do not. After enduring the trauma stemming from the self-destruction of his Christian daughter at a public institution, Steve Henderson conducted research on the impact of colleges and universities on the spiritual lives of students. The results of that research were stunning. On the one hand, the impact of non-Christian schools is so negative and so powerful that one-half to two-thirds of Christian students at those institutions will turn their backs on their faith. On the other hand, Christian schools with believing faculty members, Christian students, and an intentional effort to integrate faith and learning actually promote higher levels of commitment in the lives of their graduates.[25]

---

25. Steve Henderson wrote an article summarizing his findings: "A Question of Price Versus Cost," *Christianity Today*, March 2006, 80, 82, 86, 96, 98, 102, 106. This article may be accessed online at: www.christianconsulting.net/stats.htm. His full report is also available at that same site.

As you can see, the choice of a college/university is not just an academic or vocational decision. Because this is such a critical period in the shaping of one's spiritual development, wherever you go to school, you *must* be intentional about developing strategies to both protect and advance your spiritual life. I graduated from a Christian liberal arts college and I teach at a Bible college, and I can attest to the values of both kinds of schools. In any event, here's another assignment from the professor: Read *How to Stay Christian in College* by J. Budziszewski (Colorado Springs: NavPress, Th1nk Books, 2004) between the junior and senior years in high school.

8. Finally, here are some personal tips for Susan (and anyone like her) to consider in the process of choosing a college.

- If you don't know what you want to be when you grow up, start with a good junior college or community college and take general education courses at a cheap price. If you do know, select a college that is strong in your desired vocation.
- Talk to several graduates from each of your top three potential college choices, and ask them the strengths and weaknesses of their schools.
- Visit your top two or three potential college choices. While on campus, ask hard questions and attend as many classes as you can.
- If you choose a secular college, take pains to nurture your faith and be involved in outreach.
- If you choose a Christian liberal arts college, take extra Bible courses so you have a good grasp of the Bible.
- If you go to a Bible college (I can recommend one), get out of the bubble and into the world for active ministry.
- Make a timely decision, so you have time to pursue every scholarship and loan that you need.
- Don't borrow more than $20,000 for your education unless you are being trained for a high-paying career. Instead, stop when funds run short, work like crazy to earn more tuition money, and then go back and finish your college degree as soon as you can.

- ✦ Take a full load of courses every term and finish college as quickly as possible. Most of those who stop get entwined in life and never finish.
- ✦ The key to a good education is a thirst for learning. No one can stop you from getting a good education if you work hard and pursue the best teachers.

Case 2: The Marriage Decision for Joe and Nancy

Unlike the choice of a college, the Bible does address the marriage decision. At no point are believers told to seek the (individual) will of God regarding this (or any other matter). Paul's lengthy discussion of the relative merits of singleness and marriage (1 Cor. 7) places this non-commanded decision squarely in the laps of those involved. So Joe and Nancy are both free and responsible to make this important decision.

Personally, I have been happily single longer than Joe and Nancy have been alive, so they might not come to me for counsel. But if they did, I could help them develop a plan for decision making.[26] As one would expect, the approach would be similar to what I recommended to Susan in her choice of a college.

First, Joe and Nancy must pray for wisdom. They should do this at each step along the way, asking God for insight and for personal growth through the process.

Second, they must consult the moral will of God. In this case, the guidance is pervasive because it includes all the biblical material on God's design and instructions for marriage. Most people skip this step. But before one asks, "Should I get married?" one should ask, "What does God have in mind for marriage?" Joe and Nancy should study Genesis 1–3, Matthew 19, 1 Corinthians 7, Ephesians 5, and 1 Peter 3 to see where they will be headed if they choose marriage. If I were teaching a college course on this subject, I would

---

26. At this writing, Robin Maxson and I are working on a book for single adults on marital decision making. But Joe and Nancy probably will need to make their decision before this book is published. What is available to them is a chapter-length presentation on their decision: "Marriage and Wisdom," in *Decision Making and the Will of God*, rev. ed. (chap. 20).

require the reading of *God, Marriage, and Family: Rebuilding the Biblical Foundations* by Andreas J. Köstenberger with David W. Jones (Wheaton, IL: Crossway, 2004). *Intimate Allies* by Dan B. Allender and Tremper Longman III (Wheaton, IL: Tyndale, 1995) fleshes out the implications of God's design for married couples.

With that groundwork, Christians can seriously explore their suitability as potential marriage partners. The guidance of the moral will of God emphasizes spiritual and moral qualifications. This is wonderfully illustrated in the Old Testament book of Ruth, which gives a glimpse into what Boaz and Ruth saw in each other. From observing her in the harvest fields, Boaz knew that Ruth was a hard worker. That was significant because most of life involves work. They both saw each other reaping a harvest through diligent physical effort (Ruth 2; cf. Prov. 31:13–16). Further, Boaz witnessed Ruth's devotion to her mother-in-law, Naomi—a "bitter" woman (Ruth 1:20; 2:11). Boaz concluded that Ruth's devotion to a morose mother-in-law demonstrated that she could love him, warts and all. For her part, Ruth noted that Boaz cared for his workers and they respected him as their foreman. So Boaz and Ruth impressed each other with their diligence and their caring spirits. Finally, both were growing in faith. Boaz blessed Ruth for her faith (Ruth 2:12; cf. Prov. 31:28–29), and his workers blessed Boaz for his faith (Ruth 2:4). This triad of excellence (worker, lover, grower) is a great place to start.

It bodes well for Joe and Nancy that they have been dating for two years and that they are relatively mature (probably late twenties). In that length of time, they should know each other pretty well. Nevertheless, they would do well to consult with counselors to bring pastoral insight and objectivity to their assessments. Once again, some of this counsel can be gained by reading. My colleagues recommend the aptly titled, *How to Avoid Marrying a Jerk: The Foolproof Way to Follow Your Heart Without Losing Your Mind* by John Van Epp (New York: McGraw Hill, 2007). Additional insight is available from Neil Clark Warren's classic, *Finding the Love of Your Life* (Colorado Springs: Focus on the Family, 1992), or his more recent and comprehensive book (with Ken Abraham), *Falling in Love for All the Right Reasons: How to Find Your Soul Mate* (New York: Center Street, 2005).

But Joe and Nancy also should receive insight from people who are close to them—especially family members, friends who know both of them, and mentors. Remember, throughout human history, most marriages have been *arranged* by others—usually parents—so the perspectives of others can be very helpful.

I also agree with marriage experts who recommend *pre-engagement* counseling. The primary objective of this counseling is to help a couple assess their suitability and readiness for marriage. In particular, an experienced counselor who is trained to utilize the testing materials provided by the PREPARE/ENRICH marital enhancement program can administer and evaluate objective inventories that will help a couple identify the issues that they need to consider.[27] This will include the strengths that each brings to the relationship and the factors that may produce conflict in the marriage. They are looking not only for "deal breakers," that is, things that would warrant no further consideration of marriage, but also for the kinds of things that will require adjustment and adaptation in a future marriage. Serious issues such as relational abuse or addictions within families of origin will need to be significantly addressed in advance of a wedding. As you can see, pre-engagement counseling becomes the first level of premarital counseling for those who choose to proceed with marriage. This will take time and effort, but a lifetime is a long time to live in close connection with another person.

Much more could be said, but I conclude with this piece of advice for Joe and Nancy (and any couples like them). If you cannot give yourself fully in the covenant of marriage with this person, end the relationship. You can't date for fun when you are thirty-one. Most likely one of you is already waiting for the other. Do your homework, pray throughout the process, and decide. Then, trust in the Creator of marriage, the sovereign God, to be working out His good purposes in both of your lives.

---

27. See the PREPARE/ENRICH Web site at www.prepare-enrich.com. Other similar programs also may be helpful.

Case 3: The Choice of a Local Church for David and Rachel

This is a nice problem. When it comes to choosing a church home, Americans have the luxury of multiple options. In most places in the world, believers feel fortunate if they have one church (and a pastor) and do not have to meet underground.

Assuming that all three churches David and Rachel have examined are doctrinally sound, there are two main components to their decision, with several secondary considerations. The Bible (God's moral will) teaches that one of the primary functions of the church is the edification of believers. That means that all Christians are to *receive* upbuilding ministry from fellow believers in the church, and all Christians are to *contribute* to the mission of the church (Eph. 4:11–16). So, David and Rachel should be evaluating churches on the basis of what their family will *gain* from the local body and what they will *give* to it. And they should be seeking a balance that is appropriate for this stage in their lives. For example, if they are relatively mature, high-energy self-starters with ministry experience, they could make a significant contribution to Third Church—and they would be motivated by the challenge. On the other hand, if they are relatively new to the faith and both work full-time, they would benefit more from the more established ministries of First or Second Church.

Secondary considerations include proximity, worship style, quality of preaching, and opportunities for children. The secondary factors are important and will tip the scale if they find that two (or all) of the churches provide equal opportunities for ministry input and output.

A comparison chart is one way to wisely evaluate multiple options. The important factors of the decision can be listed, in order of preference, in one column and the options presented in parallel columns. Next, each of the options can be evaluated with respect to each factor. A comparison chart for David and Rachel's church decision could be simply constructed (see figure 2.7).

Such a list puts the most important things first and gives a good overview of strengths and weaknesses. Each member of the family (including the children) can pray about the decision for a week. The

FIGURE 2.7. COMPARISON CHART FOR DECISION MAKING

Important Factors	First Church	Second Church	Third Church
Doctrine	1	1	1
Service opportunities	2	1	1
Children's ministries	2	1	3
Preaching	2	1	2
Proximity	1	3	2
Worship style	3	2	1
Atmosphere	3	2	1

time of prayer will give everyone a chance to ask God for wisdom, asking Him to help align the family's values with the ones He has revealed in Scripture. The selection of a church can be part of every family prayer time.

If a consensus choice does not emerge after a week, then David and Rachel can determine to visit one of the churches for four months and then decide yes or no. Four months is generally long enough to gain more of an insider's view and to evaluate a church by personal values.

Whichever church is ultimately chosen will have weaknesses. But there are many creative ways to compensate for them. If the selected church is weaker in children's ministry, David and Rachel can involve their kids in programs and activities offered by other groups. If the preaching is uninspired, they can determine to learn what they can from the pastor and supplement his messages with recordings from more gifted speakers. If the driving time is longer, they can be more selective about which activities they attend.

This balanced approach is preferable to (and should not be confused with) a "consumer" mentality that "shops" for a church solely on the basis of what it has to offer. It also acknowledges that Christian families have varying needs and resources and that local congregations have strengths and weaknesses. David and Rachel (and any believers like them) should not be looking for the perfect church or God's ideal will but for a reasonably good match. Being grounded and useful in one imperfect church is better than looking for a perfect church forever.

5. A Final Word

It may be helpful to give a final summary of the way of wisdom, using practical questions as we face decisions. The wisdom view advocates decision making by asking, Which decision will help me love God and people the most? Which option will most promote the glory of God and building up of people? Is this choice moral; is it wise? Which decision will most promote the kingdom of God? Which path will facilitate being as shrewd as a serpent and as blameless as a dove? Make it your goal in life and decisions to be "full of the Spirit and wisdom" (see Acts 6:3).

A Specific-Will View Response to the Wisdom View

RICHARD AND HENRY BLACKABY

Introduction

We welcome the opportunity to dialogue with Garry Friesen on this important subject. We appreciate Friesen's desire to encourage Christians who want to live their lives in the fullest measure possible. In this volume he has characteristically written with passion and conviction. Not surprisingly, however, as we studied Friesen's presentation, we found a number of points with which we disagree. The following represents some of the major areas of difference.

Subjective Starting Point and Approach

Friesen's launching point for discovering—or inventing—the wisdom view was his own experience. He became frustrated trying to determine the college in which he should enroll. He claims of the traditional view, "I couldn't get it to work." He eventually determined that since the problem was not in God's ability to communicate, "That left only one other explanation for my difficulty:

there was something wrong with my understanding of the biblical teaching on God's will."

Friesen's eventual embracing of the wisdom view was precipitated by his own disappointing experience, which led him to look for a reason for his failure to find God's will. The danger of going from one's experience to Scripture is that we risk doing what Friesen accuses the traditionalists of doing—proof-texting. Clearly it is advisable to begin with Scripture and let it speak for itself. Then, if our experience does not match up with what is presented in the Bible, we ask the Holy Spirit to help us adjust our experience until it lines up with what the Bible teaches. But when we focus on our experience and then look to Scripture to confirm it, we open ourselves up to misusing God's Word.

Friesen asked God to tell him what he should do, and God did not; so Friesen concluded that his understanding of God was inaccurate. While we would agree at that point, there are other possible answers to his dilemma. For example, one reason for not receiving divine guidance could have been the presence of sin in his life. God withholds His assistance from those who ask for it if they insist on clinging to their sin (Isa. 59:1–3). Or perhaps God delayed His answer in order to increase Friesen's faith (John 11:4–6). While Friesen obviously has made an extensive study of biblical sources, it strikes us as being predicated by his personal, negative experience.

Also on the personal level, Friesen testifies to having received a thousand letters in response to his book on decision making, many of which are positive toward his approach. While he does not offer this as anything more than anecdotal support to his argument, perhaps we should counter by saying that our work, *Experiencing God: Knowing and Doing the Will of God,* has been met with a resoundingly positive response. Approximately eight million copies have been purchased, and countless additional copies have been acquired in over seventy languages. We could submit thousands of testimonies from Christians who say the material helped them to experience God as He specifically guided them. While the writer with the largest volume of fan mail does not necessarily win the debate, we must note that we regularly receive heartfelt stories from people whose Christian lives were radically transformed when they realized God is a person who seeks an intimate, dynamic, interactive relationship with them.

Traditional View Misrepresented

Throughout Friesen's presentation, he misrepresents the traditional view, at times resorting to *argumentum ad absurdum*. Perhaps because he once held the traditional view, Friesen believes he can speak authoritatively for it. At times, however, he appears to misrepresent the view in order to better assault it. While it may be easier to defeat a straw man, doing so makes any victory less convincing.

For example, Friesen claims, "Every day we make thousands of decisions, but most of them are so insignificant that we hardly notice them. Which seat in class? Which pair of socks? Beverage at lunch? The traditional view asserts that God cares for every detail, and so His individual will for you is very specific." He goes on to assert that "followers of the traditional view must abandon their theology for ordinary, less important decisions. . . . The traditional view paints itself into a corner by claiming that for every decision there is only one choice that is God's individual will." Friesen first creates a distorted caricature of the traditional position. Then, after inserting values not shared by those who hold the view, he targets those invented absurdities. We are familiar with many of the leading advocates of the traditional view. We know of no one who claims that God has a specific will for which beverage we select out of the soda machine and that to choose the "wrong" one is sin. Because God is omniscient, He always knows which decision for us ultimately would be best, even to the smallest degree. However, we fully recognize that numerous commonplace decisions are insignificant in their impact on our lives.

We understand that God affords people complete autonomy in these decisions. To portray people as obsessing over such mundane choices is obviously a gross misrepresentation of our view. Moreover, to acknowledge that God leaves us free to make routine decisions does not negate the fact that He wants to be involved in the weighty matters of our lives.

A clear example of Friesen's exaggeration is the "imaginative rendition" of "The First Supper." Such argumentation, while humorous, is not helpful. We could include scenarios to support our case as well, and we could do so without having to conjure up imaginary ones. Several years ago Richard needed to hire a new professor for the seminary. He interviewed a man who was qualified and seeking a position. The candidate visited the campus and met with the faculty. He was enthusiastic about the job. But then he pulled out his pros-and-cons list. He identified various aspects of the seminary mandate that greatly appealed to him. He also had some concerns, which included health care, relocating his family, the harsh Canadian climate, and the quality of the local school system. Back and forth he wavered. In a subsequent phone call, he could not say definitively that he was prepared to come to the seminary. Neither could he say the faculty position was the wrong choice for him. He simply didn't know. Eventually Richard ended the process. Three years later Richard ran into this man at a conference. He was still searching for a teaching position. He had interviewed with several other institutions but always with the same stalemated result. But, he explained, although he was frustrated at waiting for years to find the school that would best fit him and his family, he had been extremely appreciative of the wisdom approach to decision making. He kept lists of pros and cons and applied all the methodology recommended by proponents such as Friesen, and he was sure that eventually he would find an appropriate job. Presumably this man took the wisdom approach to the extreme, but rarely have we met someone more indecisive and confused.

The man did not expect direct guidance from God, so he had to rely on himself. He had dutifully itemized pros and cons, but how did he know when his list was complete? Had he overlooked a pro? Had he neglected a con? Was something he had identified as a pro in fact a con? Although there were slightly more pros, was that enough differential to address the various cons? Although fewer in number, did some of the cons carry more weight than certain pros? This man found the decision-making process overwhelming, and, since appealing to an omniscient God for direct guidance was out of bounds, he carried the full weight of choosing without having all the information he felt he needed.

Biblical Selectivity and Weak Exegesis

Despite Friesen's attempt to develop a biblical approach, he is selective in his use of Scripture. For example, Friesen comments, "The moral will of God commands wisdom in decision making," and he cites Ephesians 5:15–16. While verse 15 exhorts people to not walk as fools but as those who are wise, verse 17—which Friesen does not cite—urges, "Therefore do not be foolish, but understand what the Lord's will is." The apostle Paul was indeed advising believers to be wise, for they lived in difficult, evil times. But how were they to be wise? By understanding the Lord's will. Wisdom is not merely making the best choice on our own; it is knowing God's will.

Friesen selects several verses, such as Proverbs 3:6 and 16:9 and Romans 12:2 and then attempts to show how they have been misused or poorly translated by various Bible translations. Yet, as seen in our earlier chapter, these are not the prime verses upon which those holding the traditional view would build their case.

Friesen uses Luke 14:28–32 to advocate pros-and-cons lists as tools in general decision making, but here Jesus was clearly encouraging people to consider the significant cost before choosing to follow Him. Friesen cites the incorrect counsel given to Job by his friends, as well as the advice of the people of Malta to Paul, as evidence that the counsel of others cannot effectively exegete our circumstances. Again, such examples are a stretch. Job's counselors are notorious for their inaccurate theology (cf. Job 42:7–9). The natives on the island of Malta—who were not even believers—obviously would be unable to recognize God's activity in Paul's circumstances. Presenting these examples as evidence that godly counselors cannot aid us in interpreting our circumstances is an exegetical fallacy.

Friesen also suggests, "There is no indication in *Scripture* that the Holy Spirit leads believers in non-commanded decisions by means of inner impressions." Until Pentecost (Acts 2), the Holy Spirit did not reside within each believer. That is why much of the biblical record records God speaking to people in ways other than through an inner voice. After the Spirit descended upon believers, however, He did speak to them. Matthew 10:19 says Jesus assured His disciples they need not worry when they appeared before the authorities because the Holy Spirit would give them the words to speak. Undoubtedly, this would be internal communication. Likewise, the Spirit told Philip to approach the Ethiopian eunuch (Acts 8:29). While Scripture does not identify this as an inner impression, the only outward alternatives would be an audible voice or a visible cue. In any case, the Spirit guided Philip in a non-commanded action. Friesen does acknowledge this event later but arbitrarily places it in a convenient category of "exception." Peter also heard a voice in a trance, presumably the Holy Spirit's (Acts 10:13). Paul, Timothy, and Silas were warned by the Spirit not to preach in Asia or Bithynia (Acts 16:6–7). Again, unless these were written memos or an audible voice, they would have been inner impressions. Later Paul was "compelled by the Spirit" to go to Jerusalem and said that "the Holy Spirit warn[ed]" him about what to expect there (Acts 20:22–23).

Inadequate Pneumatology

Friesen acknowledges that he has been labeled a deist, and indeed his presentation of the Holy Spirit's work subjects him to such a label. Friesen never thoroughly addresses the fact that when people become Christians, Christ resides within them by His Spirit (Gal. 2:20). The same Christ who gave regular guidance to His disciples now dwells within each believer. Friesen leaves Christ mute in believers' lives except when affirming what they are reading in their Bibles. Claiming that God does not speak to us in our inner spirits also diminishes prayer. If the Spirit does not speak to us inwardly, our prayers are reduced to one-way conversations in which we ask for what we want and God mutely complies with or denies our requests.

Friesen claims that the primary way to receive wisdom is to pray for it. He is unclear, however, on how God grants wisdom through prayer. If the Spirit does not give direct guidance, does He suddenly increase our wisdom brain cells? Friesen also asserts that most "impressions" stem from a mixture of influences, none purely good or evil (we assume he is excluding God from these). Therefore, "wisdom doesn't waste time wondering about the source." This advice appears unwise! Even if the Spirit's voice is only one of several inner impressions we receive, the fact that God is speaking makes it foolhardy not to discern which voice is His. Excluding God (who is Spirit) from speaking directly to one's own spirit eliminates a major avenue in our communion with Him. It seems Friesen recognizes that the Spirit ought to have a significant role in the believer's life, but he is unsure how to give Him one while keeping Him silent at the same time.

Inappropriate Scientific Approach

Part of Friesen's dilemma is that he wants to develop a rational, empirical formula for decision making. This leads to what he terms the "problem of subjectivity." He notes that there is no sure way to know if the "inner voice" you hear is from God; therefore, he concludes, it cannot be authoritative. He mentions "road signs" that the specific-will view offers to verify a word is from God and then claims these signs do not provide objective criteria for evaluating inner impressions. Interestingly, he neglects to mention Scripture as a means of verifying internal messages, although this would be the first place those holding the specific-will view would turn. Scripture clearly offers authoritative, objective criteria for evaluating what people sense the Spirit is saying. Further, Friesen concludes, "The need for *clarification* from the other signs calls into question the origin of the inner voice." This is a circular argument. On the one hand, Friesen argues that because there are no objective ways to evaluate an "inner voice" (assuming we exclude Scripture), inner impressions are invalid. Then, on the other hand, he contends that because such inner impressions must be tested, they are invalid. With such reasoning, the apostle Paul's words to the Berean Christians would have been rejected because the Berean believers felt the need to confirm what he said with Scripture (Acts 17:11).

Friesen's attempt at a foolproof method for decision making overlooks the fact that Christianity is a relationship between persons. Relationships are not scientific. There are things we know about each other intuitively. Dismissing the feelings and impressions we experience turns something dynamic and growing into a sterile formula. Watch a couple that has been married for forty years. They communicate volumes without even speaking. Is that communication invalid because it is not scientifically measurable? Likewise, to mute the Spirit's voice and to consign Christians to a life of following principles and pros-and-cons lists is to rob them of the joy of relating to a person who loves them and desires fellowship with them. Because we have Scripture, supplemented by the wise counsel of godly believers, we have safeguards to evaluate what we sense God is saying to us inwardly.

Special Revelation

Friesen sidesteps the numerous scriptural occurrences of God speaking directly to people by labeling these occurrences as "special revelation" and claiming that they are not comparable to the normal decision making we do. Theologians have constructed categories such as general and special revelation, but of course, these terms are not found in Scripture. The Bible simply presents God as communicating with people in numerous ways, both general and specific. While Friesen speaks of "discovering" God's will, we recognize that you cannot discover God's will. God must reveal it. We contend that you cannot bundle up the scores of biblical examples of God speaking directly to people and classify them as "special revelation" or "sporadic" or "exceptions" that are irrelevant to modern Christians and then claim to have developed a biblical model for decision making.

Wisdom Theory

Friesen seems to suggest that because those holding the specific-will view have God to tell them what to do, they don't find a need for wisdom. In fact, we recognize and wholeheartedly affirm that Scripture exhorts people to seek and use wisdom. Friesen's theory of wisdom, however, leaves us with several questions. First, how does God grant wisdom without communicating directly with us? Friesen lists Scripture, outside research, counselors, life experience, and direct revelation as additional sources of wisdom. Regarding outside research, Friesen mentions Joshua sending spies into Canaan. What the spies gathered would be better labeled knowledge, not wisdom. What Joshua *did* with that knowledge demonstrated wisdom. Likewise, under direct revelation, he mentions the angel telling Philip to join the seeker. Was it wisdom Philip was given or a command? Was not Philip's obedience to the angel a demonstration of wisdom rather than a reception of wisdom?

Finally, principle 4 of the wisdom approach is confusing. It seems that after arguing throughout his essay that God does not tell us what to do in things not commanded in Scripture, Friesen then inserts principle 4 to tell us not to worry because, regardless of what decisions we make, God will work it all out in the end. Friesen asserts, "To Paul's piercing question, 'Who resists his will?' (Rom. 9:19), we must humbly answer, 'No one!'" Of course, people *do* resist God's will. Anyone who commits a sin resists God's will. While God does have a will for us to follow, He does not force it on us. Fortunately, God's eternal purposes do not hinge on us. His plans will be accomplished. But whether or not we will participate and enjoy the fruit of His activity are choices we make. We cannot make our decisions apart from God's active involvement and then assume God will overcome our bad choices to bring to our lives the good He intended. Such an attitude is irresponsible. If we want to be involved in God's activity in our world, we need to seek His leading at the front end and not pray for God to clean up our messes after we have acted apart from His proffered guidance.

God wants to give us far more than His wisdom or His principles or His commandments. He wants to give us Himself. Why would we settle for less than that?

A Relationship View Response to the Wisdom View

GORDON T. SMITH

In Appreciation

Garry Friesen's autobiographical references catch my attention, in part, because in many ways they reflect my own journey on this topic. I too was raised within a religious subculture that took for granted the perspective known herein as the "specific-will" view. And with my mind's eye, I can still picture the cassette tapes of lectures on the "wisdom" view given by Professor Bruce Waltke at Regent College that a friend sent to my wife and me back in the 1970s, introducing us to this perspective.

It was a perspective that, at the time, resonated deeply with us, with its affirmation of the appropriate way to read Scripture and the affirmation of the human call to grow in maturity and wisdom and to act with wisdom. I felt that through this teaching we were being called to set aside childish ways and embrace a mature vision of the Christian life and, in particular, of decision making as an integral part of the Christian life. Much of what resonated with me in those years is reflected in the content of the essay by Garry Friesen in this volume.

With his 1980 publication and with subsequent essays and updates, Friesen has effectively profiled themes and perspectives that are invaluable to this whole discussion. Indeed, in my own teaching on this subject, as a rule I spend little time providing a critique of the specific-will view; I just tell my students to "read Garry Friesen."

In particular, they will find his critique of the whole notion of "open doors" and "fleeces" especially valuable.

Beyond his excellent critique of the specific-will view, I find in Friesen's book, as in his essay here, some things that are of continuing value. First, I appreciate his rigorous approach to the Scriptures and the rightful insistence that they cannot be used (and so easily abused) in a manner that discounts or ignores the original intent. He rightly observes that many texts that have no direct bearing on the matter of specific choices and decisions are routinely used by those who are seeking to support a specific-will view. Friesen aptly calls us back to a reading of Scripture that truly honors the text.

Second, I have also valued the emphasis on wisdom in his essay and in the perspective of Friesen and others who have taught the wisdom view. It has served as an excellent reminder that, while we are children of God, we are not to tolerate childishness. Rather, the human ideal is one where the Christian grows in faith, hope, and love, and this spiritual growth is evident, over time, in wisdom. To grow old is to grow wise; and it is a deep tragedy when someone grows older but does not grow wiser. One almost feels that a life lacking wisdom is a wasted life. And this wisdom will certainly be evident in the quality of one's choices. Indeed, we are not wise *unless* we are wise in our decision making. Foolish people choose poorly; the wise, in contrast, are able to weigh considerations and options and, for themselves and for those they serve, make wise choices. And as a rule this is learned over time. One grows older and in the process learns wisdom.

In Critique

But, while I can and must affirm the strengths that Friesen brings to this conversation, I fear that this might be yet another example of the bathwater and the baby. In reading his essay, it does not take long for the reader to see that something is missing—something valuable has been thrown out. Furthermore, he needs to be challenged on another point. First, I will address what is missing and then what must be challenged.

What is missing is the power of immediacy—of intimacy and fellowship with Christ. There is nothing of this in Friesen's essay. While I would not go so far as to call this approach "cold," one wonders where God is in all of this, with so few references to the presence of Christ and the ministry of the Spirit. The distinct sense that one gets is that God provides the wisdom when we seek it through prayer, but God is not immediately present to our lives and thus not present to our decision making. Years ago, Regent College professor Klaus Bockmuehl raised a concern about those who advocated this view of divine guidance and decision making. Speaking of Jesus' relationship with the Father, he insisted that Jesus signaled "the end of the rule of religious principles that we often assume and then apply independent of God," which is nothing but another version of "self-rule," a kind of "practical deism."[28]

As I read this most recent contribution from Friesen, I did so with the following question: Does Friesen, as a representative of the wisdom view, adequately respond to this critique from Bockmuehl? I am not convinced that he does. To the contrary, I find this to be an essay that fails in the opposite way from that of the Blackabys. My concern with the specific-will view was that when it came to the twofold test of 1 Thessalonians 5—do not quench the Spirit but test everything—the Blackabys were eager to be open to the Spirit but did not have an effective approach to discerning whether something was truly from God. Friesen comes up short on the other half of the equation. The wisdom perspective is all about testing and weighing and considering, but there is not reflected here a radical openness to the Spirit, an eagerness to know Christ intimately and to respond with joy to the inner witness of the Spirit. Indeed, this inner witness, this immediacy, is discounted. And in the process what is lost is the clear expectation that our relationship with Christ would be a reflection of the relationship that Jesus had with the Father.

Thus, a whole range of the biblical witness is not accounted for, most notably those segments in the teaching of Jesus and the

---

28. Klaus Bockmuehl, *Listening to the God Who Speaks: Reflections on God's Guidance from Scripture and the Lives of God's People* (Colorado Springs: Helmers and Howard, 1990), 51.

apostles wherein this level of intimacy—an immediate, not formal relationship—is highlighted. What we urgently need is an approach to decision making that allows Christ to be fully present to our lives—not just the idea of Christ and not just the wisdom of Christ, but indeed Christ Jesus Himself, who, of course, is present to us by the power and presence of the Spirit. For the Christian, this is the very stuff of life: to know the voice of Jesus, which (especially in the gospel of John) is clearly what Jesus desires for His disciples. This is a relationship that can be described as His abiding in us as we abide in Him. In this relationship, He is our Shepherd. We live in a dynamic fellowship with Christ that is made possible through the ministry of the Spirit. The clear intent of the Scriptures is that Christ would be in immediate relationship with His disciples. And naturally this relationship has implications for how we approach the critical choices of our lives.

This gap in Friesen is reflected, in part, in the way that he speaks about prayer. In his essay he regularly calls his readers to pray, but this prayer is not the prayer of communion but merely that of asking for wisdom (and perhaps also the prayer of affirmation of the sovereignty of God). But, in this perspective, there is no real reason to pray if you already have the wisdom. If you have what you need, then you do not need God anymore. In other words, this view has not as yet responded to Bockmuehl's critique.

For example, when it comes to the case studies and the counsel he gives to the couple who are considering the choice of a church, he urges, "Each member of the family (including the children) can pray about the decision for a week. The time of prayer will give everyone a chance to ask God for wisdom." But again I ask, Why pray, and pray more, and pray yet again? Is it merely a way to keep topping off the amount of wisdom we might have? In other words, the call to prayer is commendable; but as with the specific-will view, the purpose of prayer is much too pragmatic and functional. Yes, the Scriptures urge us to seek God and to ask for wisdom; but this is only one dimension of the biblical understanding of prayer, which is most fundamentally an act of communion and fellowship with God.

This is what is missing from Friesen's presentation. There is also something in his essay that must be challenged, namely, his view of the subjective—and particularly the role of the affections (emotion)—in Christian experience and decision making.

Friesen rightly affirms the unique revelatory authority of the Scriptures over against interior impulses or movements of the heart. But then he extrapolates from this that the subjective must be marginalized since it is not authoritative and since, in his view, it cannot be trusted—specifically because it is "subjective."

There are two notable problems with Friesen's view at this point. First, he insists that the written Word is objective and therefore the only reliable guide for the Christian (not in tandem with, but over against, the subjective). But this takes no account of choices or issues we face that pit the good against the good—when two good, biblically sound alternatives represent competing values for us, when the ambiguities of life are not resolved by a verse of Scripture. The most poignant biblical example is the experience of Christ in Gethsemane. From Friesen you could think that the only problem with Jesus was that He did not read His Bible clearly, or He would not have had to wrestle so deeply with this matter of the cross.

The other problem with this is what can only be termed a naive or one-dimensional understanding of the human person. Midway through the essay, Friesen makes a series of affirmations—numbered 1 through 5—in which he "rules . . . out" inner impressions as unreliable indicators of God's (so-called) individual, specific will. He discounts them because they are subjective and not "objectively true." And thus, he argues, these are not in any way to be treated as "revelation" from God.

Can we pit the objective and the subjective against one another in this way? While the Scriptures are surely an "objective" witness, our reading of the Scriptures never is! Further, do we not need to affirm that what is happening to us emotionally, subjectively, always will be a factor in both our reading of Scripture and our response to God? All decisions—there are no exceptions—are deeply shaped by the emotional contours of our lives. There is no such thing as pure objectivity. There is no such thing as a reading of Scripture that is not informed—markedly so—by the joys and sorrows, fears and anxieties, that make up our human existence. We cannot bracket out the emotional contours of our lives. Friesen discounts the subjective but then also discounts the pervasive role of the "heart" in the experience of the believer. This is one-dimensional and, actually, not objective (as though this is possible). To the contrary, we need an approach to discernment and decision making that (1) takes account of the immediate presence of Christ in our lives and (2) enables us to respond to God, to our world, and to our circumstances with both heart and mind.

Actually, one gets a hint of the problem fairly early on in Friesen's essay when he provides his review of historical sources. He makes the remarkable claim that the desire to know the will of God for one's life is something that emerged only within the last 150 years of church history and then adds, "Prior to the writings of George Müller, there was virtually no discussion of 'how to discover God's will for your life' in the literature of the church. What I call the traditional view of guidance was an integral part of the theological culture of the Keswick Movement, which was very influential in England and America. As Keswick-trained missionaries spread across the globe, this view of guidance became part of the evangelical tradition through their teaching. I was among the recipients of that heritage."

While the particular configuration of the question, of course, is uniquely reflected in Keswick teaching, it is quite extraordinary to say that this question did not emerge earlier in the life of the church. Quite to the contrary, how to know God's will for one's life is an ancient question! And it is one that has shaped the spiritual conversation of the church from very early in her history. When Friesen speaks of a "traditional view," he does not truly capture the "tradition," which is actually much older and consistently affirms the two things that he minimizes: the dynamic, immediate, encounter with Christ and the interplay of the affections and the intellect in spiritual discernment.

In Summary

While my emphasis in these comments has been on the immediacy of Christ, it is really one's theology of the Spirit that is at stake here. Can we speak of an immediate witness of the Spirit to our hearts? And if so, how are we to test and discern if and when we have experienced this witness—the witness by which we know Christ Jesus? Friesen repeatedly appeals to the "objective" revelation as found in the Scriptures, speaking of this as the only thing that can give us certainty. Quite apart from whether such certainly is possible, what I am reminded of is this. When Jesus announced to the disciples that He would be returning to the Father, He assured them that He would not leave them orphans. But His closing line was not, "Do not worry; I will leave you the Bible"! Rather, He promised that He would send another, the Counselor, the Spirit of truth. Does this in any way minimize the role of the Scriptures in the life of the Christian? Of course not. But it does remind us that the Bible is not the central dynamic of the Christian life; it is God Himself.

The Blackabys indicate that they are open to such an inner witness, but they fail to provide an adequate basis for discernment—why this Scripture or this impression in prayer or this circumstance or this counsel from another is to be acted upon or not. In contrast, Friesen emphasizes the need for discernment without the flip side: a radical openness to the Spirit and thus to the voice of Jesus, the voice of the Good Shepherd.

Chapter 3

LEARNING TO LISTEN

The Relationship View

GORDON T. SMITH

1. Introduction

Readers working their way through this volume have already had brief exposure to my view of Christian decision making and God's will in my short responses to the larger presentations of my colleagues. Perhaps it is already abundantly clear that my view of these matters shares some things in common with each of the other views—the specific-will view and the wisdom view—and yet differs from each of those views in important ways. Likewise, I trust that it will be equally clear that my view is not simply a middle way or mediating view between those expressed by the Blackabys and by Friesen. Grateful as I am for this opportunity and forum for interacting on these matters, I want to turn now to a fuller explanation of what we are calling the relationship view of Christian discernment and decision making.

Decision Making and Relationship

One of the deep longings of the human soul is to be able to act with clarity, wisdom, and courage in making the decisions that shape the contours of our lives. And we feel this most keenly when it comes to the choices that are part of the very fabric of human life—questions of marriage, work and career, and more.

Part of what it means to grow into adulthood is that we are thrust into decision making—not only for the large, formative choices, such as marriage and vocation, but also as we try to make sense of the myriad of daily options, expectations, and problems we may face. Most decisions for children are made by parents, guardians, and caregivers; in childhood we do not need to make difficult choices. But growing up means that we take adult responsibility for our lives; we assume agency for the decisions we need to make. This does not mean that we spurn the counsel and advice of others. Rather, it means that if we are to develop into maturity, we must learn to take ownership of our choices—choices that no one else can make for us. There is something pathetic about an older person who obviously has never really left the security of the parents' home and long after "leaving" home relies on others to play the parental role—whether a corporation, business, institution, or church "family." Both good parenting and effective education empower individuals to act with wisdom, courage, and clarity and take adult responsibility for their choices.[1]

Yet this call to maturity does not mean that we function independently or autonomously. The Christian Scriptures assume, and indeed call humankind and each individual person to, an intentional response to the will of God. Our decision making occurs within the created order, that is, within the nature and purpose of God for humanity within creation and thus within God's redemptive intention. For the Christian this means not only that we pray, "Your kingdom come, Your will be done on earth as it is in heaven," but also that, as grace enables us and allows us to see, we make choices that are consistent with the reign of Christ.

Then follows the critical question. What level of involvement does God have in our decision making? Is intimate engagement possible between the Christian and Christ when we are making choices?

As already implied, divine participation in human decision making does not negate the legitimate exercise of human volition. To be

---

1. This principle applies as equally to elementary education as to graduate theological studies. Effective academic processes are not, in the end, about helping students anticipate every choice they are going to face and providing them ready-made decisions. Rather, they are processes by which students develop the capacity to choose and act with discernment in the midst of the ambiguities of life, work, and ministry.

created in the image of God means, in part, that humanity has been given the capacity to choose. Yet this capacity does not threaten the relationship that God intended to have with God's creation. To the contrary, the exercise of human volition actually strengthens that relationship. God graces us to see ourselves and our world more clearly. God did not create pawns but human beings who are capable of choice, real choice. Our acts of volition, then, are part of the way in which we fulfill the intention of God's creation. We fulfill the purpose of creation by exercising this call and capacity.

Yet the individual is not alone in decision making. It is for us to choose and the Scriptures clearly assume that in making these choices, we take adult responsibility for the decisions we make. Nevertheless, for the follower of Christ, this means that we choose and act with God, and we do so in response to the call of God. Some may wish to defer to a higher authority—be this God or an elder or religious mentor—because they fear the weight (and responsibility) of making their own choices. They want God or someone else to choose for them. This God will not do; indeed, it would violate God's very creation. But God does not leave us alone in our faulty ingenuity and frail wisdom. God grants us three gifts that empower us to choose well: the Scriptures, the community of faith, and the Spirit. The gifts do not negate true human volition and none of these "makes the decision for us." But humanity cannot choose well without the resources provided through these gifts.

This is so, in part, because of the reality of sin. Our hearts and our minds have been so infected by sin that we are easily deceived and self-beguiled and very capable of rationalization. But in the grace of God we can live in vital and intimate relationship with God, despite the reality that our lives are complicated by the presence of sin. We are invited to make our choices in response to divine initiative and counsel and in response to the presence of the Spirit, who both guides and empowers us and enables us to choose well and to act with courage.

Therefore, in the discussion about divine guidance and decision making, the fundamental issue is not so much whether there is a particular will of God for each person or whether this will can be known. Rather, the fundamental issue is whether or not there is immediacy with God—a relationship of intimacy and communion—that makes possible this kind of knowledge of the particular will of God. Isn't this the kind of relationship with God that the Scriptures and our Christian heritage assume and to which the individual Christian should aspire?

Particularity and Ambiguity

There are two words that are helpful to have in our lexicon here, words that shape our discourse about divine guidance and decision making. The first is *particularity*. God has always chosen to work within a specific time and place of human history, and God works with particular guidance and instruction for specific individuals. The wonder of God's redemptive work and the outpouring of the Spirit at Pentecost is that, now, God speaks into the specifics of our lives, into our particularity. There are obviously general principles that necessarily govern the lives of Christians. For example, the Ten Commandments apply to all Christians at all times, and the Sermon on the Mount is a powerful explication of the fundamental contours of discipleship for all who choose to follow Jesus.

However, the way in which the laws of God and the rules of the sermon are lived out is never generic. Each Christian must discern how these general principles apply and hold sway in his or her particular situation. Moreover, God's guidance in our lives is always specific and particular. We ask, "How am I, in this time and place, being called to live out my life as a follower of Christ?" It is not unlikely that two Christians, in apparently similar circumstances, will sense that God is calling them to act in remarkably different ways. Thus, Romans 14 underlines the urgent need for each Christian to live according to conscience. For example, some Christians will be led to tithe a tenth of their income, but others will sense the direction of God to contribute significantly more. Also, all Christians must participate in efforts to alleviate poverty and pursue justice, but the specific ways in which each is called to act may well be diverse.

We cannot respond to every wrong we witness or every injustice we know about. The existence of a wrong does not constitute a mandate for action. Rather, we must discern God's intentions for us as individuals. In the midst of all the brokenness in the world, in the face of the huge diversity of needs that are around me, what is the specific wrong or need to which I am to respond? How am I being called to act?

The second word needed for a discussion on divine guidance is *ambiguity*. This word is needed because we recognize, perhaps even with a mixture of frustration and anxiety, that "we see through a glass, darkly" (1 Cor. 13:12 KJV). Sin touches the whole of our lives and our world. Consequently, our own decisions are inescapably compromised by the presence of sin in our hearts and minds. Our hearts easily deceive us. We are capable of rationalizing our choices and falsely assuring ourselves (and others) that we have acted in good conscience. This uncertainty about our motives is further compounded by the fact that the choices before us are rarely clear and are usually clouded by the reality that we see only in part. There is much we do not understand, and often we are choosing the lesser of two evils, forced to make a choice that reflects profoundly the fragmented character of our world. In the words of William Williams's beloved Welsh hymn, we cry out, "Guide me, O Thou great Jehovah" because we are pilgrims in a "barren land."

But choose I must. None of us can live without choosing. However terrifying a choice can sometimes be—we imagine the potential consequences for ourselves and for those we love and for whom we are responsible—we cannot *not* choose! By not choosing to marry, we have chosen to remain single. By not choosing to move, we have chosen to remain where we currently reside. We cannot escape choices; to be human is to choose. Even procrastination is a choice—a choice to not choose. Furthermore, our choice may be the way by which we serve God and others. That is, as God enables us, we make choices that influence the lives of those whom God has placed in our path—whether as parents who offer guidance, as administrators who make corporate decisions, as teachers who choose curriculum, or as preachers who identify an approach to a text. This heightens the angst, of course. We know our choices affect not only us but also those whom we long to serve well.

The comforting news is this: in our choosing, we are not alone. We can attend to the initiative of God. Through the grace given to us through the Scriptures and the heritage of the church, we can learn what it means to be aligned with the reign of Christ in the world. And, further, even in the midst of the noise and confusion of this world, we can learn to attend to the inner witness of the Spirit. As we shall see, this is an issue of heart and mind, for we must learn to listen to the Spirit with heart and mind.

The Risen, Ascended Christ

At the heart of this discussion is a central theological theme witnessed to by the Scriptures: the risen Christ is now at the right hand of God, exercising authority over the world (establishing His kingdom) and, as High Priest, mediating for the needs of the world before the Father. One of the sad realities of much contemporary Christianity is the failure to appreciate that this position and ministry of Christ is so very present to the world, the church, and the individual Christian. It seems we've been innoculated into supposing that Christ is distant and apart, "preparing a place for us" as a kind of heavenly engineer—at work in another world but not all that present in this world. In fact, the Scriptures assume a remarkable level of immediacy. Christ is here—not visible, but no less present. Yes, one day this Regent will be seen, at the Revelation. But though unseen now, the ascended Christ is alive and dynamically present here and now.

This conviction is the basis for everything that will be said in the pages to follow. What I hope we will see is that Christ is so present to our lives that we simply cannot choose "on our own." Our choices become one of the critical ways by which we live in communion with Christ, and our capacity to choose well stands in direct proportion to the quality and depth of this relationship. Yet, as we shall see, it does not then follow that all we need to do is have a daily devotional time.

Culitivating a relationship with Jesus involves and includes learning the art of decision making. We foster the capacity to discern well as an essential part of living in communion with the living Christ.

2. The Testimony of Scripture

Do the Scriptures speak to this possibility of intimacy with Christ, this kind of immediacy to our relationship with God, particularly in our times of choice? Indeed, the biblical writers assume, and summon us to, this as the very goal of the Christian life: a union with Christ that is so intimate as to necessitate divine participation in our decision making. The New Testament obviously is our primary source in this regard; but we appreciate this message in the context of the witness of the Old Testament, with its affirmation of the God who speaks but also of the need for discernment.

Old Testament Prophets

Any consideration of divine guidance and decision making must be located within a basic affirmation that God speaks and that the entreaty of the Scriptures is simply that we would learn how to listen. We will consider further the "how" of this listening and, if—or rather, when—God speaks, whether or not He is specific regarding the details of our lives. What cannot be discounted, however, is that the Scriptures assume that God is one who speaks and that we live by attending to the word and will of God and by learning to discern the voice of God from false voices or witnesses.

For believers under the Mosaic covenant, this meant learning to attend to the message of the prophets. Moses himself was the first in a line of prophets who spoke for God. And of paramount importance to those living under this covenant was the discernment question, the matter of true and false prophets and who speaks for God. The nations surrounding Israel had their prophets, soothsayers, and diviners; but for Israel, a people chosen to live in covenant with the living Creator God, it was to be solely through God-appointed prophets that they were to know the will and purposes of God.

Thus, Deuteronomy 18:14 denounces divination and sorcery. Israel instead was to live by the word of God as communicated through the office of the prophet. Prophecy, then, was a gift of God to His people, a means by which the people of God could know the life-giving word of God.

Not only were they to turn from divination and magic, but they also needed to be alert to false prophets, those not sent from God. The covenant people of God needed discernment to recognize a true prophet. This was of no small consequence for they were bound by their covenant with God to listen to and obey, and thus to be attentive to, the prophet or prophets whom God had sent. It was a life-and-death matter.

It was also a question of much gravity to accept the call to be a prophet, to speak on behalf of God, and to presume to have such authority. Deuteronomy 13:1–5 and 18:20 spell out the severe outcomes when such authority was claimed but had not been given by God.

Jeremiah puts the discernment question on the table (cf. Jer. 20:7–18; 23:18–40). What emerges here for the prophet is the charismatic experience—a profound spiritual encounter with God—that became the basis for the prophet's speaking (see especially Isa. 6 and also Mic. 3:8). This profound encounter and call then empowered the prophet with a willingness to bring bad news when this was required and to be terribly unpopular; the prophet's accountability was to the divine call (that is, to Yahweh). A sure sign of a false prophet was that the prophet told the people (or the king) only what the people wanted to hear.

And so the people of Israel were taught discernment. They learned to recognize a true prophet by attending to several critical indicators of authenticity:

+ Faithfulness to the Torah (see Deut. 13:1–5). Indeed, this is why Jesus had to regularly demonstrate that He (and not His contemporary opponents) was a true interpreter of the Torah in the prophetic tradition (for example on the matter of Sabbath observance).

+ Their prophecies came true (Deut. 18:21–22). This needs qualifying, however, for in a sense the prophecy of Jonah regarding Nineveh did not come true, and this was precisely because Jonah was a true prophet. Prophecies often had a built-in conditional or repentance clause, as with Jonah, whose prophecy would come to pass only if the people of Nineveh did not repent.
+ The content of the prophecy. It is, for example, the false prophet who preaches peace when there is no peace (Jer. 6:14).
+ The moral life of the prophet (Jer. 23:14). Here again we note a qualification in that Matthew 7:22–23 suggests that God can speak through less-than-perfect spokespersons.

While we have a couple of qualifiers, taken together these four criteria provide us with a mind-set, a way of thinking about God's "speaking," that demonstrates the need for discernment. This mind-set begins to provide us with the contours that will eventually shape our response to God under the new covenant.

God Speaks Through the Son

The dramatic shift to the New Testament and the new covenant is captured vividly by the opening words of the epistle to the Hebrews, which tell us that God spoke through the prophets in times past, but now God has spoken through the Son. What the New Testament portrays from beginning to end is that now the revelation of God—the disclosure of the will and purposes of God—is centered in Christ Jesus.

This is not to the exclusion of the Old Testament and the prophets; they continue to be God's word, but now only insofar as they enable the reader to hear the voice of Jesus. Indeed, even Christ, the Word incarnate, appointed apostles who wrote with divine authority, for they spoke not on their own but under inspiration of the Spirit. Yet here, too, these writings are a means to an end (not the end); they enable us to attend to the voice of Jesus. God speaks through the Son.

Jesus, then, stands within the prophetic tradition, but clearly He is unique as the embodiment (literally) of the word of God. When we listen to Jesus, we listen to God, and this listening is for us the very life of God, that which animates our lives.

Thus, Jesus speaks of His disciples as those who listen and obey. And, specifically, they listen to *Jesus*. At His transfiguration something profound happens: Jesus is confirmed as the Messiah of God. The voice from heaven resounds, "This is My Son, My Chosen One; listen to Him!" (Luke 9:35 NASB). And then throughout the Gospels, we see Jesus again and again making it abundantly clear that this is, indeed, the heart and soul of Christian discipleship: the "sheep" of the Good Shepherd listen to His voice (John 10:16).

This immediacy between Jesus and His disciples is not reserved for those who heard Him speak during His earthly life prior to the resurrection. To the contrary, attending to the words of Jesus remains the central dynamic of the Christian life. Furthermore, John 15 highlights that this engagement with the words of Jesus is located within a dynamic and intimate relationship—we abide in Christ even as Christ abides in us. Indeed, Jesus insists that we are not mere servants with marching orders; we are "friends." And we, the branches, bear much fruit as we live in the Vine, Jesus.

There is also the remarkable exchange between Jesus and the early church as portrayed in the opening chapters of the book of Revelation. There in the words spoken to the church in Laodicea (Rev. 3:20), we see that Jesus is "at the door," eager for the church to listen; if they hear the voice of Jesus, they will know the fellowship with Jesus (represented by a meal) for which every Christian longs.

The Gift of the Spirit

This then leads us to the exchange between Jesus and His disciples in what is commonly called the "Upper Room Discourse" (John 14–16). Here Jesus advises the disciples that He will be returning to the Father. He explains that this will be a temporary arrangement. For now, He will be with the Father, but He will "return" to consummate His reign. In the meantime, He will send the Spirit, who will be their Counselor, convict the world of sin, and lead the disciples into all truth (John 16:7–15).

It is clear that we live now in the era of the Spirit, wherein Christ is known and experienced by the presence of the Spirit. The life and ministry of the Spirit is the central dynamic of this period in redemptive history. And so the call to "listen to the Son," by whom and through whom God has spoken, is made possible by the Spirit. This is *the* dynamic of the Christian life—its energy, its animating force, its power—without which this redeemed life would neither make sense nor be possible. In other words, the presence of the Spirit is neither incidental nor secondary, but central to the experience of the Christian disciple.

The Spirit generates the enabling grace of God by which the Christian knows the salvation of God and is able to grow in faith, hope, and love. This is the enabling by which the Christian lives in the world but not of the world—able to respond to temptation and trial in such a manner that incrementally and surely leads to spiritual maturity.

At this point Jesus becomes not only the means by which the salvation of God is experienced but also the model or paradigm of this experience. By this I mean that just as Jesus exemplifies what it means to live in a manner that is attentive and responsive to the Father, even so He demonstrates for His disciples what it means to be attentive to Himself as they respond to the presence of the Spirit in their lives.

But then comes the obvious question: What does this mean for the daily experience of the Christian? What implication is there for how the Christian faces transitions in the course of relationships, work, and career? What does it mean, in practical and concrete terms, to speak of the "voice" of Jesus through the witness of the Spirit? And how far does this apply; that is, how extensive is this witness in our lives? Does it—to go to the heart of the matter for this essay—include guidance in times of choice?

On the one hand, this cannot mean new scriptural revelation. The Spirit given at Pentecost is the same Spirit who has inspired the biblical text. Thus with confidence the Christian can know that the inner witness of the Spirit will never contradict the written witness. It makes more sense and is more helpful, though, to state this positively and specifically: the guidance of the Spirit will be the application—the *particular* application—of the biblical text to this time and place, within the life of this individual, family, business, or church community.

Furthermore, the provision of the Spirit is one that necessarily takes account of the community of faith. Pentecost is at one and the same time the coming of the Spirit and the birthday of the church. The grace of the Spirit is certainly known by the individual believer, but it follows that the individual believer is in community, a participant in the fellowship of the Spirit.

We will return to both of these markers—Scripture and community—below, but for now what needs to be emphasized is that life in the kingdom of God, under the reign of Christ, is one that is experienced through the grace of the Spirit. And our question here is, Does this grace include the provision of guidance in times of choice?

For this question, the rest of the New Testament—following the Gospels—is tremendously instructive. The book of Acts is a powerful case study and example of the Spirit's active presence in the life and ministry of the apostles and the early church. The Epistles also provide critical guidelines for how this witness is discerned and known, picking up some of the same themes found in the Old Testament, where the key question was the authenticity of a prophet.

The book of Acts portrays a remarkable intimacy between the work of the Spirit and the work of the apostles. For example, in Acts 13:1–4 we see that the resolve to set aside Paul and Barnabas as missionaries to Asia Minor is clearly derived from the immediate call or witness of the Spirit. Then, in Acts 15 we have the description of a church council where the final decision is introduced with the compelling words, "It seemed good to the Holy Spirit and to us" (v. 28).

The example provided by the book of Acts is matched by the call of the Epistles. Most noteworthy is Paul's urging of his readers to not "quench" the Spirit (1 Thess. 5:19 KJV, NASB, ESV). To do so would be to smother and marginalize the witness and initiative of

God! If we "quench" the Spirit, we lose connection with the life and grace of God, for it is precisely through the ministry of the Spirit that Christ is present to His church.

But then Paul just as quickly insists that while we must not obstruct or limit the Spirit, we must be discerning. "Test everything," he says to the Thessalonians (1 Thess. 5:21). In theological reflection on the practice of discernment and decision making, the church has always recognized that Christians must be eager in their attentiveness to the Spirit but they also must be discerning. We must be open and receptive but also wise and discriminating.

Finally, we need to mention that the initiative or witness of the Spirit is experienced when Christians intentionally and readily respond with heart and mind. The question of how intellect and emotion intersect in the Christian life is a huge one, of course, and this is especially so when it comes to decision making. Indeed, this question has been a recurring theme in the history of the church with regard to the matter of decision making. We will explore this interplay of heart and mind—affect and intellect—and demonstrate how the church has consistently insisted that we cannot conclude that decision making is simply about making careful rational choices. Such thinking overlooks both the nature of the human person—we never are purely cerebral—and the nature of relationship, particularly in the case of one's relationship with Christ. Even a cursory reading of the New Testament reminds us that we must attend to matters of affect and emotion if we are going to choose well. This theme is picked up, as we shall see, by the historic witness of the church to discernment and decision making.

3. Our Spiritual Heritage

While it has become accepted language among many contemporary Christians to speak of the "traditional view" of divine guidance as that which arose within the last century or two, in actual fact there is a much longer and more ancient "tradition." It is a tradition that goes all the way back to the early church, such that in each chapter of church history there is a consistent witness to the imperative of listening and discernment or, as it has typically been called, "the discernment of spirits."

Consistently the wisdom of our Christian heritage affirms the need to attend with heart and mind to the presence of the Spirit in our lives. Our response to the Spirit is not purely cerebral or merely emotional; it is not one of either pure analysis or of untested spontaneity or impulse. Rather, the response to God is one in which emotion plays a crucial part (indeed, the affections are at the very heart of authentic Christian experience), but this is always an experience informed by the "renewing of the mind."

It is only in what might be called "rationalist" or "scholastic" periods of the church's history that emotion or the affections have been discounted. Both the testimony of the Scriptures and the continous witness of the church point to the critical place of the affections in discernment and decision making. The great contribution in the history of the church in this regard is the "Rules of Discernment," taking up a few pages of the devotional prayer guide of the sixteenth century, Ignatius Loyola's *Spiritual Exercises*.

While this call for discernment and the particular application of what it means to discern with heart and mind is masterfully presented in the "Rules of Discernment," this understanding is not unique or original to Ignatius. He clearly stands within a tradition of critical reflection on the matter of discernment, one that was initiated in the first century. Further, we find that the issues at stake in Ignatius's "Rules of Discernment" are reiterated by subsequent contributors to the discussion on both the Protestant and the Catholic sides of the Reformation, most notably in the writings of Francis de Sales in the seventeenth century and Jonathan Edwards and John Wesley in the eighteenth century.

Two representative voices prior to Ignatius will suffice for our purposes here: Origen of Alexandria and Bernard of Clairvaux.[2]

---

2. In the course that I teach on "Divine Guidance and Spiritual Discernment" at Regent College and other seminaries, I draw not only on the works of Origen and Bernard, but of others as well, including Catherine of Siena, Julian of Norwich, Francis of Assisi, and the Brethren of the Common Life (notably the *Imitation of Christ*). For post-Ignatian sources, I draw on both Calvin and Luther, Ignatius Loyola's contemporaries, and then also Francis de Sales, Jonathan Edwards, John Wesley, and others.

Then we will comment more specifically on Ignatius and look at the contribution of John Wesley two centuries later.

Origen of Alexandria (185–254)

Many consider Origen of Alexandria to be the greatest theologian of the church prior to Augustine. Most of what we know of him comes through the ecclesiastical history of Eusebius, who helps us appreciate that Origen's immediate context was the persecuted church and, within this, his own experience of tribulation. Origen's most significant consideration of discernment is found in two works: *Spirit and Fire* and *On Prayer*, where he insists that prayer is not merely petition but actual participation in the life of God. I will concentrate here mainly on what he says in *Spirit and Fire*.[3]

Noteworthy in Origen is the conviction that the human person is capable of making judgments and that this is part of what it means to be human. We make choices; what is crucial is that we learn to make good choices. This challenge is one of motivation and disposition. We discern well only when we are able to cultivate a freedom from preoccupations and prejudices that unconsciously govern our attitudes and responses. While sin is powerful, we can learn to make good judgments through discipline and training. This discipline and training begins with attending to what motivates our thoughts and proclivities. Only then can we learn to be more open to the Spirit of God.

Further, Origen stresses that discernment requires that we locate ourselves within the broader, cosmic vision of God's work; we need to see our lives and our work in the context of what God is doing in the world. Our human choices, in other words, have broader implications. He observes that the angelic host notes our actions and choices. When speaking of our judgments, Origen writes, "Either the angels in heaven will cheer us on, and the floods will clap their hands together, and the mountains will leap for joy, and all the trees of the field will clap their branches—or, may it not happen, the

---

3. Origen, *Origen, Spirit and Fire: A Thematic Anthology of His Writings*, ed. Hans Urs von Balthasar, trans. Robert J. Daly (Washington, DC: Catholic University of America, 1984). All further references are to paragraph numbers in this edition.

powers from below, which rejoice in evil, will cheer."[4] Mark McIntosh observes that, in Origen, "a more conscious scrutiny of one's views and motivations sets one free to discern the wider cosmos within which one's life takes place; and conversely, a growing awareness of the eternal implications of one's choices alerts one to the bias and narrowness at work in one's views." He notes further, "Cosmic drama is always unfolding even in the smallest choices. Discernment teaches one to recognize those wider and eternal dimensions in everything."[5]

So we see that in Origen there is a critical interplay between the inner examination of our motives and the external or overarching cosmic vision of God's work in the world. Yet in both cases we are consciously and deliberately opening ourselves up to the Holy Spirit. The inner examination and the outward vision of God's work in the world enable us to discern the Spirit.

Origen speaks of the "discernment of spirits," perhaps the earliest source we have that uses this language or phrase. He speaks of two "spirits" and suggests that each person has something like a good angel and a personal devil, a kind of particular expression of the Spirit of God who calls us to the good and the "satanic spirit" who would destroy us. His particular emphasis is that the fruit of the "good spirit" is peace and the actions that arise from peace. And thus peace—he actually uses the language of "consolation"—is the true home, the resting place of the soul.[6] In peace we have, as he puts it, "a vision into the true nature of things." In peace we see rightly.

It is important also to note Origen's observation that the way that leads to life is difficult and strenuous and that in this world we will experience "bitter herbs." Thus, "peace," or consolation, does not presage an easy way.[7] Rather, peace can be found even in tribulation and suffering; and what sustains us in these times is an awareness of the love of God.[8]

---

4. Quoted by Mark A. McIntosh, *Discernment and Truth: The Spirituality and Theology of Knowledge* (New York: Crossroad, 2004), 27.

5. Ibid.

6. Origen, *Origen, Spirit and Fire*, #561, 566, 568–573.

7. Ibid., #581.

8. Ibid., #584.

The crucial question for Origen is the disposition of the heart. He contrasts the hard heart (with reference to Rom. 2:5) with the heart that "accepts the seal of the divine image," a heart that "is made to rise like incense before the Lord."[9] The challenge with regard to true affections or emotion is that our hearts are "impeded by their passions." Thus, if we do not know the peace of the Spirit, it is because we are not pure in heart. This impurity, in turn, is due to disordered longings, which arise when we do not appreciate that all the treasures of God and of life are found in Christ.[10]

While all of this may seem overwhelming, Origen at more than one point reminds his readers that we learn the way of the Spirit over time and that we learn in the turmoils (and temptations) of life.

Bernard of Clairvaux (1090–1153)

Bernard was the most influential theologian and churchman of his generation. His impact on the theology and spirituality of the Middle Ages is huge. What is noteworthy about Bernard is that he was both a theologian and a mystic (the words of the hymn, "O Sacred Head, Now Wounded," are attributed to him), as well as an active administrator whose most important contribution was the reformation of the monastic orders.

While many of Bernard's writings address the matter of decision making and discernment, the most notable is his *Five Books on Consideration* ("consideration" is his term for discernment).[11] In this work, as in all his writings, we see a remarkable emphasis on both heart and mind. Bernard's emphasis on the vital place of the heart and affections in Christian experience is cogently captured in the oft-quoted line, "Instruction makes us learned, but feeling makes us wise."[12] For Bernard the goal of theology is not ultimately an

---

9. Ibid., #588, 591.

10. Ibid., #596, 597, 599.

11. Bernard of Clairvaux, *Five Books on Consideration: Advice to a Pope*, trans. J. D. Anderson and E. T. Kennan (Kalamazoo, MI: Cistercian Publications, 1976). This work was essentially written as spiritual counsel for Pope Eugene III.

12. Ibid. Sermons 23.14; see also Sermons 16.1.

intellectual knowledge of God but the *experience* of God and, particularly, the experience of the love of God. For Bernard the heart's true home is found in loving God. We were designed to love God, and thus our good is found in loving God.

Yet the challenge is that we are so easily drawn aside from this true home. In words that seem to anticipate Bunyan's *Pilgrim's Progress*, Bernard speaks of the Christian life as fraught with danger, and he states that our only hope is to be assiduously careful and alert. He reminds us that we cannot be naive to the power of spiritual evil in our hearts and in the world.

It is critical, then, that we have hearts that are eager and open, characterized by what Bernard calls "fervour." The spiritual life arises from a passion to know God and to do the will of God. Yet passion without discernment is dangerous. Thus we must seek *discerning* passion. Without actually referencing 1 Thessalonians, Bernard captures the similar dual call: to be open (do not quench the Spirit) but to "test everything" (cf. 1 Thess. 5:19–22). It is not a matter of either/or but of both/and, for true discernment arises from a passionate heart, and true passion is regulated by discernment.

Reflecting the language of Origen and his prompting to discern by looking to the interior—to the heart and to the motivations or dispositions of the heart—Bernard makes the all-important observation that, in "consideration" (or discernment), we begin with ourselves. To discern it is necessary to know oneself, and particularly to know what one is experiencing emotionally. He cautions his readers to be alert to anger and "softheartedness," for anger leads to excess and the "soft" heart— a lack of critical reflection on what is happening to one emotionally—weakens one's capacity for good judgment.

Finally, the central question for Bernard is one's relationship with Christ. If a believer is able to discern well, this capacity is derived from that person's union with Christ. And the evidence of this union is humility, a major theme in Bernard.

This then leads us to the definitive voice in discernment, Ignatius Loyola and the "Rules of Discernment."

Ignatius Loyola (1491–1556)

Ignatius is best known as the founder of the Society of Jesus (the Jesuits), an extraordinary missionary order with a remarkable emphasis on the value of scholarship and learning (evident in the number of Jesuit universities around the world). He is the author of the spiritual classic and guide to directed prayer, *The Spiritual Exercises.*

Ignatius himself did not begin his adult life with such missionary and educational aspirations. Rather, he longed to become a famous knight in the service of the king of Spain. He served for a time in the court of the king of Spain and later came into the service of the Duke of Najera, who employed him to put down regional rebellions and to fight off foreign invaders. It was in Pamplona, as Ignatius and others were defending the fortress against French invaders, that a cannonball shattered his left leg and injured his right knee. While recuperating he chose to read what was available, and this included the life of Jesus and the lives of the saints. This reading eventually compelled him to dedicate his life, not to romantic chivalry, but to service as a "knight" of Jesus Christ.

More to our point, while in convalescence Ignatius began to note that he had two distinct visions or powerful daydreams: one of serving Christ the King and the other of the old attraction to be a gallant knight. He was impressed with the contrary emotional experiences that corresponded to these visions. Notably, the desire to be a chivalrous knight left him feeling "desolation," whereas the vision of service for Christ left him in "consolation." Thus, the "Rules of Discernment" emerged from what he learned on the emotional terrain of consolation and desolation.

Yet the "Rules" need to be located within the overall vision of the Christian life to which Ignatius felt called and, more particularly, within the perspective on prayer that is encouraged by his *Spiritual Exercises.* There are three essential parameters of the spiritual life that provide the framework for appreciating the "Rules for Discernment."

The first parameter is the emphasis on a personal and immediate encounter with Christ. For Ignatius, discernment—and thus, decision making as the capacity to know the mind of God in a matter—is specifically the fruit of an encounter with Christ. The spiritual exercises are intentionally structured as a liturgy by which the one who prays is brought into an experience of the life, death, and resurrection of Christ—not just an appreciation for, but an identification with, the life, death, and resurrection of Christ. The exercises are a guide to prayer that are meant to foster, as it were, a continual conversion in which the individual's life is brought into alignment with the life of Christ, conformed to the image of Christ. This is the goal of the whole Christian life and, thus, it is the specific goal of both prayer and discernment.

This is done not through thinking *about* Jesus—the idea of Jesus or even the powerful idea that Christ died and is risen—but by an actual *encounter* with the ascended, risen Christ who is revealed to us through the depiction of the life, death, and resurrection of Jesus in the Gospel narratives. And thus the one who prays seeks to know Christ and have his or her mind saturated by the Spirit of Christ, the same Spirit who enabled Jesus to do the will of the Father.

Through prayer the Christian has an encounter with Christ. This is an immediate, real-time encounter with the risen and ascended Christ made possible by, and grounded in, the Scriptures and experienced by the believer who is in community with Christ's body, the church. This is not a spirituality of meditation on Christ and His life as a kind of supreme ethical model, a "what-would-Jesus-do?" kind of spirituality based on Jesus as the supreme model for the Christian life. Such guidance in the Christian life is simply a matter of determining what Jesus would do in a given situation. Rather, our decision making in the world arises out of an immediate and intimate experience of Christ. We know the mind of Christ because we have met Christ. As a parallel in the experience of a Christian community, a worship service is not an encounter with an idea but with a person, the Lord Jesus Christ, and our encounter is real and in real time.

For Ignatius, the evidence that one has met and knows Christ is joy. Indeed, his vision of the spiritual life is a mysticism of joy in the world. This is often captured in the phrase "contemplative in action." We are called to live in the world, but we are in the world as those who have known and encountered the risen Christ in prayer; we are contemplatives who are called to make a difference for and with Christ in the world. On the one hand, this bespeaks the priority of prayer. There is no effective decision making or discernment without prayer. On the other hand, it also just as surely speaks of a crucial attitude. Our being in the world is marked by a particular expression of the heart—namely, the experience of joy.

In other words, discernment enables us to live in the world with integrity and courage—to know and do the will of God regardless of the cost. But there is more. It is also a matter of joy; we embrace God's will with joy.

The second essential parameter central to Ignatius's educational vision, as well as his spiritual or contemplative ideal, is the principle captured in the wonderful phrase, "finding God in all things." Briefly put, to "see God in all things" is to appreciate the diverse ways in which the Spirit of Christ is so very present in our world. We discern our own call to act in the world as we "see" how God is already at work in every sphere and dimension of our lives, the church, and the world. We learn to ask, "Where is God in this?" even as we seek to discern, "How is God calling me to respond?"

The third essential parameter of the spiritual life for Ignatius is probably familiar to those who have studied at Jesuit schools or universities. Somewhere on their school buildings would appear the defining banner statement, *ad majorem dei gloria*—"to the greater glory of God." In the particular challenge of discernment, this motive and goal finds expression in the call within *The Spiritual Exercises* to experience the grace of "holy indifference." This indifference is not apathy or lack of passion, but rather an active orienting of one's life in terms of the glory of God and the cross. It is not indifference but a passionate engagement in and with the world governed by the reign of Christ. The evidence of this orientation is that we are "indifferent" to, quite literally, everything else. And this is freedom. It is a freedom from inordinate attachments, most notably riches, honor, and pride.[13] It is the freedom of true humility, a humility that comes from being with Christ. Humility is critical here. It is no co-incidence that the reflection on humility in *The Spiritual Exercises* is found immediately prior to the "Rules for Discernment." But what catches our attention is that it is the humility of being *with* Christ—in union with Christ.

Therefore, it is secondary if we are poor or rich. If we are honored or dishonored, this, in the end, is neither here nor there. What truly matters is that we are with Christ. This suggests, of course, an ordering of our affections. For indeed, the challenge of life and Christian witness is that we wrestle with conflicted "loves" or desires. Thus, discernment arises out of a reorientation of our desires so that our wills and the will of God are in communion. Herein lies inner integrity and spiritual freedom.

Within this framework—the transforming encounter with Christ (contemplatives in action), a longing to find God in all things, and the spiritual freedom that comes through holy indifference—we are able to make sense of the movements of the heart and discern how God is at work in our lives and through our lives in the world.

This discernment does not happen in isolation from the world, as though prayer and worship are an escape from the world. Rather, it is as those who are very much in the world that we are urged to be attentive to the call and purposes of God for our lives. Indeed, as I will stress below, we cannot discern well if we do not have a good "read" on our circumstances—opportunities, challenges, and potential problems or obstacles. Students of Ignatius know that hearing the call and will of God is not something that is experienced when we are naive to the reality of our situation. To the contrary, the guidance of God is particular, and therefore we need to be astutely aware of our particularity if we are truly to be contemplatives in action.

Finally, we come to the actual "Rules for Discernment." As is clear, discernment for Ignatius is a matter of paying attention to

---

13. Spiritual exercise #142. There are many good contemporary translations of *The Spiritual Exercises*; a good option is that of Louis J. Puhl, *The Spiritual Exercises of St. Ignatius* (Allahabad: Allahabad Saint Paul Society, 1975).

what is happening to us emotionally, especially the experiences of consolation and desolation. And here we find the simple yet profound guidelines that have been such an important source of encouragement and wisdom for Christians of every generation since and in many different spiritual traditions. The "rules" capture something of enduring value that all Christians can appreciate and apply— especially when it comes to the need to be attentive to Christ and responsive to the Spirit by giving careful attention to the emotional contours of our lives.

More on this after we consider the contribution of John Wesley.

John Wesley (1703–1791)

For many evangelical Christians, John Wesley is the primary voice when it comes to an appreciation of the vital place of the "witness of the Spirit." This eighteenth-century evangelist and popular theologian was profoundly indebted to two great streams in Christian theology. First was his own heritage, mediated though the Church of England and the English Puritans, that linked him with the Protestant Reformation. Second was the mystical heritage of the church, particularly those spiritual writers who enabled him to appreciate that the spiritual life is one of *devotio* and deep interiority, of the Spirit witnessing with our spirits that we are children of God.

Wesley, like Ignatius, was deeply committed to the integration of heart and mind in the spiritual life. He affirmed the vital place of reason and rationality and the critical use of the mind in responding to truth and in living in the truth. Yet this was matched by his equal insistence that our Christian faith is a matter of the affections; indeed, he spoke of his own experience of the gospel as one in which he felt his "heart strangely warmed." This attention to the emotional life was not incidental or secondary to the spiritual but the heart of the matter (pun intended) for the Christian.

Yet, while Wesley spoke of the witness of the Spirit to the heart of the Christian, he was not a sentimentalist. He insisted on the need for discernment. On the one hand, the witness of the Spirit was located within the broader provision of God for Christians, which includes their rational capacities, the church's continuing teaching (the tradition), and, of course, the Scriptures. If a Christian were to discount or ignore critical thinking or the Scriptures or the ongoing witness of the church to the faith, that Christian could not hope to be in communion with Christ.

On the other hand, there was also for Wesley the immediate test—disclosing the marks of authenticity—by which the Christian could discern whether the perceived interior experience of the Spirit was truly of God. The test is twofold. First, the authentic witness or experience of the heart would be evident in transformed character, or moral reform, in behavior that reflected the will of God. Second, and just as important, joy would be a crucial indicator of the Spirit's witness. It is necessarily both. Joy without moral reform is mere sentimentality, and moral reform without joy is nothing but burdensome legalism. Christians reject both legalism and sentimentality, Wesley would insist. Rather, we seek an experience of the Spirit by which we are enabled to live transformed lives. And in all of this, joy is not incidental.

Spiritual Heritage Conclusions

What do we make of this historical overview as we consider the contributions of Origen, Bernard, Ignatius, and Wesley? While it is just a sampler, I have sought to demonstrate that there is a distinctive "tradition," a thread that runs through the spiritual heritage and collected wisdom of the spiritual masters who are our teachers in this regard. What they point to, on the one hand, is the possibility and priority of an immediate relationship with Christ, the ascended Lord. The obvious conclusion, then, is that we need to learn how to listen, how to be attentive to Christ, as an immediate experience and as a dynamic of our Christian experience. And what the church has always recognized is that the capacity to listen is fostered by silence. We learn to hear God only when we cultivate the capacity to be still in the presence of God. This is not a mindless or even contentless experience of silence; to the contrary, it is the silence that is filled by the Christ who is revealed to us in the Scriptures. Noise distracts us and clutters our hearts. It is the silence that gives Christ space in our lives and enables us to know the beauty, love, and direction of the One who is Lord.

One of the abiding themes of this overview—heard from both the biblical witness and from voices in the history of the church—is the crucial place of the affections. It is clear that the genius of those who learn how to discern—how to respond to the risen Christ who is present to us by the Spirit—is the willingness and ability to listen with heart and mind. We often urge people to choose rationally, whether they are buying a home or going to war. And by this we often press them to bracket out emotion so that they can make a wise decision "objectively," not influenced by emotion or passion. What the biblical witness and the spiritual heritage of the church would tell us is that this is naive. It is misguided on two fronts, both with regard to the nature of the human person and with regard to the nature of discernment.

The crucial need of the church is to empower and enable Christians to choose well. This means that we must help all believers cultivate the capacity to process what is happening to them emotionally. Effective Christian living is a matter of integrating heart and mind; effective decision making is a matter of using one's head and attending to one's heart. And ultimately these are not in tension.

What strikes me in this historical review is the remarkable relevance to the contemporary church. Ignatius and these other voices offer the contemprary generation of Christians the wisdom for which they have a palpable longing: a way to integrate heart and mind, intellect and affect. We have a generation of Christians who know that emotional intelligence is not incidental but essential to the capacity to choose well. In these historic spiritual masters, today's believers have guidance for the very integration for which they long. And what they discover is that neither intellect nor affect can be isolated from the other. They are interdependent and interactive; they each inform the other. We cannot assume that rationality or reason and the critical application of universal principles are all that is needed for effective decision making. In actual fact, all choices are influenced by the affectives. And, if we are naive about this or deny it, as often as not we will only be more vulnerable to our emotions' negative involvements in our decisions (note, for example, how fear can subtly affect our choices). We claim to be choosing solely on the basis of good judgment, but it is very easy to rationalize a choice when it is actually fear or anger that lies behind the conclusion to which one has come. Norms, principles, and logical analysis play vital roles in good decision making. My point is that the spiritual heritage of the church offers a continual reminder that these intellectual elements by no means exhaust the challenge of discernment and choosing well.

Further, we need a method of decision making that will allow for surprises. The church and the world so urgently need individuals who will not act merely in obvious ways but will bring creativity, courage, and innovation to their actions. And this requires that we tap into their deep passions and hopes and dreams and not merely into what might be termed "good judgment." We need an approach to decision making that will take account of our intuition and imagination as well as careful and logical processes of analysis. And for this we will need to integrate heart and mind.

There is no doubt that any overview of the historical perspective on this matter needs to take account of the input of the Reformers. Both John Calvin and Martin Luther were skeptical of an immediate experience of God, and their reservations in this regard have had a lasting impact on evangelicals and Protestants. Luther had his ongoing battles with Thomas Muntzer, one of the fringe leaders of the Anabaptist movement. They differed on a number of points, but most notably Luther was disturbed by Muntzer's insistance that the Christian is to live by a daily inner experience of God's word. Luther expressed his concern that the Anabaptist movement was characterized by a lack of attention to the objective witnesses of the Spirit: the Scriptures on the one hand and "brotherly conversation" on the other. Any inner subjective experience would need to be evaluated in the light of the Scriptures and the community of faith. Luther was right on this; in truth, this twofold "check" on the inner witness is utterly fundamental.

John Calvin similarly recoiled from the radical fringes of the Reformation, the spiritualists, who sought inner illumination without attending to the Scriptures. With Luther, Calvin would insist that our comprehension of the Scriptures comes through the illuminating grace of God. But he could not accept that there is a direct, unmediated, witness to the heart and mind of the Christian.

While, in my estimation, Calvin and Luther overreacted to the extremists of their day, together they provide an essential element to any discussion of spiritual discernment and divine guidance, namely, that the inner witness of the Spirit can be comprehended only within the framework or context of the written witness (Scripture) and the fellowship of the Spirit, that is, the community of faith. Thus, one of the most critical signs indicating that we are capable of listening to the voice of Jesus and choosing well is that we are people of the Word who live in mutual submission within Christian community. With respect to Scripture, this is so because the inner witness of the Spirit will never contradict the inscripturated witness; and, further, this inner witness essentially is the application of the written witness to the particulars of our lives and our work. Moreover, discerning people are those who are in community and who have patterns of mutual submission, accountability, and service within the church.

4. The Ascension, the Gift of the Spirit, and the Call to Discernment

What forms the dynamic center of the Christian's spiritual experience? How can it not be the reality of the risen, ascended Christ who is fully present to His people? In other words, while the Scriptures and the church are indispensable to Christian identity and calling, so much so that we cannot conceive of the Christian life apart from our identity in community as the people who gather for the fellowship of the Word, the critical and dynamic center is the ascended Christ. We could press this even further and affirm that we cannot know the ascended Christ in isolation from community and without the preaching of the Scriptures. Yet, the dynamic center remains—not the Scriptures and not the church, but the Lord Christ. Our identity is not, in the end, that we are a "people of the book," or even a people marked by religious affiliations and community. We are rather a people marked by our identification with and allegiance to the ascended Christ.

Thus we ask, Can Christians live in intimate communion with Christ, and can Christians live in the world as those whose choices and decisions are deeply informed by their very communion with Christ? The answer to both, of course, is yes, for God has sent the Spirit. It is by the Spirit that we know intimacy with Christ and by whom we know Christ's guidance in times of choice. The ascension has little if any meaning and no immediate relevance without Pentecost. Our affirmation that Christ is the risen and ascended Lord is then necessarily matched by our intentional and deliberate response to the One who has been sent to be with us—the Comforter, the Counselor, the One who convicts the world of sin and guides the church into all truth (John 16:7–15).

In this way the genius of living in alignment with the ascended Christ is that we have the capacity to discern the Spirit, to recognize the presence and movement or witness of the Spirit, and to be open to the Spirit ("do not quench"), but also to be discerning ("test everything").

The apostle's instruction to test everything includes weighing the movements of our hearts against the standard of Scripture (the written witness) and the church (the living body). But then there is also the internal dimension of discernment, that is, the inner attentiveness or *listening* to Christ—seeking to know Christ personally and intimately, seeking an enounter with Christ that infuses our choices and indeed the whole of our Christian experience.

This listening, then, is the foundation of our Christian experience—a listening evident in our attentiveness to the inner witness of the Spirit. This is the heart of the matter. And here is where the "Rules of Discernment" as found in Ignatius Loyola's *Spiritual*

Exercises are so pertinent.[14] These "rules" are a concise guide to discerning and choosing well, and what we learn from them is that we discern well and choose well by giving attention to what we are experiencing emotionally. We take note of the movements of the heart. We recognize that what is happening to us emotionally is not secondary or incidental to the presence of God in our lives but the locus of God's immediacy to us. Religious experience is located in the affections.

As already alluded to above, the "Rules of Discernment" suggest that we grow in understanding of our affections by observing where we might be experiencing *desolation* and where we are experiencing *consolation*. By desolation, Ignatius means all movements of the heart that draw us away from Christ, whether despondency, fear, anger, or any "negative" emotion that, in essence, is a reminder that we live in a fallen and broken world. In some cases, this desolation may be entirely legitimate. We experience fear when our lives are threatened; we are angry in response to an actual wrong committed against us or those we care for. As legitimate, genuine, and justifiable as these emotions may be, they are still desolation, experienced because we live in a sin-damanged world.

Consolation, by contrast, speaks of the emotional contours of our hearts when we are in alignment with Christ. It is the joy or peace, the serenity of heart and mind, that is congruent with the reign of Christ in our world—reflecting a heart that is as it was created to be, governed by joy and peace.

The "Rules of Discernment" assume this basic distinction between desolation and consolation and then insist, first, that we must not make decisions in desolation. Many Christians recognize instinctively that they are to make decisions in "peace," and this intuitive awareness is rooted in wisdom. We are right to say, "God gave me peace that I was to . . ." marry, or accept an appointment, or choose a particular course of action. What we do not mention is the converse: that we must not choose in desolation (that is, in the lack of peace). We must not resign in anger; we must not choose a course of action

---

14. Ignatius, *Spiritual Exercises*, #313–336.

when our heart is caught up in fear or despondency. The anger or fear may be an honest reflection of our circumstances and certainly will reflect the state of our hearts. But the fact remains that in desolation we cannot trust our hearts to choose well—to act in a manner that is congruent with the reign of Christ in the world. When we choose in desolation, we will almost inevitably be guided by such emotions as anger and fear rather than by the Spirit of God.

For example, the resolve to act only in peace means that we will choose not to discipline our children in anger, knowing that even if discipline is called for, our anger will distort our capacity for appropriate measures. We do not resign from a job or committee position in anger about some circumstance there, knowing that in such emotional situations, our judgment is distorted.

Rather, we learn to recognize the lack of peace and slow down, responding with care and sensitivity to what is happening to us emotionally. If our desolation is due to the neglect of spiritual discipline, then we can attend to the practices that bring us into alignment with Christ. If our desolation is due to our being wronged, we can learn to cast our cares upon Christ or learn to let the edge of anger pass and then, later, when our hearts are in peace, act with patience, courage, and wisdom. A resolve to choose only in consolation can also guard us against acting impulsively, when we might not even be aware of what we are experiencing emotionally.

The first rule of discernment, then, is, do not act or make a choice or decision in desolation. However, the second rule of discernment is equally important: If we are experiencing consolation, the consolation must be tested. If we feel peace about something or a potential decision, we cannot necessarily assume that it means that God is guiding us. Christians frequently have acted inappropriately on the false assumption that "I feel peace about this." Typically, when someone says this, we assume the discussion is over. The whole tradition of discernment, however, insists that we must ask the follow-up question, "How do you know this peace comes from God?"

Spiritual masters of each generation have recognized that the Evil One is capable of masquerading as an angel of light. But lest we give more credit to the Evil One than is deserved, we should remember we are quite capable of rationalizing our decisions by ourselves around untested emotions. If it feels right, then we very easily assume it is right. But the "Rules of Discernment" rightly challenge us at this point. Just because we have peace does not mean we can act with confidence. The great challenge of the spiritual life when it comes to decision making is that we need to discern whether this peace comes from God or from misguided motives or desires.

Many have recognized that the most fruitful way by which we can "test the peace" and confirm that this consolation is truly from God is by a rigorous examination of motive. Indeed, the capacity to examine our hearts and to be ruthless with ourselves when it comes to assessing our motives is certainly one of the most critical capacities or skills for the maturing Christian.

We can and must ask some challenging and probing questions of our lives. And for many, the most productive questions are those that reflect the temptations that Jesus experienced when He was drawn into the desert following His baptism (Luke 4:1–13). For example, in simple form, we can ask, Is the peace that I feel about this potential decision driven by an inordinate longing for wealth or financial security (cf. vv. 3–4), or an inordinate desire for power (cf. vv. 5–8), or a longing for affirmation and recognition (cf. vv. 9–12)? In themselves, neither money nor honor nor power are evil or wrong—not in themselves. But when our choices are shaped by an inordinate desire for any of these, we can see that this "peace" we feel is not from God. And in this encounter with the Evil One, we see how Scripture actually can be used to distort the will of God. So frequently we think that if someone has a verse to substantiate something, this must mean the impression has come from God. The use of Scripture by the Evil One belies this kind of thinking. When a text of Scripture impresses us, even in our prayers, we still must be discerning and not make premature assumptions.

One can readily—and correctly—make the observation that our motives are seldom pure. But what a maturing Christian comes to see is that we can recognize when our decisions are not motivated by the "greater glory of God," to reference the Ignatian line noted earlier. We get to know ourselves and to know our hearts, and we can tell when decisions are being driven by the desire for honor, wealth (or financial security), or power. What we long for is the grace to accept honor if it comes, but also to accept the freedom that comes with living and working in obscurity. We know that the longing for affirmation causes us to do things that respond to our craving for this recognition. We also know that we can easily rationalize our need to be "sensible" about financial matters when what is really at stake is the longing for wealth and the untenable desire for financial security. As we mature in our faith, we see that what really makes a difference is not "power" or positions of supposed power but rather the capacity to serve and to empower others. And so we can and must ask how each of our choices enables us to serve others.

Asking these kinds of questions is just one way to test the feeling of peace one has about a decision, but the main point remains: we cannot make the assumption that if we feel good about something, if we are experiencing consolation, this settles the matter. In actual fact, it means nothing in itself. The peace must be tested. We need to be able to answer both questions: What is Jesus saying to me at this point in my life? *and* How do I know that it is Jesus?

In the end, though, the principle remains the same. While careful reasoning is essential to the process of discerning well, what we are experiencing emotionally is decisive. It is naive to think that our decisions can ever be matters of pure reason. When we think this is the case, we frequently fail to recognize that choices are actually rooted in such emotions as anger or fear. But, positively, there is no reason to think that the emotional factor is problematic. Human life was so designed! We have been created to live in joy. When we are in fear and anxiety, we must learn what it means to transition from this fear to the peace that "transcends all understanding" (Phil. 4:6–7). This is where we find life; this is our true home. It is not wrong to be angry, per se (see Eph. 4:26), but we don't live in the house of anger. We do not act out of anger or fear or discouragement. Rather, our lives and our choices arise from a heart that is settled on the reality of the ascended Christ. This is the fundamental orientation of our hearts. And only as our hearts are aligned to the reality of the ascension—the glory of the risen Christ—can we think clearly and act rightly.

5. Some Practical Considerations

So, with this as a backdrop, how might we counsel those who are making critical choices? Here I consider the case studies presented in this volume's introduction—a question of career, a question of relationship, and a question regarding stewardship.

Susan needs to make a decision regarding higher education, as she considers her options for where she should apply and enroll. She wonders whether she can "absolutely know" the will of God for her future studies.

Joe and Nancy are considering marriage but recognize that this will have potential implications for their careers. How do they discern their future together against the backdrop of their career questions?

And then we have David and Rachel, who need to make a decision about church affiliation, a choice complicated by competing values. There is good preaching in one church, but they wonder if the criteria for their decision should be shaped by opportunities for service. Their decision will be further influenced by opportunities for their children.

How might I advise these decision makers? How can I encourage them as they seek to consider how Jesus is speaking to them at these particular transition points in their lives? How might the wisdom of their Christian heritage be applicable to their circumstances? By way of counsel and encouragement, I offer the following working principles that might be pertinent to these three case studies (and, of course, other situations like these).

(1) There must be clarity about one's ultimate allegiance. This is the first and most fundamental principle of decision making. In each case study presented, we can and must take it as a given that

each party truly wants what is good and true, that each *wants* what honors Christ and what most enables them to fulfill *God's* call on their lives. Yet this cannot be taken for granted. Spiritual counsel for those in decision making always needs to reference "the greater glory of God" (to use the language of Ignatius Loyola). Romans 12:2 follows on 12:1: if we are able to discern the will of God (v. 2), it is in large measure because we have clarity about our ultimate allegiance (v. 1). Simon Peter hears the call of Jesus to "feed" and care for the Lord's "sheep" *after* he responds to the question, "Do you truly love me more than these?" (John 21:15–19). And in our decision making, we are wise to ask ourselves pointed questions in this regard, questions that probe, as best we can, what it is that motivates us. The examination of motive is an essential part of all effective decision making. As a variation on the test put before Jesus in the wilderness (Luke 4), we can ask, How might an inordinant longing for wealth or financial security be influencing this choice? or How might a desire for honor, recognition, or affirmation skew my capacity to choose well? or How might a misguided pursuit of power (rather than a call to service) mislead me in my time of choice?

The evidence of clarity in our allegiance is a radical openness to the call of God, a willingness to do what Christ would have us do. When we are facing a choice, time spent clarifying our commitment to Christ is always time well spent. And it is reasonable to expect that this cannot be done effectively when we are caught up in the business of life and work; we need time and space, sometimes even the time and space afforded us in a retreat setting.

(2) It is essential that we attend to what is happening to us emotionally, as the history of the spiritual practice of discernment reminds us. In the case studies that have been presented, we are reminded that the decision makers can choose well only if there is a fundamental honesty about what they are experiencing emotionally. This means that they acknowledge how fear or fears might shape their choices and inadvertently undermine their capacity to choose well. They also need to identify whether anger or frustration or discouragement might factor into their choosing. Might Susan

be inclined to choose a college as a way of "proving" herself to her father? Or might David and Rachel be coming into this choice having just left a church that was filled with conflict, perhaps even a set of dynamics that left them emotionally wounded? In other words, we never make decisions in isolation from the emotional contours of our lives. So we are wise to enter into our choices with truthful awareness of our emotional state.

I can hardly overstate how important it is not to be naive about the significance and power of emotion. If our hearts are in desolation—fear or anger or discouragement—we simply cannot choose well. We must discern the will of God in peace, and this may well mean that we learn to wait. We must first resolve the matters, as God enables, about which we are anxious or angry. This will position us to discern the mind of God as those who are not worried but rather know "the peace of God, which transcends all understanding" (Phil. 4:7). This will position us to discern as those who are slow to anger and receive the Word of God with meekness (James 1:19–21).

(3) God leads one step at a time. There is such wisdom in this simple phrase; yet so often we are stymied in our decision making because we are asking more of God than God will provide us. The process of discernment requires both a deep trust in the providential care of God and a confidence in God's greater wisdom and long-term perspective. So, then, we trust God for this day and seek the mind of the Spirit for *this* chapter of our lives. And in so doing we make no assumptions about what might happen five, or ten, or twenty years down the road.

This one-step-at-a-time living does not mean that we are shortsighted or that we do not consider the long-term implications of our choices. We will have fruit in a decade only if an orchard is planted now; the housing we purchase now must be sustainable in the years to come. Indeed, we urgently need to attend to the long view of things—both in Christian ministry and mission as well as in the pattern of routines and rhythms to our daily lives and relationships. How many have regretted that they did not create a better foundation in their early years—whether for the (literal) house they have built or for the lives they have constructed (perhaps with more time given to study and reading). Despite the well-intentioned admonition of some, we simply cannot live under such threats as "the Lord may return at any moment" with the assumption that this is a good referent for decision making. To the contrary, we must take the long view. The choices we make affect, not just ourselves, but also our children and their children, and the generations that follow. We make choices now but with attention to long-term implications—for the environment, for our families and friends, for the work to which we are called.

But in all of this, Christ *leads* us one step at a time. For example, while we might choose to embrace medical studies now in response to God's leading, we do not know all of where God intends this to lead. So we should be careful about assuming what our medical studies will mean to us ten, twenty, or more years down the road. This brings us to a fourth crucial principle of effective decision making.

(4) We need to sequence our decision making, attending to what needs to be decided first. Wise Christians recognize that people often are perplexed and confused as they face necessary decisions because two or more previous choices have muddied the waters. Thus they cannot choose well now because they have not attended to first things first, or because they are trying to resolve too much at one time.

Take the case of Joe and Nancy with their decision about marriage and how this crucial choice is influenced by career issues. In this case, two things merit our attention. First, marriage necessarily takes priority over career in our choosing; as a state of life, it is far more important. And, regarding marriage, people choose well only if they first discern whether they are called to be single or called to be married. After this, they can discern whom they might marry as the opportunity arises. Marriage is a covenant relationship; we must first discern about this fundamental state of life and then discern about potential partners. But second, the priority of the decision about marriage over career is based also on the practical reality that we simply do not know how our careers might play themselves out. There are too many uncertainties about the future for us to make marriage choices based on speculation or assumptions about career or work or vocation.

So, rather than choosing a life partner in light of our current careers, we must decide the life partner question first. Is this the love of my life? And, if God would have it, is this the person I want to spend the rest of my life with? Is this the one I would like to have as a life companion to join me in the process of making choices and decisions about my work, my career, and the vocation that God has and will give me?

Paul's words in 1 Corinthians 7 are a reminder that marriage takes priority over career. If we discern that vocation and career come first, then we should remain single and accept this as the call of God. But if we marry, then our responsibility is to our spouse— to live for the other, to submit to the other, and to discern how we are called to live and work in the world with this as a "given," as a marker and necessary "limit" on our work in the world. We cannot be married and live as though we are single. To put it forthrightly, if a married couple says that God has guided them to live separately, the one in San Francisco while the other pursues a career in New York City, then something was skewed in their discernment process. If we are married, then God expects us to live as those who are married.

In *The Spiritual Exercises*, Ignatius says that God's leading in our lives will always take account of the fundamental givens of our lives, including, most notably, our covenant relationships. This is a further reflection of the principle that we need to sequence our decisions.

Many people cannot discern what God is calling them to do until they have felt peace that they are to conclude what they are *now* doing. Some cannot discern whether God is calling them to accept a new appointment until God has first given them peace to leave where they are now employed. Many spiritual counselors, therefore, suggest that all discernment questions should be "yes or no" questions, keeping it simple. Determine what choices must be resolved first, and then take on the sequence of questions one at a time. This leads us naturally to the next working principle.

(5) We need to be clear about our circumstances. It is basic to discernment and decision making that we keep in mind that when God speaks, it is always to the particular—to this time and place. God speaks not into situations as we wish they were but as they actually are. If we are married and have four children, this is the context in which we pray and listen to the call of God. We must be honest, not nostalgic for a former time and place or dwelling in an illusion about the actual circumstances of our lives. Wise Christians know that they must name reality; knowledge of our situation, our *actual* situation, is essential to good discernment.

Therefore, we never merely say, "Pray about it, and God will show you the way." Life is never that easy. Furthermore, this belies a false notion of how we honor God. God speaks into the particular, and thus we honor God by knowing the particular situation. For example, for a church to discern how God is calling them to be the church in their neighborhood means that they do their research, including a social and cultural analysis of the community. God-honoring discernment also means that we identify honestly, and as thoroughly as we can, the potential obstacles as well as the opportunities represented by a choice we are facing.

A person truly in relationship with God is not naive about our world—the economic, political, social, and cultural dynamics of our lives. Yet, these factors are never determinative. God can call us and work through us in ways that confound these realities. But these realities are always the context in which God speaks to us.

(6) We need time and space to choose well. We can discern well only if we take the time to do so, only if we approach our decision making with an intentionality evident not merely in our assessment of our circumstances but also in the extended time of prayer and reflection that we take prior to coming to a decision. If we are to hear the voice of Jesus in the midst of our lives, we need to move apart from the frenetic pace of our lives and find space for quiet, where,

in a period of thoughtful prayer, meditation, and a weighing of our circumstances, we can attend to the witness of the Spirit.

In the quiet of solitude we know the joy and power, the comfort and guidance that come from Christ. Our time of extended prayer has a twofold agenda: to cultivate our relationship with Christ (so that we might, in the language of the medieval saints, *know, love, and obey* Christ) and to discern out of this union with Christ how we are being called to act in the world.

It would be difficult to overstate how important this is. Well-intentioned Christians make poor decisions for a whole host of reasons, no doubt. But the most common misstep is that they simply do not take the time for prayer or they do not know how to make such a time of solitude fruitful. Discernment is a learned art; we learn what it means to be alone with Christ and we learn how to discern the prompting of the Spirit in this time of solitude.

(7) Finally, there is the need for accountability. What we discern in solitude needs the counterbalance or affirmation that comes through the words of others. While we may be alone in our prayers, we are not alone in our decision making. Our decisions are never purely our own. If we are married, we make our decisions in tandem with a spouse. This is obvious. Yet, in fact, all of our decisions involve others and have implications for others. Thus, it is wise and good to actually bring others into the process so that we strengthen our capacity to choose well.

Sometimes the patterns of accountability are clear. For example, a pastor may discern the calling of God to start a new church program, but this choice needs to be vetted and approved by a council or board of elders. This is as it should be. No one should claim unique capacity to know God's voice or God's will. We discern as best we can, but we live and work in communities that include structures of accountability. Beware of the pastor, for example, who claims to be accountable only to God. This is naive and thus dangerous. True discernment is tested within the structures of accountability that are vital for congregations, mission agencies, schools, and businesses.

If these structures are not in place, then we are wise to create them. David and Rachel are seeking to discern what church they should attend and join. As part of the process, why not create a small listening group of four or six persons whom they bring into the conversation? These friends can listen and ask questions and provide David and Rachel with a sounding board for the reflections that are part of the decision-making process.

We need other voices and perspectives, in part because we recognize our capacity for self-deception and rationalization. And what we often need are people who will not be worried that they will hurt our feelings or crush our spirits. We need those who will speak compassionately and sincerely, but truthfully.

However, what is critical is that these co-discerners, as they might be called, not have a vested interest in the outcome. They need to be able to help David and Rachel hear what God is saying without presuming to know what they should do or, I would say, without even offering an opinion of what choice would be best. Here is where a young person often needs the input of an adult other than his or her parents—a spiritual mentor and friend, who will free the person to hear God without the pressure or expectations that so frequently accompany a parent-child relationship.

Further, I also should note that our own process of discernment never obligates another. Joe and Nancy are considering marriage, but they discern this both in their own individual solitude and prayers and then also together. One cannot say to the other, "I have discerned that we are to marry, so now you do not need to pray about this." Rather, what one might discern is that a proposal of marriage should be made, while leaving the other, before God, to discern if this proposal is to be accepted.

6. Conclusion

In all of this, nothing is so pivotal to our capacity to discern well, and then to choose well, as the character and quality of our relationship with Christ. Therefore, nothing so prepares us to make critical life decisions as does the time and discipline we spend in cultivating this relationship. The theological vision that guides our lives and specifically our decision making is the ascension: Christ, the crucified and risen Lord, stands at the door and knocks, and if we will invite Him in, He will enter into our lives and commune with us.[15]

When we meet the risen Christ, the Lord's first and last word is consistently, "Do not be afraid." This was His word to the disciples when they first embarked on the adventure of being His disciples (Luke 5:10), and it is His ongoing word to them following the resurrection (Matt. 28:10). Furthermore, this call is complemented by the words of assurance that God is with us and that in our choosing we are not alone. As often as not, it is in the times of choice that we feel most keenly our vulnerability and radical aloneness. So the promise of Christ is of utmost significance when He assures His disciples that, while He is returning to the Father, He will not leave them orphaned (John 14:16–18). He will send them the Spirit— the Comforter, the Spirit of truth—to be with them. Their intimate working with the Spirit is, without surprise, evident in the pages of the book of Acts.

Therefore, few things are so pivotal to Christian discipleship as the capacity to listen well, to attend to the presence and prompting of the Spirit. It is the most fundamental posture of the follower of Jesus. Of course we listen that we might obey, for we live and walk in the truth only if we obey. But first we learn to listen.

In so doing, we live in the reality that the ascended Christ, by the Spirit, has a real-time connection with our lives. This does not mean that we dispense with critical thinking or that organizations no longer attend to strategic planning. It is, rather, that thinking and planning are not the sole determiners of the direction and outcomes of our thought processes. It means that our decisions are not purely secular or rational matters, and it means that the decisions we make as churches or even as businesses are not ultimately governed by mere pragmatics. Rather, the driving energy that shapes our lives and thus our choices is the real-time connection we have

---

15. The allusion here is to Revelation 3:20, where the context is clearly one in which Christ is welcomed and received by a congregation, in this case by the church in Laodicea. But I reference this text on the assumption that this principle is equally applicable to our individual circumstances and the eagerness of Christ to participate in our individual lives.

with the risen Christ. We live not just with the idea or the principle of Christ, for it is not just a Christology that shapes our decision making. It is Christ Himself.

Therefore, in order to discern well, we must attend to christological perspectives. First John 4 reminds us that if we do not see and appreciate the incarnation, we will not discern well, if at all. But further, it is not merely the person of Christ but the *reign* of Christ that shapes our discernment. We see and discern how the reign of Christ (i.e., the kingdom of God) is taking shape in our world, both globally and in the communities, neighborhoods, and organizations of which we are a part. Discernment is not merely about our own personal issues. It is about us, but it is much more than this; it is about seeing and appreciating how the reign of Christ is present and then asking, in the company of Christ Himself, how we are being called to choose and act. And the kingdom of God is about mission. It is about feeding and advocating for the poor; it is about caring for creation; it is about the nurture and cultivation of healthy congregations. And we long for our personal lives to somehow witness to the reign of Christ. Discernment is about asking Christ to enable us to choose well, or, better put, it is about inviting Christ to speak to us, into the particularity of our lives. The genius of the history of the Christian practice of discernment is that this process of decision making is made in communion with Christ Himself.

This means that the primary purpose of the Scriptures is not to provide us with specific guidance for a particular problem or issue or decision. It may provide us with this on occasion, but this may not be the primary grace that we receive from the Scriptures. Indeed, how we use the Bible is a key question. We need to beware of the temptation and proclivity, so dominant within many Christian communities, to treat the Bible as a kind of data answer sheet. Far more beneficial is that we learn to live our lives within the world and message of the biblical narrative, the story of God and the story of God's Son. We read the biblical text—indeed, we immerse ourselves in the text—so that we are enabled to live our lives in a similar vein, seeing life and seeing the world through the lens of the gospel. And this means that we read the whole of Scripture in light of the gospel so that our vision of life and of the world and of our decisions in the world are shaped by the good news. We enter into the story, as it were, choosing to live within the big picture, the metanarrative. As we read the biblical text, we long for our imaginations and our vision of life to become shaped, formed, and reformed by a continual engagement with the ancient story so that, in the words of Romans 12:1–2, we are no longer conformed to this world but are transformed as our minds are renewed by the biblical narrative. In this way, we come to a growing appreciation of Christ and the reign of Christ, which should be the context for all of our decisions.

A Specific-Will View Response to the Relationship View

RICHARD AND HENRY BLACKABY

Introduction

The relationship view advocated by Gordon T. Smith provides helpful insight into a Christian's decision making. We applaud Smith's emphasis on the immediacy of Christ in believers' lives as they make choices. We affirm his emphasis that the Christian life is an outgrowth of one's relationship with Christ. The following paragraphs contain our reflections on some of the statements with which we wholeheartedly concur as well as our responses to some aspects of Smith's presentation we might question.

Responsible, Mature Choices

Smith claims the mark of maturity is one's ability and willingness to take ownership of personal choices. He mentions the pathetic nature of grown adults who continue to rely upon others to perform a parental role for them. We agree that people must take responsibility for their decisions. A day of accounting is coming when all people will answer for their choices (2 Cor. 5:10). Of course it is difficult to find one analogy that completely and accurately defines the Christian experience. No human relationship can perfectly parallel our relationship to God. In one sense people remain absolutely dependent upon their Creator. Jesus claimed that apart from Him we can do *nothing* (John 15:5), even as He claimed His own dependence upon God the Father (e.g., John 15:9–10; cf. 5:30; 6:38; 12:49–50). The Lord formed us out of dust. He knows us better than we understand ourselves. He sees our future. Therefore humans have an inherent dependence upon the heavenly Father. While it is abnormal for adults to remain reliant on their parents, Christian adults living in dependence upon their Lord is another matter.

Smith raises the critical question: "What level of involvement does God have in our decision making?" On the one hand, Smith notes that God has created us to make responsible choices that glorify Him. On the other hand, passages such as Galatians 2:20 indicate that the goal of the Christian life is absolute surrender to their Lord. Verses such as these seem to be crucial to developing a relationship view of decision making but were not addressed by Smith.

Free Choices by Faith

Smith also notes that people do have the capacity to choose, for we have not been created as pawns. Again, we agree. However, there is also the reality that God is not only our Creator but also our Lord. While we are free to choose, Christ's lordship ought to directly influence our choices. These two truths are integrated when we freely choose to submit our will to God's. Smith notes that some people want to defer all their decisions to God in order to avoid having to make their own choices. Such people represent the opposite end of the spectrum from those who insist on making every choice independently. The Christian life involves a balance between humble, loving submission to God and a sense of personal accountability for our actions.

According to Smith, God speaks both into the particularity as well as the ambiguity of our lives. Why does God allow ambiguity? Why doesn't He make every issue crystal clear for us? Friesen views this ambiguity as evidence that God does not have a specific will for people. Those holding the wisdom view must ultimately face life's unknowns and make the best decisions possible. But Smith inadequately addresses the question of why a person who is enjoying an intimate relationship with Christ faces abstruse situations. We feel it is because God wants us to live by faith, for without faith it is impossible to please Him (Heb. 11:6). The nebulous aspects of life invite us to develop faith in the one who sees all things clearly.

The Place of Peace

Smith presents Ignatius Loyola's *Spiritual Exercises* as a tool to guide Christian decision making. Loyola uses the concepts of "desolation" and "consolation" as guideposts in making choices. If a decision leads us to experience desolation, or if we are trying to make a choice while in the midst of an experience of desolation, we should be cautious. Conversely, if we make a decision that leads us to experience consolation, it may indicate we are on the right path. Smith argues that good decision making must take into account, not only the facts we know cognitively, but also our emotions. Smith claims that despite the traditional suspicion of emotions when making decisions, they actually have an important role to play. We concur. Because we are holistic people, we cannot make decisions based solely on reason apart from our feelings, nor should we.

Our concern with Smith's presentation is not so much with what he says but with what he does not say. It is certainly important to know our state of mind as we face decisions. A sense of peace following a decision is significant. However, for a Christian, there is another side to the decision-making process. It is the Holy Spirit's active role in our lives as we make choices. Smith advocates a relationship view of decision making, but much of his discussion focuses inwardly on the decision maker and his or her feelings and appears to neglect the relationship aspect of the relationship view.

Smith notes that "the very goal of the Christian life [is] a union with Christ that is so intimate as to necessitate divine participation in our decision making." Smith has presented a valuable approach to Christian decision making by using our walk with Christ as the context of our choices. Yet, when Smith utilizes Ignatius Loyola's guidelines of consolation and desolation, the model seems to focus primarily on the decision maker. We wonder whether a preoccupation with our feelings of consolation or desolation could lead to an inward-gazing approach. While we should know our state of mind as we make decisions and recognize the motives that lie behind our decisions, focusing on how our decisions affect us emotionally or cognitively only helps us to understand half of the issue. It excludes God. We would expect that a relationship approach—one that views our lives as intricately entwined with Christ—would help Christians better recognize the thoughts and feelings of Christ concerning possible decisions they faced. How do we know if Christ is pleased with an option we are considering? How do we recognize when the Holy Spirit is convicting us of prideful (selfish, or otherwise sinful) options we are contemplating? It is important to know ourselves. It is critical to know God.

While it is true that people often lack self-awareness, there is a plethora of books, seminars, and programs available to focus on this area. We contend that people's major disorientation is not to themselves but to God. Believers acknowledge that Christ lives within them, and Christians often glibly announce that Jesus is their "best friend," but the reality is that many believers do not know how to recognize the Holy Spirit convicting them or instructing them in truth. We would appreciate further writing from Smith outlining specific ways to discern the activity of the Holy Spirit in our lives and helping us know how to identify His voice when He is speaking. We do not advocate a scientific formulaic study that tries to isolate a specific, predictable method by which God speaks. We have found, however, that many Christian writers affirm that God speaks to people and is active in people's lives, but they do not provide their readers with practical guidelines to recognize when God is doing it.[16]

---

16. We attempted to do this in our books—see Henry and Richard Blackaby, *When God Speaks: How to Recognize God's Voice and Respond in Obedience* (Nashville: LifeWay, 1995); Henry and Richard Blackaby, *Hearing God's Voice* (Nashville: Broadman & Holman, 2002)—but we are certain Gordon T. Smith would add much to the discussion.

A second question regarding Ignatius's use of consolation and desolation involves making difficult decisions. We believe the Holy Spirit grants peace when we make decisions that are in God's will. As Smith readily acknowledges, however, our feelings of peace ought to be tested in order to be sure they are from God. Simply experiencing a sense of consolation, or peace, is not incontrovertible proof that we have made the right decision. Neither do feelings of desolation or lack of peace indicate we are making a mistake. Feelings alone often can be unreliable.

For example, there could be times when a particular decision appears to lead to joy and contentment yet is not the path Christ would have us take. Conversely, Jesus commands us to deny ourselves, take up our cross, and follow Him. From a human perspective this looks like desolation, yet it is the correct decision. We can see this example clearly in Jesus' life. When Jesus prayed in the garden of Gethsemane, He was not experiencing a sense of peace. He was deeply troubled. Should His sense of desolation have alerted Him that His choice to allow Himself to be arrested and crucified were giving Him a troubled spirit? Recognizing and understanding our feelings must be coupled with an awareness of the Holy Spirit's leading in our lives. We must be in tune with the Spirit's voice as well as the testimony of our own spirit.

Recognizing Motives

Smith notes that to properly make decisions, we must clearly recognize what is motivating us. It is true that we can easily deceive ourselves by rationalizing selfish motives so as to view them as being pious. We question, however, whether people can ever fully discover and identify their motives. Scripture declares that our hearts are desperately wicked and deceitful (Jer. 17:9). While we affirm the importance of searching our hearts, we wonder how much of the deceit of our hearts we can uncover apart from the convicting work of the Spirit of truth (cf. John 14:15–18; 16:8–11). It would have been helpful if Smith had elaborated on how the Holy Spirit, who resides within us and knows us better than we know ourselves, helps to expose those dark and shadowy aspects of our motivations that we might not recognize on our own.

Garry Friesen criticizes the assertion that we must test our sense of peace concerning decisions. He argues that, because we must test our inner impressions, they are too subjective and therefore unreliable. We, however, do not take our critique of Smith this far. For the Bible acknowledges that Christians will receive many impulses and information from various sources—such as sinful desires and false prophets—that must be measured against the objective truth of God's Word. Just because false prophets abound, that does not mean we must reject all prophecy. Rather, we evaluate prophets by how their life and message align with the unerring Word of God. Likewise, we can measure any impulse or feeling against Scripture to know if it is verified by what God has clearly said.

Prayer

Smith says, "Through prayer the Christian has an encounter with Christ." We enthusiastically affirm this. Prayer is more than reciting a litany of requests and complaints and hoping God has heard and will respond. Prayer is an interactive process between creatures and their Creator. It involves God communicating as much as the person praying. Perhaps Smith could have explained further how God specifically uses prayer to guide us in our decision making. When he examined the case studies, prayer did not seem to play as prominent a role as we would have expected.

Recognizing God in All Things

Smith also presents Ignatius Loyola's notion of "finding God in all things." Smith claims we always need to be asking, "Where is God in this?" and "How is God calling me to respond?" This corresponds with one of the seven realities we identify in our book *Experiencing God*: God is always at work around you.[17] The key is always whether we recognize Him and His activity in our circumstances. Just because you are Jesus' disciple, that does not mean you

---

17. Henry Blackaby, Richard Blackaby, and Claude King, *Experiencing God: Knowing and Doing the Will of God*, rev. ed. (Nashville: LifeWay, 2007).

naturally recognize when He is at work around you. When Jesus' twelve disciples failed to understand what He was doing, He rebuked them, saying, "Do you not yet perceive or understand? Are your hearts hardened? Having eyes do you not see, and having ears do you not hear? And do you not remember?" (Mark 8:17–18 ESV). The challenge for Christians is to develop their spiritual senses so they can perceive when the Lord is at work in the world around them and then join Him.

Relationship Is Central

Smith states, "Our choices become one of the critical ways by which we live in communion with Christ, and our capacity to choose well lies in direct proportion to the quality and depth of this relationship." To that we say amen! Decision making is more than an opportunity to make mature, independent choices; it is the means by which we interface our love for, trust in, and dependence on Christ with our life circumstances.

We agree with Smith that "the presence of the Spirit is neither incidental nor secondary, but central to the experience of the Christian disciple." We find this emphasis underdeveloped in Friesen's presentation. We also agree that Christ's utter dependence upon His Father is the paradigm by which we understand our relationship to Christ.

Regarding Ignatius's teachings, Smith observes, "Thus, discernment arises out of a reorientation of our desires so that our wills and the will of God are in communion. Herein lies inner integrity and spiritual freedom." We see this as a sorely needed corrective to much that is currently taught and practiced on the subject of decision making. While seeking God's guidance for decisions has a long tradition, practicing a self-focused Christianity in which God serves as our trustworthy life consultant is a more recent trend. Asking, "What is God's will for my life?" is a relatively recent focus. Asking, "What is God's will?" is not. Smith's emphasis on relationship, on intimate communion with Christ and an agreement of purpose with the Lord, is the antidote to a modern pandemic of self-centered Christianity.

Specific Steps

In the discussion of the specific case studies, Smith offers a sevenfold guide to decision making. These can be summarized as follows: (1) Have clarity about our ultimate allegiance; (2) pay attention to what is happening to us emotionally; (3) take a one-step-at-a-time approach; (4) sequence our decision making; (5) be clear about our circumstances; (6) take time and space to choose well; and (7) seek feedback from others. These are helpful steps in the decision-making process. What seems lacking in this view, however, is specificity concerning the direct role of the Holy Spirit in helping someone arrive at the proper decision. Coming from a relationship view, we would expect more guidance in knowing how one's relationship with Christ directly affects the decision-making process.

For example, steps 1 and 2 suggest that we identify our motives and feelings. While these are important, they focus on us, not on Christ. To really know ourselves, we must know what the Spirit says about our motives. Smith makes it clear from his presentation that Christ plays an integral role in the Christian life, yet these first two steps appear to advocate "know thyself" rather than knowing what the Spirit thinks or sees in our lives.

Step 5 tells us to be clear about our circumstances. In other words, do our homework. The example given is of a church doing a demographic study of its neighborhood. While we would not disparage the gathering of information, we assert that the most important data we can collect is that which comes from God. For example, in Mark's gospel we are told that Jesus spent an evening healing people in the city of Capernaum (Mark 1:32–34). We read, "The whole town gathered at the door." The next morning the crowds were reassembling to receive Jesus' healing ministry, and it was patently obvious to Peter and the other disciples where Jesus could experience an effective ministry. Yet Jesus had gone to seek additional information. He was praying. He knew that despite the pleas from the crowd, another voice was far more important. It would have been easy for Jesus to establish His whole ministry in that city and to bask in the popularity and success He was experiencing. Yet, as Jesus prayed, His Father made it clear that His assignment was to preach in *all* the towns and villages. Incredibly, Jesus walked away from the appreciative crowd that day and carried His ministry to other locations. When a church does a community survey, it finds out what the people are like and what they want, but it has not necessarily heard from God. God may (and probably does) have an entirely different agenda than the people in the community, many of whom will not be believers. While it is good to familiarize ourselves with the needs of our community, it is always far more important to know what is on God's heart for that locality. To thoroughly understand our circumstances, we must gain God's perspective on our situation.

Step 6 calls for finding the time and space to choose well. Smith mentions getting away to a quiet place to hear from God. He says, "Discernment is a learned art; we learn what it means to be alone with Christ and we learn how to discern the prompting of the Spirit in this time of solitude." Here Smith comes closest to addressing our concern of identifying the specific role the Spirit plays in our lives as we make choices. We would have liked for Smith to expand this section to explain how taking time with Christ in solitude and prayer helps Christians learn to recognize the Spirit's voice. How does spending time in prayer allow us to hear God's thoughts? Step 7 addresses the need for accountability. We agree and have included this aspect in our own approach to decision making when we suggest that the Spirit can speak to us through other believers.

In the end, this seven-step process focuses on what *we* do but does not describe how to recognize what God is doing and saying. While it is clear that Smith believes God communicates with Christians, the reader could benefit from some general examples or guidelines on how to recognize God's voice, especially since this is a relationship view.

Summary Critique

Overall we appreciate Smith's contribution to this study and particularly his emphasis on relationship, which is central to the

Christian life. Our criticism is not so much with what he said as with what he omitted. We wanted Smith to tell us more about how our relationship with Christ affects us practically in our daily lives. Nonetheless, we affirm his position that the safest place from which to make a decision is when we are walking closest to our Lord.

A Wisdom View Response to the Relationship View

GARRY FRIESEN

Introduction

Gordon T. Smith's essay is not only about guidance; it is also a powerful devotional or poignant message on knowing Christ personally. Everyone says that Christianity is not a religion but a relationship, and Smith inspires us to really believe and seek such a relationship. My presentations have always been criticized for not clearly showing where fellowship with Christ and the Spirit relate to decision making. Though I see the moral will of God as primary and its primary command is to love God with all your heart, Smith is much better at keeping this heart emphasis at the center of his presentation, and it is a good corrective in emphasis from which I can learn.

On my Web site, I critique his book *Listening to God in Times of Choice*, and I find it to be clearer on how this viewpoint actually makes decisions.[18] While his essay in this book is better at urging us to have a relationship with the living Christ, it is often very general about how that works out in specific decision making. I will assume that both presentations accurately reflect his viewpoint and sometimes refer to his book as well as his essay.

---

18. See http://www.gfriesen.net/sections/review_gordon_t_smith.php.

Specific Will?

Smith seems to assume a specific will when he says, "The fundamental issue is not so much whether there is a particular will of God for each person or whether this will can be known. Rather, the fundamental issue is whether or not there is immediacy with God—a relationship of intimacy and communion—that makes possible this kind of knowledge of the particular will of God." I think this quote means that he is going to assume the concept of a specific will and not talk much about it. Rather, he will talk about how intimacy with Christ makes it possible to know. This is a nice, quick way to avoid one of the key weaknesses of his viewpoint. A major question is whether there is such a biblical concept of a specific will of God. If God does not have a specific will, who cares if we have enough intimacy with God to learn it (if it existed)?

In many ways, Smith's view would be better if it denied the concept of a specific will and just said that God can sovereignly step in whenever He wants and give specific guidance. The wisdom view argues this. It takes the supernatural examples of guidance like the Macedonian vision and concludes that God can give such direct revelation whenever He wants. He has not promised to do this, but when God does give revelation, it is supernatural and perfectly clear. Smith wants to avoid the discussion of a specific will of God, and I recommend he do that by dropping the concept altogether.

Smith does not discuss the specific will very much in this essay, but he does more so in his book. Indeed, in *Listening to God in Times of Choice*, he thinks that the specific-will view undercuts "the presence and voice of God in the times of choice," but his terms sound exactly like the specific-will view.[19] He speaks of "prompting," "impressions," "still small voice," "inner witness," "subjective" speaking, and the "peace of God." "God does not have a mouth; he does not speak audibly. Rather, God 'speaks' to us through our feelings, impressions left on our minds."[20]

---

19. Gordon T. Smith, *Listening to God in Times of Choice: The Art of Discerning God's Will* (Downers Grove, IL: InterVarsity Press, 1997), 16.

20. Ibid., 52.

Smith avoids saying that God's specific will applies to every decision by limiting God's will to "choices or decisions that shape the fundamental parameters and direction we will take."[21] This limiting of the concept is not proven from Scripture and appears to be based on practical necessity. Who can find God's specific will for every decision?

More surprising, Smith undercuts another key point of the specific will of God. He does not believe that you can know God's specific will with certainty. In the essay he used the word "ambiguity" to describe this uncertainty, because in this life we see through a glass darkly (1 Cor. 13:12). In his book he is more pointed: "In this life we will not have absolute, unambiguous peace and rational certainty that we have divine guidance."[22] Instead of telling believers to wait if they do not have certainty of His will, he says we should "trust God and make our choices despite the lack of absolute certainty. We cannot wait until every question is resolved before we act."[23] Smith is a realistic mystic. He knows that his method is subjective and, with consistency and honesty, he does not claim certainty. This uncertainty protects his mysticism from foolishness. Discussing the peace of God, he says, "But, consolation may be from God, or it may reflect the deceitfulness of the Evil One, masquerading as good. Or it could reflect our own confused desires and misguided motives. It may even reflect nothing more than what we had for breakfast."[24] When you are uncertain, you are encouraged to check your feeling or impression by other sources, including the wisdom of God's people.

Smith has accepted one of the greatest weaknesses of his mysticism. The specific-will view and the relationship view are seeking guidance information from a subjective source, and no subjective source can provide certainty. The Blackabys claim certainty and clarity in guidance, but Smith is more consistent in admitting "ambiguity." However, this honesty leaves Smith with a specific will of

21. Ibid., 52–53.
22. Ibid., 56.
23. Ibid., 67.
24. Ibid., 57.

God for important decisions, not all decisions. It leaves him seeking specific guidance on decisions, but knowing that in this life he cannot have certain knowledge of God's specific will.

Scripture

Smith's main example of evidence for God's intimacy in the Old Testament was the prophet. God gave specific, direct revelation to the prophets, but Smith never claims that we receive similar revelation. Indeed, the New Testament clearly states that only some are gifted as prophets and apostles. This kind of intimacy experienced by a prophet or apostle is clearly not God's gift to every believer. Christ is the revelation of God, but the closest He comes to promising more revelation is His promise to the apostles to teach them all truth (John 16:8–15). The apostles received direct revelation, but we are not the apostles. First Thessalonians 5:19 urges us not to quench the Spirit, but this seems to refer to prophecy (v. 20) and testing to be sure the prophet and his words are from God (v. 21). There are examples of God giving specific revelation to individuals in both Testaments, but Smith does not claim that we have the same experience. Rather than receiving revelation, we are reading our emotions, or impressions, to discern God's "voice."

The History of Mystical Believers

I will assume the accuracy of Smith's survey of spiritual history. I have read very little of the books he reviews and will be a learner, not a critic. I found this history interesting but helpful only when he discussed the biblical views of the individuals involved. When he gave details about how they made decisions, it was not convincing as a biblical argument. These may be great men, but they are men, not authorities. The summary of Origen, Bernard, Ignatius, and Wesley would interest me only if they made convincing arguments from Scripture for their viewpoints. In the summaries, there was very little of such argument. Smith does show a thread through history for a mystical camp, but he would agree that such a line is not biblical proof of anything. The history of the mystical, wisdom, or specific-will views is not the deciding factor.

Hearing the Voice of Jesus

Smith is hard to pin down, but it seems he also uses expressions like God "speaking" and the "voice of Jesus" in a misleading way as the Blackabys did. To say God "speaks" to a prophet means one thing. To say God "speaks" through an evaluation of my inner emotional life is something different. The word *speaks* has gone from direct revelation to interpreting impressions.

Smith views the witness of the Spirit as another way of describing our inward impressions. The "witness of the Spirit," however, is better used of the Spirit's work to give inner conviction of the outward message of Christ. We are convinced of the objective, clear words of the gospel by the subjective convicting and convincing work of the Spirit in our hearts. The objective words and the inward convincing work in tandem.

I once asked an apologist who was an evidentialist, "Are you 99 percent or 100 percent sure that Christ was raised from the dead?" To my surprise, he answered 99 percent. He knew that historical evidence is very helpful and garners high probability for the resurrection, but historical evidence can never reach 100 percent. But, I'm 100 percent sure of the resurrection. How is that possible? By the witness of the Spirit in the proclamation of the resurrection, I become 100 percent certain. The witness of the Spirit takes the truth of Christ's resurrection and fully convinces me. This witness is in accordance with the evidence but goes beyond it. In my deepest being, the Spirit takes the gospel of Christ and gives me full assurance that Jesus has been raised from the dead after dying for my sins. This doctrine should not be watered down into a view that some of my impressions are equal to God speaking to me. The witness of the Spirit takes the words of Christ and convinces me fully. This "subjective" convincing work combines with the objective speaking of God's Word to create faith and full assurance. Once the subjective "voices" are separated from the objective revelation, however, the result is subjective uncertainty.

Discernment Emphasis

In my review of *Listening to God in Times of Choice*, I concluded that Smith has so laced his doctrine of guidance with wisdom that it could not be ruined by his mysticism. His mysticism has so much muscle that it is almost palatable. He takes his mystical impressions and runs them through a rigorous one-hundred-point inspection. By the time the actual mysticism kicks in, he has already narrowed the options down to ones that are moral and wise. So I recommend him strongly to those who believe that impressions are equal to the pure voice of God. His process will help filter out the sinful and the foolish impressions so that only the wise and godly ones are left. The end result is not revelation, but anything wise and moral will be profitable in decision making.

It is the discernment emphasis that makes his mysticism workable. Those who don't follow his testing procedures will be led by impressions that feel like they are from God. Those who think God is speaking to them intimately without testing will go astray, but those following Smith will do fine. All of this, however, is in stark contrast to the prophets and apostles. They knew clearly and decisively when God gave them miraculous, direct revelation. They were not mystics but prophets and apostles.

Heart and Mind

Smith has a wonderful emphasis on both heart and mind. He sets this emphasis over against rationalism, cerebral decisions, and, by extension, the wisdom view. But wisdom in the Bible is not rationalism, and the "fear of the LORD" is at its beginning (Prov. 1:7). The wisdom view begins with loving God and your neighbor (moral will of God) and then asks God for wisdom in doing that. It asks tough-minded questions to seek the best way to serve God. It seeks its goals from God's moral will, its means from the Spirit's power, and its wisdom from God (James 1:5).

Smith makes a good point in saying that we should not make a decision when we are angry, depressed, or in desolation, and I'm sure all the views would agree. Anger is usually sin and will just lead to more sin. Smith also seems to be saying that consolation is a form of God speaking and saying yes, while desolation is God saying no. This is a different issue and again turns subjective feelings and impressions into "voices." This is not helpful. Peace is a fruit of the Spirit, which should always be experienced (Gal. 5:22–23), not a mystical voice saying yes. A lack of peace manifested in anxiety is a lack of faith and is not a divine voice authoritatively saying no. Impressions are often a source of wisdom, and each impression should be judged by God's moral standard and wisdom. If impressions are so judged, they often yield much help. We should ask, "Why do I feel peace?" or "Why do I feel uneasy about this decision?" The answer to these questions will yield guidance in the form of moral understanding and wisdom.

The Christian life, of course, involves both heart and mind. God wants to revolutionize our affections and longs for us to learn to love everything He loves and to hate everything He hates. He is transforming our hearts to desire His moral will. The affections are at the heart of our growth. A wild horse of lust will be slowed down by legalistic fences, but sooner or later the wild horse will crash through, run around, or jump over any fence. The wild heart of the horse must be changed. Only God's grace is powerful enough for that work. What is not helpful is claiming that impressions in our heart are coded messages from God that must be identified and then interpreted to get at the authentic voice of God.

Indeed, it is helpful to take our emotional life into consideration when making a decision. How much pressure can we handle? Are we emotionally stable enough to sustain a difficult ministry? Are our children emotionally mature enough to handle living in the inner city? Wisdom must ask these kinds of questions. Our emotions are a significant part of the context of any decision, but they are not cryptic messages from God.

Case Studies

In comparison to his full-length book, Smith gives less specific help in his essay here in this volume. It almost appears that in the case-study section of his essay, he just continued to argue for communion as the key to the decision. In essence, he says that God is going to make the decision; you must be listening and you will get your answer. A process does come through by combining ideas from the essay and the book: (1) make rational evaluation of the options, context, and obstacles; (2) devote extended time to prayer and consideration; (3) have accountability and discussion with others in the body of Christ, including a "clearness committee"; and then (4) the mystical voice of God will confirm the final decision. I am confident that if someone follows the first three steps, he or she will have godly and wise options from which to choose. The final mystical confirmation will not be able to steer someone wrong, because there are only good options left on the table.

The kind of mysticism that scares me is that which really believes that God is directly telling a person what to do, the kind that talks like a prophet. Those who adopt this kind of mysticism are sure they hear God's voice, and so it is that impressions are thought to carry God's authority and serve as final judge. Such mystics are not persuaded by wisdom because they presume to have direct, divine guidance on the subject. They do not listen to other believers who question their choices because they must obey God rather than people. They do not need to do research because God is omniscient and (they claim) He reveals decisions directly to them. This kind of mysticism is more consistent with its theology, but it is, of course, more dangerous. Giving mystical feelings the same authority as the pure voice of God scares me. Smith, however, teaches mysticism with mettle. I recommend him to all those who choose his mystic path, since his form of the view is filled with moral and wisdom muscle. If you take away the moral and wisdom safeguards, however, guidance turns into a subjective process that often will end in foolishness. The new believer or the emotional believer especially will be prone to its dangers.

I recommend to the reader that you pursue a heart like Smith's, which seeks a personal relationship with God, but don't describe that relationship as centered in subjective impressions or feelings. Center it on a profound faith in God's love for you, and reflect that love back to Him. The moral will of God is the foundation for relationship. "Love the Lord your God with all your heart and with all your soul and with all your mind" (Matt. 22:37). Focus this relationship on His revealed scriptural truth, which is able to equip you "for every good work" (2 Tim. 3:17).

CONCLUSION

I Still Have Decisions to Make!

DOUGLAS S. HUFFMAN

1. The Task of the Editor

In the first place, we need to recognize that we do not find God's guidance for our lives by reading a book on guidance!
—SINCLAIR B. FERGUSON[1]

The readers who have worked their way through this volume to this point may well be a bit dizzy from the discussion. Many have likely had the typical pendulum experience of reading such multiple-view books: the first author is completely convincing, and the reader adopts that view; the second author writes so clearly and convincingly that the reader must change and adopt that view; the third author ingeniously dissolves the arguments of the others, and the reader must change again to adopt that view. Of course, in multiple-view books that offer minor responses to each of the major chapters (as this one does), several rounds of the pendulum ride can be experienced. Thus, by this point in such a book, the reader is looking to the editor (sometimes viewed as the referee of the discussion) to sort through the jumble of arguments, declare a "winner," and point the reader back to the real world with the correct view in hand.

---

1. Sinclair B. Ferguson, *Discovering God's Will* (Carlisle, PA: Banner of Truth, 1982), 11. Ferguson says further, "Time and time again people who have read the 'standard' books and booklets on guidance complain that they did not really find them helpful. What they often mean is that they did not discover their personal calling by reading a booklet on guidance! As if God would deposit his personal, eternally purposed will for the life of every Christian in a booklet! No, his will cannot be known apart from the process of discovering it as time unfolds" (p. 78).

If that were the role of this volume's editor, however, the editor might not be me. In fact, this volume is not likely to definitively solve the debate regarding decision making and the will of God. My refusal to declare a winner may be somewhat frustrating; after all, the readers of this book (and even its nonreaders!) still have decisions to make (like career and college selections, marriage partners, and ministry involvements). If this book does not solve the "how do I find God's will" question, how can such decisions be made?

Well, I can assure you that I certainly am not going to make individual decisions for individual readers. Nevertheless, I would like to take the final pages of this volume on decision making and presume to offer a contribution to the discussion. While I might not finally resolve this dispute, I would like to point the reader back to the real world with some sense of resolve for living there.

2. Reflections on the Discussion

If you are willing to follow [God], he will lead you exactly where he wants you to go. There is nothing controversial about that statement. All Christians would agree with it. The problem comes at the next level—the level of practical application.
—RAY PRITCHARD[2]

Before I try to add anything to the discussion, let me make a few reflective comments on it. Our contributors, while representing the three different schools of thought on guidance, have several points of agreement with one another. Furthermore, they are each successful in avoiding the potential extremes of their own views, and they are even complimentary of one another's views. Let's review some of these items.

Points of Agreement

The representatives of the three different views on God's will and decision making are all sincere, passionate, committed evangelical

---

2. Ray Pritchard, *Discovering God's Will for Your Life* (Wheaton, IL: Crossway, 2004), 38 (emphasis in original).

believers who wish to be dependent upon God's Word and who desire to lead lives pleasing to our Lord and in submission to His Holy Spirit. They all agree that decision making is an important discipline in the life of a Christian; they merely disagree on how this important discipline is to be carried out. They all agree that God provides guidance; they merely disagree on how believers ascertain that guidance.

There are other points of agreement among these representatives of different decision-making paradigms. They all agree that God's Word is the primary source of guidance and that no other form of guidance for any specific action will go against an explicit command or an implicit teaching of the Bible. They all agree that God promises to guide believers (cf. Ps. 32:8), that the Holy Spirit plays a role in the guidance of believers (cf. Rom. 8:14), and that willingness (cf. Phil. 2:13; Matt. 6:10) and obedience (cf. John 7:17) are two highly important factors in guidance. They all agree that believers are to be entirely devoted to God (cf. Rom. 12:1–2), that prayer for direction is to be an ongoing part of the believer's life (cf. Col. 1:9; James 1:5–7), and that God is to be trusted to give believers the guidance they need.

It is especially significant to note the agreement all three schools of thought—as represented by our contributors—have with particular regard to key elements in each other's paradigms. Note that all three viewpoints agree that

+ God can give specific—even miraculous—direction to individual believers if and whenever He chooses;
+ God wants His followers to make wise choices;
+ having a relationship with God through faith in Jesus Christ is of utmost importance.

Avoidance of Extremes

For the most part, the representatives of the three schools of thought have successfully avoided the overly extreme claims that are sometimes associated with their views. For example, the Blackabys avoid the extreme position taken by some proponents of the specific-will view who suggest that believers must seek out

God's specific plan for every detail of life before taking any action at all. Friesen avoids the extreme position sometimes projected onto wisdom-view authors who seem to give the impression that God has no specific plans for humanity and that we are left to fend for ourselves. And Smith avoids the potential extreme position of some with the relationship view who might give the impression that relationships matter apart from any and all behaviors. Likewise, in their responses the contributors are largely successful in avoiding the corresponding straw man charges against their colleagues. Thus, the discussion here tends to be fair-minded and aimed at the real points of disagreement rather than the imagined extremes.

Complimentary of One Another

Furthermore, I find it quite instructive to note that the contributors to this volume are complimentary of one another's expressions of their views. In describing each other's work—in whole or in part—they use such terms and phrases as "impressed," "more convincing," "formidable," "apt," "appropriate," "rightly affirming," "appreciate," "invaluable to this whole discussion," "of continuing value," "helpful insight," "affirm his emphasis," "inspires us to really believe," and "a good corrective in emphasis from which I can learn." Some have even said that they recommend each other's books to students. To be sure, they take one another to task on points of disagreement, but their points of agreement are nicely matched by their mutual admiration.

Complementary with Each Other?

On the one hand, we note that the contributors to this discussion are complimentary to one another on the places where they can agree. On the other hand, these three schools of thought on God's will and decision making are somewhat mutually exclusive—each one calling the other two views incorrect. Nevertheless, I would like to contend that there are times when the viewpoints also seem to be complementary with each other, fitting together in some way.

Note, for example, how Smith comes to the defense of the Blackaby position over against Friesen. Friesen argues that because searching for God's specific will for one's life is a recent concern un-represented in Scripture, it is actually an illegitimate worry for be-lievers. Without taking the specific-will view, Smith disagrees with Friesen. Smith is troubled that Friesen has wrongly foreshortened the true history of believers searching for God's will for their lives. Rather than being something of a fad of the last 150 years—since the time of George Müller, as Friesen claims for the specific-will view—Smith gives evidence that the question of finding God's will for one's life is an ancient concern. Smith does not embrace the specific-will view's approach to discovering God's will, but Smith's relationship view sees great value in and a longer history to the search.[3] In this way, the Blackabys and Smith agree over against Friesen.

In fact, it is clear that two of the three camps sometimes agree together over against the third view. In particular, each of the three schools of thought has a position on (1) the nature of God's will for individuals (a specific plan for each life and/or general moral principles for everyone), (2) the individual Christian's need to search (or not) for a specific plan of God, and (3) the nature of the indi-vidual's responsibility (characterized by concern for wise choices or by concern for relationship). Each school of thought finds itself in agreement with one of the others over against the third, but all on different issues. It is this observation that leads me to suggest a way of diagramming all three positions together.

3. The Geometry of the Discussion

The more some people talk about God's will, the more confusing it becomes.

—HOWARD WHALEY[4]

It must be admitted that a system of only three schools of thought on God's will is perhaps all too tidy. There are scores of

---

3. For a very brief and readable history of the church's interest in discerning God's will, see particularly Danny E. Morris and Charles M. Olsen, *Discerning God's Will To-gether: A Spiritual Practice for the Church* (Nashville: Upper Room, 1997), 29–41.

4. Howard Whaley, "This Way to God's Will," *Moody Monthly*, March 1973, 104–6.

books on guidance. While some writers may clearly fit into one camp or another (e.g., our representative contributors), many writers on guidance and decision making display elements from two or all three perspectives. Given the points of agreement and disagreement among the three schools of thought on this issue, I find that the illustration of a triangular-shaped, two-dimensional continuum can help bring clarity to our understanding of the potential connections between the three views (see figure C.1).

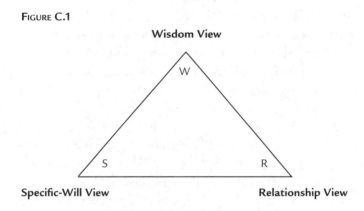

FIGURE C.1

Wisdom View

W

S   R

Specific-Will View   Relationship View

The appropriateness of a triangular-shaped, two-dimensional continuum becomes clear when we recall the rudimentary geometry principles used to describe a triangle. Just as the line shared between points S and R is opposite point W on the triangle, so the specific-will and relationship views share a position opposite the wisdom view, namely, that God does have a knowable and specific plan for each individual. Of course, the specific-will view and the relationship view differ as to what to do about the specific plan, but they both acknowledge it. Opposite this position, the wisdom view claims there is no specific individual will and searching for it is a recent and fallacious fad (see figure C.2).

In the same way, just as the line shared between points W and R is opposite point S on the triangle, so the wisdom and the relationship views share a position opposite the specific-will view, namely, that God's specific will for the individual does not need to be sought

FIGURE C.2

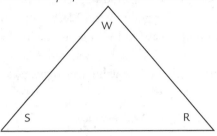

Wisdom View

"There is no specific individual will to be discovered."

Specific-Will View   *"God does have a specific*   **Relationship View**
will for each individual."

out as some sort of undiscovered plan. Granted, the wisdom view and the relationship view differ as to why God's individual will is not to be sought out in this manner, but they do share the position. Meanwhile, the specific-will view claims that believers should search to know God's individual will—God's plan—for them (see figure C.3).

Finally, just as the line shared between points S and W is opposite point R on the triangle, the wisdom and specific-will views share a position over against the relationship view, namely, that doing what God wants is largely about making right choices. In some

FIGURE C.3

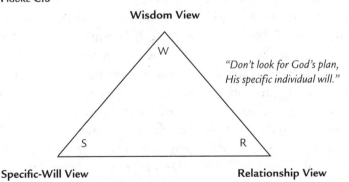

Wisdom View

*"Don't look for God's plan,
His specific individual will."*

Specific-Will View   **Relationship View**

*"Look for God's plan,
His specific individual will."*

sense, the wisdom view and specific-will view differ only with regard to the means for right choices—the prior view stressing wisdom and the latter stressing choice of God's specific plan—but they agree in their emphasis upon right choices. Meanwhile, the relationship view says that doing what God wants means emphasizing a right relationship with Him, with right choices following from the discernment learned in that relationship (see figure C.4).

FIGURE C.4

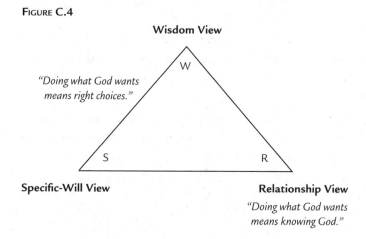

We must note immediately that few authors on the subject of God's will and decision making—including the contributors to this volume—can be plotted to an extreme corner of the triangle diagram. As already noted above, I appreciate the care with which our contributors have avoided extremes while still representing the viewpoints of their respective corners. It is this appreciation that lends itself to the further observation that other writers on the subject of God's will and decision making can be plotted on the triangular diagram, noting nuances in their respective positions. The position represented by X on the diagram is that of one who holds mostly the specific-will view but also some wisdom-view ideas (see figure C.5). Someone in position Y holds mostly to the specific-will view but shares ideas from both of the other two camps as well. In reality, we might guess that few writers hold positions on the border lines (like that of X) and even fewer are in an extreme corner. Most writers on guidance and the will of God express themselves such that their position would be plotted like that of Y (or Y^2, or Y^3, etc.), gravitating toward a particular corner but still sharing some ideas from both of the other views.[5]

FIGURE C.5

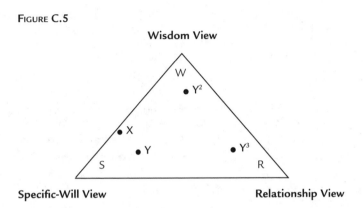

What intrigues me about this geometrical way of thinking is the possibility of a centrist position. What I am suggesting, of course, is something of a balance of the three schools of thought. It seems to me that the balance to strive for is that of the position in the center of the triangle, represented by Z on the diagram (see figure C.6). In the middle, possible errors of the extreme corners can be avoided (e.g., "God has no specific plans for humans, and we are left to fend for ourselves"; "Believers must seek out God's specific plan for every detail of life before taking any action"; and "Relationships matter apart from any and all behaviors"). But, in the middle, the positive views of the connecting lines still can be held in harmony (e.g., "God does have plans for His people"; "We need not overburden ourselves with searching for God's plans when we are trusting God to guide us"; and "Right decisions must be made"). This idea seems promising, but is such a centrist position possible, proper, and practical? I suggest that it is worth pondering.

---

5. Working with this idea, I have plotted the locations of dozens of books on this topic on this triangle diagram in the bibliography to this volume, "God's Will and Guidance: A Categorized Bibliography."

Figure C.6

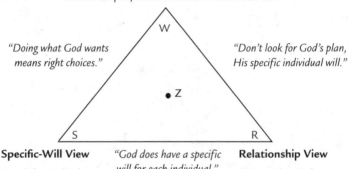

Wisdom View

"There is no specific individual will to be discovered."

W

"Doing what God wants means right choices."

"Don't look for God's plan, His specific individual will."

•Z

S R

Specific-Will View

"Look for God's plan, His specific individual will."

"God does have a specific will for each individual."

Relationship View

"Doing what God wants means knowing God."

4. Some Other Questions to Ponder

Misunderstandings and mistaken beliefs about guidance, or more generally about God and communications between Him and His creatures, make impossible a right walk with Him. This is no less true if we "don't want to think about it." I have seen repeatedly confirmed, in often tragic cases, the dire consequences of refusing to give deep, thoughtful consideration to the ways in which God chooses to deal with us.

—Dallas Willard[6]

There is always more to think about. In addition to the suggestion of a balance of the three positions on God's will and decision making, let me offer some additional questions to ponder. In particular, let me suggest that future studies might ask how these three different schools of thought on guidance fit with different categories of decisions, different individual personalities, and/or different stages of Christian maturity.

---

6. Dallas Willard, *In Search of Guidance: Developing a Conversational Relationship with God* (Ventura, CA: Regal Books, 1984), 224.

First, could it be that the different views of Christian decision making are each proper and appropriate but for different kinds of decisions? For example, might a person use the wisdom approach to select an institution of higher learning but a relationship approach to select a spouse? What effect would this modified perspective have on the arguments given by our contributors against one another's views?

Second, might different models of decision making be useful for different kinds of personalities? In asking this here, I am not invoking a postmodern turn away from absolute truth and toward a subjective relativism (i.e., "If it works for you, then it must be true for you even if it is false for me"). Such disrespect for truth is a disrespect of God's Word and would be a violation of the shared convictions of this volume's contributors. These things I do not want to do. Rather, I am asking whether the three very different views on God's will and decision making argued in this volume are really just three different models, each of which works fine for a particular kind of person. As Paul Helm observes, "Yet it is obvious that while the *fact* that God providentially guides the Christian can be deduced from the fact that he guides the church (for the Christian is a member of the church), *how* he guides cannot be deduced. For Christians have only to glance around them, or to have the faintest inkling of the history of the church, to see that the circumstances of Christians differ markedly. It is thus quite implausible to suppose that there is one uniform pattern of providential guidance for every Christian."[7] Charles Coleman makes a similar statement: "The truth is that God uses, for each of us individually, the kind of guidance which suits our need, our faith, and our personality."[8] Could it be that different schools of thought are correct for different kinds of people?

Finally, could it be that different models of decision making are used at different levels of Christian maturity? Does one method

---

7. Paul Helm, *The Providence of God*, Contours of Christian Theology (Downers Grove, IL: InterVarsity Press, 1994), 122.

8. Charles G. Coleman, *Divine Guidance: That Voice Behind You* (Neptune, NJ: Loizeaux Brothers, 1977), 43. Cf. F. B. Meyer, *The Secret of Guidance: Guideposts for Life's Choices* (repr., Greenville, SC: Ambassador, 2000), 10.

characterize a young believer's decision-making approach, while another method is more indicative of a mature faith? I realize that asking this question brings a new dimension to the debate and, if asked earlier, would have required our contributors to haggle—perhaps immaturely?—over which view is most mature. But it occurs to me that all three views may well have immature versions: the specific-will camp might have those who insist that they will not eat (or sleep, or work, or move, etc.) until God gives a supernatural sign of direction for a particular decision; the wisdom camp has those who (perhaps for the same decision) would insist they can do it all by themselves, and the relationship camp has those who insist that their behavioral choices don't matter as long as there are good relationship feelings. Since immaturity is a possibility for each of the views, I'm not suggesting that one view avoids immaturity better than the others. Rather, avoiding the ditches of juvenile leanings all along the path of life, do the three views on decision making naturally line up in a progressive order for the maturing believer?

5. Some Reassurances as You Decide Which Option to Choose

At the end of the day, we will have to decide what the will of God is!

—SINCLAIR B. FERGUSON[9]

With a little irony we can observe that, at the end of the day, readers will need to make their own decisions about decision making. Believers need one another for support and accountability, for encouragement and challenge. These are, in fact, some of the motivations for producing a book such as this one. But ultimately each person must face God alone, with no other advocate than Jesus. So with Him we must decide about decision making.

Herein, however, is reassurance. Jesus Christ is not only the means to a right relationship with God but also the prime example

---

9. Ferguson, *Discovering God's Will*, 78.

of living that relationship in the will of God. He perfectly lived in God's will (in both the sense of God's moral desires for Him as well the sense of God's specific plans for Him). Believers are to become more like Christ, taking on His character (cf. Rom. 8:29; 2 Peter 1:3-4). In getting to know God in worship, study of His Word, and obedience to His commands, Christians develop the characteristics of Christ, who always did God's will. As believers become more like Christ, they will find themselves more often in God's will (in any sense of the term). When they come to difficult decisions, they ask God for wisdom. Then, in faith, they make choices for God's glory, trusting God has provided all the appropriate information to lead to the right decisions.

Some of life's decisions are very difficult and must be made prayerfully and carefully, but always with the goal of glorifying God. The believer's obligation is to live faithfully by God's moral will revealed in Scripture and to trust God to work providentially for the completion of His specific will in the individual's life. The believer's task is to seek to know God better; God's task is to guide. In seeking to know God better, it is more than appropriate to ask for wisdom from Him to help in making a decision, but then the believer must trust that God will provide the information needed (cf. James 1:5–8). It is not too hard for God to guide—Christians must seek Him and trust Him.

God will provide the help and guidance necessary, whether that is wisdom, circumstances, or assurance. On the other hand, the guidance may not include any flashes of insight or feelings of certitude. God's people do not go through life getting minute-by-minute direction from God in every detail. We must make decisions with the information already at hand, as guided by God's Word and empowered by His Spirit. But if God's will has to do with a righteous character (cf. 1 Thess. 4:3; 5:16–18), we do not fail in our relationships with Him or exit God's will simply because we do something without being specifically instructed to do it. We are expected to make wise choices and to do so trusting God (cf. Eph. 5:15–20).

There will be some decisions for which believers want more specific directions from God. But we must trust God to provide what we need, even if it is not what we want. "The life of faith means liv-ing with uncertainty even in the midst of doing God's will."[10] God will provide enough information to make the right decision. The information may not be complete—the believer's grasp of it may even be incorrect—but it will be enough of the appropriate type of information to help make the right choice. What the believer must do is communicate with God, know Him, and live for Him. God is faithful to do His part.

A college friend of mine once observed that if there is anyone anywhere who really wants us to do God's will, it is God. Or as Arthur Holmes puts it, "God is far more concerned that we do what is right than we are, and he is perfectly able to make things clear."[11] The point is that God can communicate His will to any of us regarding any decision. For each of our many decisions, if we are desiring to do His will, reading His Word, living in step with His Spirit, and communing with His people, we will be in a better place to know which option to choose.

If you always will do the will of God as you know it, you will always know the will of God that you might do it.

—ANONYMOUS

---

10. Pritchard, *Discovering God's Will for Your Life*, 44.

11. Arthur Holmes, "Building on the Will of God," *HIS*, June 1973, 19. See also Pritchard, *Discovering God's Will for Your Life*, 50: "God wants you to know his will more than you want to know it."

A CATEGORIZED BIBLIOGRAPHY

God's Will and Guidance

DOUGLAS S. HUFFMAN

The books listed in this bibliography are plotted on the triangular continuum introduced in the conclusion of this volume (see figure B.1). Each of the three schools of thought regarding God's will and decision making presented in this book is represented by a corner of the triangle: S = specific-will view; W = wisdom view; and R = relationship view. Three in-between zones along the sides of the triangle represent mediating views between two of the positions: SW = mediating between the specific-will and the wisdom views; WR = mediating between the wisdom and the relationship views; and RS = mediating between the relationship and the specific-will views. The central zone of the triangle represents centrist positions (C) that draw—consciously or not—on all three of the main schools of thought on this issue.

FIGURE **B.1**

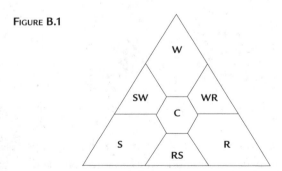

Few of the books in this bibliographic listing actually identify the name of the schools of thought to which their authors consciously (or subconsciously) attach their views about God's will and guidance in decision making. The assessments here are mine; and yet I trust that, after reading this volume, the authors mentioned here would agree that their works should be so plotted. I am, of course, willing to be corrected.

Furthermore, the seven zones of the diagram are not to be thought of as distinctly unified schools of thought. That is, each of the zones has room for variation, and books within the same camp will have points of disagreement with one another. Each camp will have a representative who is more extreme (diagrammed toward the outer edge of that camp's portion of the triangle) than the conservative members of the group (diagrammed toward the middle of that camp's zone). All this is to say that the reader must not assume that all the books grouped in this bibliography into one particular camp say the same things in the same way with the same emphasis. In fact, if we represent each of the almost one hundred books in this bibliography with a dot on the triangle diagram—positioning each dot in proximity to how extreme or centrist or borderline—the diagram might look something like figure B.2.

Figure **B.2**

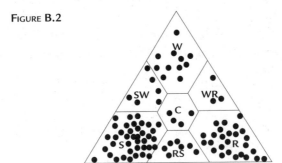

Of interest to future studies might be the tracking of any adjustments to the views of these scholars represented in new editions of their books or additional writings. Significant changes in perspective might cause their corresponding dots to move on the diagram (e.g., note my slotting of Charles Swindoll's two books on guidance—written almost two decades apart—in two different zones).

Of course, our thinking about God's will and guidance might itself develop beyond the margins of this triangular diagram. Only time will tell. And we should say about this matter as well, may God's will be done.

ZONE	AUTHOR, TITLE, PUBLICATION INFORMATION
WR	Ashcraft, Morris. *The Will of God.* Nashville: Broadman, 1980.
W	Barclay, Oliver. *Guidance: What the Bible Says About Knowing God's Will.* Downers Grove, IL: InterVarsity Press, 1978.
R	Barry, William A., and William J. Connolly. *The Practice of Spiritual Direction.* New York: Harper & Row, 1982.
S	Baxter, J. Sidlow. *Does God Still Guide? Or, More Fully, What Are the Essentials of Guidance and Growth in the Christian Life?* London: Marshall, Morgan & Scott, 1968.
S	Bayly, Joseph, et al. *Essays on Guidance.* A HIS Reader. Chicago: InterVarsity Press, 1968.
R	Benner, David G. *Desiring God's Will: Aligning Our Hearts with the Heart of God.* Downers Grove, IL: InterVarsity Press, 2005.
R	Bernard of Clairvaux. *Five Books on Consideration: Advice to a Pope.* Translated by J. D. Anderson and E. T. Kennan. Kalamazoo, MI: Cistercian Publications, 1976.
S	Blackaby, Henry T., and Richard Blackaby. *Hearing God's Voice.* Nashville: Broadman & Holman, 2002.
S	Blackaby, Henry T., Richard Blackaby, and Claude V. King. *Experiencing God: Knowing and Doing the Will of God.* Rev. ed. Nashville: LifeWay, 2007.
SW	Blamires, Harry. *The Will and the Way: A Study of Divine Providence and Vocation.* London: SPCK, 1957.
R	Bockmuehl, Klaus. *Listening to the God Who Speaks: Reflections on God's Guidance from Scripture and the Lives of God's People.* Colorado Springs: Helmers and Howard, 1990.
RS	Carlson, Dwight L. *Living God's Will.* Old Tappan, NJ: Revell, 1976.
R	Carter, Mack King. *Interpreting the Will of God: Principles for Unlocking the Mystery.* Valley Forge, PA: Judson, 2002.
S	Clark, Steve. *Knowing God's Will.* Ann Arbor, MI: Servant Books, 1974.
S	Cleave, Derek. *How to Know God's Will.* Phillipsburg, NJ: P & R, 1985.
S	Coder, S. Maxwell. *God's Will for Your Life.* Chicago: Moody, 1946.

S   Coleman, Charles G. *Divine Guidance: That Voice Behind You.* Neptune, NJ: Loizeaux Brothers, 1977.

S   Deere, Jack. *Surprised by the Power of the Spirit: Discovering How God Speaks and Heals Today.* Grand Rapids: Zondervan, 1993.

S   Deere, Jack. *Surprised by the Voice of God: How God Speaks Today Through Prophecies, Dreams, and Visions.* Grand Rapids: Zondervan, 1998.

S   Devine, James D. *A Journey with Jonah to Find God's Will for You.* Glendale, CA: Regal Books, 1977.

RS   Dobson, James. *Finding God's Will for Your Life.* Life on the Edge Series. Nashville: Word, 2000.

R   Dubay, Thomas. *Authenticity: A Biblical Theology of Discernment.* Rev. ed. San Francisco: Ignatius, 1997.

S   Elliot, Elisabeth. *God's Guidance: Finding His Will for Your Life.* Grand Rapids: Baker, 2006.

R   English, John J. *Spiritual Freedom from an Experience of the Ignatian Exercises to the Art of Spiritual Direction.* 2nd ed. Guelph, Ontario: Loyola House, 1979.

C   Ferguson, Sinclair B. *Discovering God's Will.* Carlisle, PA: Banner of Truth, 1982.

S   Flynn, Leslie and Bernice. *God's Will: You Can Know It.* Wheaton, IL: Victor Books, 1979.

W   Friesen, Garry, with J. Robin Maxson. *Decision Making and the Will of God.* 2nd ed. Sisters, OR: Multnomah, 2004.

R   Green, Thomas H. *Darkness in the Marketplace: The Christian at Prayer in the World.* Notre Dame: Ave Maria, 1981.

R   Green, Thomas H. *Weeds Among the Wheat: Discernment: Where Prayer and Action Meet.* Notre Dame: Ave Maria, 1984.

WR   Guinness, Os. *The Call: Finding and Fulfilling the Central Purpose of Your Life.* 2nd ed. Nashville: Nelson, 2003.

S   Hagin, Kenneth E. *How You Can Know the Will of God.* 3rd ed. Tulsa, OK: Kenneth Hagin Evangelistic Association, 1974.

S   Hosier, Helen Kooiman. *How to Know When God Speaks.* Irvine, CA: Harvest House, 1980.

SW   Howard, J. Grant, Jr. *Knowing God's Will—and Doing It.* Grand Rapids: Zondervan, 1976.

R   Ignatius of Loyola. *The Spiritual Exercises of St. Ignatius.* Translated by Louis J. Puhl. Vintage Spiritual Classics.

Preface by Avery Dulles. New York: Random House, 2000.

S   Jeffress, Robert. *Hearing the Master's Voice: The Comfort and Confidence of Knowing God's Will.* Colorado Springs: WaterBrook, 2001.

R   Johnson, Ben Campbell. *Discerning God's Will.* Louisville: Westminster/John Knox, 1990.

R   Johnson, Ben Campbell. *To Pray God's Will: Continuing the Journey.* Louisville: Westminster/John Knox, 1987.

R   Johnson, Ben Campbell. *To Will God's Will: Beginning the Journey.* Louisville: Westminster/John Knox, 1987.

W   Kincaid, Ron. *Praying for Guidance: How to Discover God's Will.* Downers Grove, IL: InterVarsity Press, 1996.

S   Kise, Jane. *Finding and Following God's Will.* Minneapolis: Bethany House, 2005.

S   LaHaye, Tim. *Finding the Will of God in a Crazy, Mixed-up World.* Grand Rapids: Zondervan, 2001.

R   Lake, Kyle. *Understanding God's Will: How to Hack the Equation Without Formulas.* Lake Mary, FL: Relevant Books, 2004.

S   Lang, G. H. *Divine Guidance: Its Reality, Methods, Conditions.* Rushden, England: Stanley L. Hunt, 1947; first American ed., Fort Washington, PA: Christian Literature Crusade, 1970.

R   Larkin, Ernest E. *Silent Presence: Discernment as Process and Problem.* Rev. ed. Denville, NJ: Dimension Books, 2000.

S   Little, Paul E. *Affirming the Will of God.* Downers Grove, IL: InterVarsity Press, 1971.

SW   MacArthur, John, Jr. *Found, God's Will: Find the Direction and Purpose God Wants for Your Life.* Rev. ed. Colorado Springs: Cook, 1977.

S   Maston, T. B. *God's Will and Your Life.* Nashville: Broadman, 1964.

S   McDowell, Josh, and Kevin Johnson. *God's Will, God's Best for Your Life.* Minneapolis: Bethany House, 2000.

R   McIntosh, Mark A. *Discernment and Truth: The Spirituality and Theology of Knowledge.* New York: Crossroad, 2004.

S   McLarry, Newman R. *His Good and Perfect Will.* Nashville: Broadman, 1965.

W   Meadors, Gary T. *Decision Making God's Way: A New Model for Knowing God's Will.* Grand Rapids: Baker, 2003.

S   Meyer, F. B. *The Secret of Guidance.* Guideposts for Life's Choices. Reprint, Greenville, SC: Ambassador, 2000.

S   Morgan, G. Campbell. *God's Perfect Will.* Chicago: Revell, 1901.

R   Morris, Danny E. *Yearning to Know God's Will: A Workbook for Discerning God's Guidance for Your Life.* Grand Rapids: Zondervan, 1991.

R   Morris, Danny E., and Charles M. Olsen. *Discerning God's Will Together: A Spiritual Practice for the Church.* Nashville: Upper Room Books, 1997.

S   Müller, George. *The Autobiography of George Müller.* Edited by Diana L. Matisko. New Kensington, PA: Whitaker House, 1985.

RS   Murray, Andrew. *Not My Will.* Translated by Marian Schoolland. Grand Rapids: Zondervan, 1977.

RS   Murray, Andrew. *Thy Will Be Done: The Blessedness of a Life in the Will of God.* Chicago: Revell, 1900.

S   Myers, Warren, and Ruth Myers. *Discovering God's Will: Experience Afresh How Good God Is.* Rev. ed. Colorado Springs: NavPress, 2000.

S   Nelson, Marion H. *How to Know God's Will.* Chicago: Moody, 1963.

R   Ogilvie, Lloyd John. *Discovering God's Will in Your Life.* Eugene, OR: Harvest House, 1982.

R   Origen. *Origen, Spirit and Fire.* Edited by Hans Urs von Balthasar. Washington, DC: Catholic University of America, 1984.

SW   Packer, J. I. *Decisions: Finding God's Will.* Christian Basics Bible Study. Downers Grove, IL: InterVarsity Press, 1996.

SW   Packer, J. I. "Thou Guide." In *Knowing God.* Downers Grove, IL: InterVarsity Press, 1973; reprinted as *Finding God's Will.* Downers Grove, IL: InterVarsity Press, 1985.

R   Page, Kirby. *The Will of God for These Days: In Personal Relations, Economic Life, Political Action, Race Relations, International Affairs.* La Habra, CA: n.p., 1945.

S   Palms, Roger C. *God Guides Your Tomorrows: How to Be Confident That God Is Leading Your Life.* Rev. ed. Downers Grove, IL: InterVarsity Press, 1987.

W   Petty, James C. *Guidance: Have I Missed God's Best?* Resources for Changing Lives. Phillipsburg, NJ: P & R, 2003.

W   Petty, James C. *Step by Step: Divine Guidance for Ordinary Christians.* Phillipsburg, NJ: P & R, 1999.

C   Pritchard, Ray. *Discovering God's Will for Your Life.* Wheaton, IL: Crossway, 2004.

S   Rasnake, Eddie. *What Should I Do, Lord?* San Bernardino, CA: Here's Life, 1992.

RS   Redpath, Alan. *Getting to Know the Will of God.* Downers Grove, IL: InterVarsity Press, 1954.

R   Riffel, Herman H. *Voice of God.* Wheaton, IL: Tyndale, 1978.

W   Robinson, Haddon. *Decision Making by the Book: How to Choose Wisely in an Age of Options.* Reprint, Grand Rapids: Discovery House, 1998.

S   Shepson, Charles W. *How to Know God's Will.* Beaverlodge, Alberta, Canada: Horizon House, 1981.

R   Sine, Christine, and Tom Sine. *Living on Purpose: Finding God's Best for Your Life.* Grand Rapids: Baker, 2002.

WR   Sittser, Gerald. *The Will of God as a Way of Life: How to Make Every Decision with Peace and Confidence.* Rev. ed. Grand Rapids: Zondervan, 2004.

R   Smith, Gordon T. *Courage and Calling: Embracing Your God-Given Potential.* Downers Grove, IL: InterVarsity Press, 1999.

R   Smith, Gordon T. *Listening to God in Times of Choice: The Art of Discerning God's Will.* Downers Grove, IL: InterVarsity Press, 1997.

R   Smith, Gordon T. *The Voice of Jesus: Discernment, Prayer and the Witness of the Spirit.* Downers Grove, IL: InterVarsity Press, 2003.

SW   Smith, M. Blaine. *Knowing God's Will: Finding Guidance for Personal Decisions.* 2d ed. Downers Grove, IL: InterVarsity Press, 1991.

W   Sproul, R. C. *God's Will and the Christian.* Wheaton: Tyndale, 1984.

S   Stanley, Charles. *How to Listen to God.* Nashville: Oliver-Nelson, 1985.

W   Staton, Knofel. *How to Know the Will of God.* Cincinnati: New Life Books, 1976.

W   Swavely, Dave. *Decisions, Decisions: How (and How Not) to Make Them.* Phillipsburg, NJ: P & R, 2003.

S   Sweeting, George. *Discovering the Will of God.* Chicago: Moody, 1975.

S   Swindoll, Charles. *God's Will: Biblical Direction for Living.* Portland, OR: Multnomah, 1981.

RS   Swindoll, Charles. *The Mystery of God's Will: What Does He Want for Me?* Nashville: Word, 1999.

W   Waltke, Bruce. *Finding the Will of God: A Pagan Notion?* Grand Rapids: Eerdmans, 1995.

S   Water, Mark. *Knowing God's Will Made Easier.* Peabody, MA: Hendrickson, 1998.

S   Weatherhead, Leslie. *The Will of God.* N.p.: Whitmore & Stone, 1944; reprint, Nashville: Abingdon, 1972.

S   Weiss, G. Christian. *The Perfect Will of God.* Lincoln, NE: Good News Broadcasting Association, 1950.

C   White, John. *The Fight: To Know God's Word, to Share the Faith, to Communicate with God, to Know God's Will.* Downers Grove, IL: InterVarsity Press, 1976.

S   Wight, Fred Hartley. *The Secret of Divine Guidance.* Epic Books. Los Angeles: Cowman, 1960.

C   Willard, Dallas. *Hearing God: Developing a Conversational Relationship with God.* Downers Grove, IL: InterVarsity Press, 1999.

R   Wolff, Pierre. *Discernment: The Art of Choosing Well: Based on Ignatian Spirituality.* Rev. ed. Liguori, MO: Ligouri, 2003.

RS   Wright, Henry B. *The Will of God and a Man's Life Work.* New York: Association Press, 1909.

SCRIPTURE INDEX

SUBJECT INDEX